ACKNOWLEDGMENTS

We gratefully acknowledge the help of our representatives for their efficient and perceptive inspections of the lodgings listed. Forbes Travel Guide is also grateful to the talented writers who contributed to this book.

Some of the information contained herein is derived from a variety of third-party sources. Although every effort has been made to verify the information obtained from such sources, the publisher assumes no responsibility for inconsistencies or inaccuracies in the data or liability for any damages of any type arising from errors or omissions.

Neither the editors nor the publisher assume responsibility for the services provided by any business listed in this guide or for any loss, damage or disruption in your travel for any reason.

Front Cover image: ©Getty Images/Steven Puetzer
Back Cover images: Fremont Street Experience © LVCVA
ISBN:9780984433605
Manufactured in the USA
10 9 8 7 6 5 4 3 2 1

CONTENTS

STAR PROPERTIES 4
STAR ATTRACTIONS 5
BEST BETS 8
HISTORY 13
AT A GLANCE 20

WHAT TO SEE 24
The Strip 25
Off-Strip 39
Downtown 41
Suburbs 42

SHOPPING 45
The Strip 46
Downtown and Off-Strip 52

SPAS 55
Star-Rated Spas 56
Other Spas 62

WHERE TO STAY 67
The Strip 68
Off-Strip 87
Downtown 93
Suburbs 94

WHERE TO EAT 97
The Strip 98
Off-Strip 127
Suburbs 131

NIGHTLIFE 133
The Strip 134
Off-Strip 150

ARTS & CULTURE 154
Art 155
Comedy 156
Music 157
Theater 160
Sports 163

BEYOND 165
Hoover Dam and Lake
    Mead 166
Valley of Fire 167
Death Valley National
    Park 169
Grand Canyon 169

KNOW BEFORE YOU GO 172
MAPS 177
INDEX 181

☆☆ **Forbes**
TRAVEL GUIDE

LAS VEGAS STAR PROPERTIES

FIVE STAR HOTELS
Skylofts at MGM Grand — *page 77*
Tower Suites at Encore Las Vegas — *page 79*
Tower Suites at Wynn Las Vegas — *page 79*

FIVE STAR RESTAURANTS
Alex — *page 98*
Joël Robuchon — *page 104*

FIVE STAR SPAS
The Spa at Encore Las Vegas — *page 58*
The Spa at Mandarin Oriental, Las Vegas — *page 59*
The Spa at Wynn Las Vegas — *page 61*

FOUR STAR HOTELS
Bellagio Las Vegas — *page 68*
Encore Las Vegas — *page 69*
Four Seasons Hotel Las Vegas — *page 70*
The M Resort Spa & Casino Las Vegas — *page 89*
Mandarin Oriental, Las Vegas — *page 72*
The Palazzo Las Vegas Resort Hotel Casino — *page 74*
The Signature at MGM Grand Las Vegas — *page 76*
The Venetian Resort Hotel Casino — *page 82*
Wynn Las Vegas — *page 83*

FOUR STAR RESTAURANTS
Aureole — *page 98*
Bradley Ogden — *page 100*
Le Cirque Las Vegas — *page 106*
Michael Mina — *page 106*
Mix in Las Vegas — *page 107*
Picasso — *page 110*
Restaurant Guy Savoy — *page 111*
Twist — *page 114*

FOUR STAR SPAS
Canyon Ranch SpaClub at The Venetian/The Palazzo — *page 56*
Spa Bellagio Las Vegas — *page 61*
Spa Mio — *page 62*
The Spa at Trump — *page 60*
The Spa at Four Seasons Hotel Las Vegas — *page 59*

STAR ATTRACTIONS

If you've been a reader of Mobil Travel Guide, you will have heard that this historic brand partnered in 2009 with another storied media name, Forbes, to create a new entity, Forbes Travel Guide. For more than 50 years, Mobil Travel Guide assisted travelers in making smart decisions about where to stay and dine when traveling. With this new partnership, our mission has not changed: We're committed to the same rigorous inspections of hotels, restaurants and spas—the most comprehensive in the industry with more than 500 standards tested at each property we visit—to help you cut through the clutter and make easy and informed decisions on where to spend your time and travel budget. Our team of anonymous inspectors are constantly on the road, sleeping in hotels, eating in restaurants and making spa appointments, evaluating those exacting standards to determine a property's rating.

What kinds of standards are we looking for when we visit a property? We're looking for more than just high-thread count sheets, pristine spa treatment rooms and white linen-topped tables. We look for service that's attentive, individualized and unforgettable. We note how long it takes to be greeted when you sit down at your table, or to be served when you order room service, or whether the hotel staff can confidently help you when you've forgotten that one essential item that will make or break your trip. Unlike any other travel ratings entity, we visit each place we rate, testing hundreds of attributes to compile our ratings, and our ratings cannot be bought or influenced. The Forbes Five Star rating is the most prestigious achievement in hospitality—while we rate more than 5,000 properties in the U.S., Canada, Hong Kong, Macau and Beijing, for 2011, we have awarded Five Star designations to only 54 hotels, 23 restaurants and 20 spas. When you travel with Forbes, you can travel with confidence, knowing that you'll get the very best experience, no matter who you are.

With our City Guide series, you can also count on a local perspective, in the form of a fresh, witty, insider voice. We employ local writers and inspectors who are well-connected in their respective cities to give you the very latest information on what's going on around town. As you are reading these pages, we hope you get a real flavor of the city and that you feel even more inspired to visit and take it all in. All of our books in the City Guide series include vibrant photos and easy-to-use maps to help you find your way to the city's best attractions. We understand the importance of making the most of your time. That's why the most trusted name in travel is now Forbes Travel Guide.

STAR RATED HOTELS

Whether you're looking for the ultimate in luxury or the best value for your travel budget, we have a hotel recommendation for you. To help you pinpoint properties that meet your needs, Forbes Travel Guide classifies each lodging by type according to the following characteristics:

★★★★★These exceptional properties provide a memorable experience through virtually flawless service and the finest of amenities. Staff are intuitive, engaging and passionate, and eagerly deliver service above and beyond the guests' expectations. The hotel was designed with the guest's comfort in mind, with particular attention paid to craftsmanship and quality of product. A Five-Star property is a destination unto itself.

★★★★These properties provide a distinctive setting, and a guest will find many interesting and inviting elements to enjoy throughout the property. Attention to detail is prominent throughout the property, from design concept to quality of products provided. Staff are accommodating and take pride in catering to the guest's specific needs throughout their stay.

★★★These well-appointed establishments have enhanced amenities that provide travelers with a strong sense of location, whether for style or function. They may have a distinguishing style and ambience in both the public spaces and guest rooms; or they may be more focused on functionality, providing guests with easy access to local events, meetings or tourism highlights.

Recommended: These hotels are considered clean, comfortable and reliable establishments that have expanded amenities, such as full-service restaurants.

For every property, we also provide pricing information. All prices quoted are accurate at the time of publication; however, prices cannot be guaranteed. Because rates can fluctuate, we list a pricing range rather than specific prices.

STAR RATED RESTAURANTS

Every restaurant in this book has been visited by Forbes Travel Guide's team of experts and comes highly recommended as an outstanding dining experience.

★★★★★Forbes Five-Star restaurants deliver a truly unique and distinctive dining experience. A Five-Star restaurant consistently provides exceptional food, superlative service and elegant décor. An emphasis is placed on originality and personalized, attentive and discreet service. Every detail that surrounds the experience is attended to by a warm and gracious dining room team.

★★★★These are exciting restaurants with often well-known chefs that feature creative and complex foods and emphasize various culinary techniques and a focus on seasonality. A highly-trained dining room staff provides refined personal service and attention.

★★★Three Star restaurants offer skillfully prepared food with a focus on a specific style or cuisine. The dining room staff provides warm and professional service in a comfortable atmosphere. The décor is well-coordinated with quality fixtures and decorative items, and promotes a comfortable ambience.

Recommended: These restaurants serve fresh food in a clean setting with efficient service. Value is considered in this category, as is family friendliness.

Because menu prices can fluctuate, we list a pricing range rather than specific prices. The pricing ranges are per diner, and assume that you order an appetizer or dessert, an entrée and one drink.

STAR RATED SPAS

Forbes Travel Guide's spa ratings are based on objective evaluations of more than 450 attributes. About half of these criteria assess basic expectations, such as staff courtesy, the technical proficiency and skill of the employees and whether the facility is clean and maintained properly. Several standards address issues that impact a guest's physical comfort and convenience, as well as the staff's ability to impart a sense of personalized service. Additional criteria measure the spa's ability to create a completely calming ambience.

★★★★★Stepping foot in a Five Star Spa will result in an exceptional experience with no detail overlooked. These properties wow their guests with extraordinary design and facilities, and uncompromising service. Expert staff cater to your every whim and pamper you with the most advanced treatments and skin care lines available. These spas often offer exclusive treatments and may emphasize local elements.

★★★★Four Star spas provide a wonderful experience in an inviting and serene environment. A sense of personalized service is evident from the moment you check in and receive your robe and slippers. The guest's comfort is always of utmost concern to the well-trained staff.

★★★These spas offer well-appointed facilities with a full complement of staff to ensure that guests' needs are met. The spa facilities include clean and appealing treatment rooms, changing areas and a welcoming reception desk.

FREMONT STREET EXPERIENCE

GAME ON

In Las Vegas, it's not whether you win or lose, but how you play the game. These days the "game" extends well beyond the betting tables. New hotels and restaurants continue to crop up everywhere. Retail therapy has become a spectator sport for the rich and famous. Nightclubs are some of the swankiest in the nation. And the shows keep getting better and better. So, before you get comfortable at that slot machine, see what all the buzz is about on and off the Strip.

WHAT ARE THE BEST HOTELS IN LAS VEGAS?

It wouldn't be Las Vegas without bigger and better projects on the horizon. The highly anticipated **CityCenter** finally opened in December 2009, adding more than 5,000 hotel rooms to the Strip with hotel giants like **Mandarin Oriental, Las Vegas** *(page 72)* and new names such as **Vdara Hotel & Spa** *(page 86)* and **Aria Resort & Casino** *(page 83)*, joining the fray.

Wynn Las Vegas *(page 83),* has redefined the concept of personalized service and customer care, particularly at its hotel-within-a-hotel **Tower Suites at Wynn** *(page 79)* and continues to wow guests with its lavish interiors and top-notch amenities. From the Tom Fazio-designed 18-hole championship golf course to the Penske-Wynn Ferrari Maserati dealership in front, Wynn covers all of its luxury bases. Be sure to stroll through Wynn's newest sister property, **Encore Las Vegas** *(page 69)* for a slightly more intimate take on lavish Las Vegas. Its **Tower Suites at Encore** *(page 79)*, with its own entrance and ultra-personalized service, takes the luxe level one step further.

Right next door, **The Palazzo Resort Hotel Casino** *(page 74)* offers elegant suites with European flair and cutting-edge bells and whistles including LCD TVs in the bathroom and "touch-control" curtains. Its sister hotel, **The Venetian Resort Hotel Casino** *(page 82)*, has more than 4,000 swank suites to retreat to.

Staying at the **MGM Grand Hotel & Casino** *(page 72)* has always been a pleasant experience, but if you're looking to up the ante, the **Skylofts at MGM Grand** *(page 77)* is the destination for you. Try 24-hour personal concierge service; dream, spa and music butlers; luggage unpacking; and customized stationery.

It started many trends when it opened in 1998 (outrageous street-side entertainment in the way of its fountains, a fine arts gallery and fine dining to match), and **Bellagio Las Vegas** *(page 68)* is certain to continue leading the pack when it undergoes a complete refresh in 2011. In the meantime, elegant rooms and plenty of shopping keep Bellagio as busy as ever.

WHAT ARE THE BEST CASINOS FOR BEGINNERS?

There is no doubt gambling is the name of the game in Las Vegas, and the reason that more than 36 million people visit each year. You'll have no trouble finding a casino willing to deal you in—if the slot machines in the airport weren't enough of a hint. Serious card sharks know where they're headed (most likely because they have a players card at a specific casino and all of the perks that go with it). But if you're hitting the tables for the very first time, or still perfecting your math skills, we recommend you start slow. **Excalibur** *(page 35)*, **MGM Grand** *(page 72)* and **Caesars Palace** *(page 69)* all offer roulette, craps and blackjack lessons daily. **Treasure Island**

WHERE IS LAS VEGAS'S BEST NIGHTLIFE?

Whether you're looking to grab a relaxing after-dinner drink with friends or dance your way to dawn in the clubs, Sin City will not disappoint. Bathed in a chocolate brown, olive and metallic color palette, **Blush** *(page 135)* at Wynn is an intimate boutique nightclub, that exudes warmth with its sleek décor, plush seating and 300 lanterns hanging from the ceiling. Those looking to crank it up a notch can head to nearby **XS** *(page 149)* at Encore Las Vegas. A magnet for celebrities and those looking to party with them, this posh spot pulls out all of the stops from crocodile-embossed leather VIP booths to big name DJs to an outdoor pool area (for wading only). Or head to Encore's newest nightclub, **Surrender** *(page 144)*, a swank indoor-outdoor venue.

It doesn't get more tech-chic than at **Eyecandy Sound Lounge & Bar** *(page 138)* at Mandalay Bay. From the table-to-table instant messages to the touch-activated LED dance floor to the iPod request system, you'll have plenty to keep you occupied.

For dancing, the best spots are at celeb-centric **Pure** *(page 141)* at Caesars Palace and the cavernous and decadent **Tao Nightclub** *(page 145)*—don't mind the 20-foot hand-carved Buddha—at the Venetian. The dance floors are enormous and the DJs are top-notch, pulling in hundreds of revelers nightly.

(page 81) and **Flamingo Las Vegas** *(page 85)* also often carry lower table minimums than some of their neighbors on the Strip. If you think poker might be your game, head to **Bellagio Las Vegas** *(page 68)*, as its casino devotes more than 40 tables to the sport. **Wynn Las Vegas** *(page 83)* and **The Palazzo** *(page 74)* cater to more seasoned players, but that can be half the fun—watching somebody toss $500 chips with sheer abandon.

WHAT ARE THE TOP SHOWS IN LAS VEGAS?

The masterminds who grew a multimillion-dollar playground out of an arid desert certainly haven't stopped at the slot machines. Las Vegas also carries quite the reputation for entertainment. From multiple iterations of the larger-than-life modern circus that is **Cirque du Soleil** *(page 158)*, to comedy any way you like it, to classic Vegas entertainment featuring magicians, showgirls, A-list superstars and big-time boxers, the shows of Las Vegas have only gotten bigger and more diverse over the years. There's no need to get tickets beforehand (unless you're dead set on a hot boxing match or a one-night-only engagement); just visit your concierge when you arrive and they'll be able to steer you straight into the aisles of **Jersey Boys** *(page 161)* or **Celine Dion's** return to Caesar's Palace *(page 69)*. For a taste of old Vegas, snag a seat for **Jubilee!** *(page 29)* at Bally's to watch showgirls strut their feathers. Or snag a ticket to see country crooner Garth Brooks at **Encore Las Vegas** *(page 161)*.

WHAT ARE THE BEST RESTAURANTS?

Once upon a time, a celebrity chef would merely put their name on a Vegas outpost only to never return. However, those days are long gone. Today, Vegas is a who's who of celebrity chefs–including Wolfgang Puck, Tom Colicchio, Bobby Flay, Emeril Lagasse, Joël Robuchon, Thomas Keller and Todd English–who actually care about the food that's being served, making Las Vegas one of the top food cities in the United States. The problem is choosing two or three while you're here.

One of the world's greatest chefs, **Joël Robuchon** *(page 104)* has come

LAS VEGAS STRIP

to epitomize fine, French cuisine. The dining room at his eponymous restaurant inside the MGM Grand is regal, and the 16-course tasting menu is exquisite.

Another top-notch restaurant that recently opened in Las Vegas is chef Pierre Gagnaire's **Twist** *(page 114)*, located inside the opulent Mandarin Oriental, Las Vegas within the sleek CityCenter. The restaurant is the famous chef's first stateside foray. Besides Twist, CityCenter is Las Vegas' newest nexus of fine dining. You'll find outposts from star chefs such as Jean-George Vongerichten (**Jean George Steakhouse**, *page 119*), **Julian Serrano** *(page 119)* and Masatakayama (**Bar Masa***, page117)*

If you're looking for steakhouse fare, you have plenty of great options. In Las Vegas, no simple filet will do. Find a seat at Wolfgang Puck's **CUT** *(page 102)* at the Palazzo and treat yourself to one of the tastiest dry aged steaks around, as well as Puck's delicious appetizers, such as the pork belly with Asian spices and sesame-orange dressing. You also can't go wrong at Tom Colicchio's **Craftsteak** *(page 101)* at MGM Grand, where its more about a good cut of beef than a fussy sauce or fancy preparation.

For some unparalleled ambience with your fare, no place carries more clout than **MIX in Las Vegas** *(page 107)* atop THEhotel at Mandalay Bay. From the modern white décor and sweeping staircase to the view of the Strip and the stunning Murano chandelier (comprising 15,000 hand-blown glass balls), you'll be awed from the moment you step inside. For ambience with a more artistic bent, **Botero** *(page 118)* at Encore Las Vegas is a must. The expansive poolside restaurant boasts a museum-worthy collection of Fernando Botero's paintings and sculptures, displayed beautifully against the sleek black and white interior.

If you're pining for a four-hour gastronomic feast, **Alex** *(page 98)* at Wynn is the place to go. The sense of grandeur in the dining room (replete with a grand staircase) is only trumped by the exquisitely executed entrées that float from Alessandro Stratta's kitchen. If you have the desire to try Stratta's cuisine but lack the time, his other Wynn venture, **Stratta** *(page 125),* is a more casual choice, with wood-burning pizzas and hearty Italian comfort dishes.

High-brow Asian cuisine seems to have become as popular on the Strip as celebrity birthday parties and palatial suites. **Red 8** *(page 122)* inside Wynn Las Vegas is a far cry from your neighborhood take-out joint. This red-and-black-lacquer enclave merges flavors from Southeast Asia under the skillful hand of chef Ray Kwong, who succeeds with dishes like braised beef brisket with turnip and bean curd skin. Feeling adventurous? Don't miss out on his more exotic dishes, such as jellyfish marinated with sesame oil, braised abalone with seasonal greens and braised pork knuckle noodle soup with fermented bean curd.

And what's a great meal without an equally great vintage to accompany it? Hot spots like **Aureole** (complete with a 42-foot wine tower and wine angel aerialists; *page 98*) and **L'Atelier de Joël Robuchon** *(page 105)* boast wine lists not soon forgotten.

WHERE IS THE BEST SHOPPING IN LAS VEGAS?

In Vegas it's not why you shop, it's where. Each shopping "mall" has its own reason for being, be it animatronics, live statues or stunning architecture. For the average browser, the experience is more about what you see than what you buy.

That's because buying often requires a limitless credit card account and exponential funds to back it up. Over the past decade, Las Vegas has redefined high-end shopping with the likes of a Ferrari-Maserati dealership and Alexander McQueen's second shop in the U.S. at the **Wynn Las Vegas Esplanade** *(page 52)*. The recent addition of the Encore Esplanade has upped the ante further with the addition of edgier, high-end shops like In Step and Shades, where a new pair of sunglasses will have you rockstar ready in no time.

The Shoppes at The Palazzo *(page 50)* offer über-luxe fashions from Burberry and Coach to Jimmy Choo and Christian Louboutin. Head down the Strip to **Via Bellagio** *(page 46)* for more high-priced power-players including Fendi, Dior, Prada, Gucci, Tiffany & Co. and Chanel.

The new **Crystals Retail and Entertainment** complex at CityCenter *(page 46)* is devoted to high-end retailers including Louis Vuitton, Tom Ford and Miu Miu, and features a number of equally glamourous places to dine.

The recently redesigned, contemporary **Miracle Mile Shops** *(page 49)* inside Planet Hollywood are flanked by nearly a dozen restaurants and anchored with stores such as French Connection, White House Black Market and Bebe. Just down the Strip is the **Fashion Show** mall *(page 47)*, which mixes high-end department stores (Neiman Marcus, Saks Fifth Avenue, Nordstrom) with more affordable retail therapy (Macy's, Dillard's). An 80-foot long runway in the middle of the mall hosts fashion shows and private events.

VALLEY OF FIRE

In a town where newer is better, not much time is spent on sentimentality towards the past. Casinos are imploded with fanfare once their luster has faded, and new ones are designed to be bigger, flashier and more cutting-edge than their just-opened neighbors. Still, Las Vegas does have a history that stretches back to America's pioneer days, when the desert that's today part of the city was little more than a crossroads. Here is a look at Las Vegas' hidden past.

HOW WAS LAS VEGAS FOUNDED?

Perhaps it was the enthusiasm of youth that led Rafael Rivera, the teenage Mexican scout, to name this fertile valley "Las Vegas" when he discovered it in 1830. Spanish for "the meadows," it was a generous moniker for a natural green oasis amidst a sea of sand. The sight of any freshwater spring and surrounding plant life in the middle of the Mojave Desert was certainly cause for celebration.

No matter how much today's casinos' elaborate fountains and their hotels' lush gardens try to convince you otherwise, Vegas is in the middle of a desert, which explains why the history of this thriving city is so much more brief than most of the rest of the country. Modern civilization didn't really crop up here until the early 20th century, spurred by the attempt to create a railroad town (one that didn't find its purpose until several decades later). Simply put: The ecosystem didn't previously support life on such a large scale.

All of this makes the prehistoric period of Las Vegas so much harder to imagine. About 25,000 years ago, the land was at the bottom of a 20-mile-deep lake, a basin filled with fresh water from glaciers left behind by the last ice age. Around 13,000 B.C., Paleo-Indians lived near the shrinking lake's shore, hunting caribou, bison and woolly mammoth for sustenance. The region became a desert 10,000 years later, but some of the water that had once covered the land was still flowing underground, creating natural wells and small springs. Archaic Indians settled into the valley, lured by its artesian water, which ultimately flowed into the Colorado River about 30 miles away.

WHO LIVED IN SIN CITY FIRST?

In approximately 500 A.D., the Anasazi established the first true civilization in the area, developing adobe, a clay-based construction material. Over the next several hundred years, they created elaborate multi-tiered pueblos; they also mastered irrigation, allowing them to farm sustainable crops of corn and beans. By 1150, the Anasazi had vanished; no one knows why. Disease? Famine? War? (Though we're likely never to understand why they left, we can discern a good deal about how they lived, thanks to the "Lost City," uncovered in 1924.) More than seven centuries would elapse before human beings would again learn how to live so prosperously in the desert.

Flash forward: In 1829, Mexico had recently won its independence from Spain. A trading party of 60 Mexican men led by Antonio Armijo set out from Santa Fe, seeking a way to connect New Mexican pueblos to those in Southern California. On Christmas Day, the Armijo caravan camped out about 100 miles northeast of the future Sin City and a scouting expedition was launched. As the story goes, Rivera veered off alone and, in early January 1830, camped on a mesa overlooking the valley; from that vantage point, he easily spotted "the meadows." Historians generally agree he was

SPRING PRESERVE LAKE

the first non-Native American to set foot on the land. (Today, the scout is honored in Las Vegas with a statue in front of the eponymous Rafael Rivera Community Center.) At the time, the discovery was hugely significant for Los Angeles and Santa Fe, which could now be linked via this route, which came to be known as the Old Spanish Trail. The oasis provided the only source of fresh water within a day's travel, thus serving as a vital way-station for caravans crossing the desert. The Mexicans were soon joined by Mormon missionaries, who stopped at the meadows as they journeyed between L.A. and Salt Lake City. Travel significantly increased after 1845, when John Charles Fremont arrived with a crew to survey the area for the Army Topographical Corps. His subsequent map—Congress printed 20,000 copies of it—became an invaluable tool for anyone heading west.

By 1855, Mormons decided to colonize Las Vegas. Their missionaries built a fort, dug ditches for irrigation and befriended some nearby Paiute peoples, yet they couldn't sustain a community. Crops failed but they discovered lead nearby, which lured miners from Salt Lake City in hordes too great for the struggling colony to support. The Mormons abandoned their Vegas venture in 1858; the remains of their fort are the city's oldest structures.

HOW DID THE RAILROAD JUMPSTART LAS VEGAS?

For the rest of the country, the 1860s brought tumult (the Civil War) and progress (the first transcontinental railroad), but inside the small fertile valley hidden within a desert, life remained quiet. A settler named Octavius Decatur Gass and his family claimed the old Mormon fort and managed to build a ranch, successfully irrigating crops and raising cattle while helping other homesteaders. The following decade, ownership of the Las Vegas Ranch fell to Archibald and Helen Stewart; even after Archibald's murder, Helen kept things going as she raised her children into the 20th century. She also insisted on friendly relations with the Paiute.

VINTAGE LAS VEGAS

The flip of the switch that finally turned Las Vegas into a town occurred in 1903, when Stewart sold most of her land for $55,000 to the San Pedro, Los Angeles and Salt Lake Railroad, which aimed to lay its tracks directly through the ranch as it connected L.A. to Salt Lake City. Fully aware of the changes trains would herald, Stewart bought up another 924 nearby acres and lived in the growing town until she died in 1926, by which point she was known as "the First Lady of Las Vegas."

Vegas was created suddenly—a town where none had existed, built by the railroad company with a basic infrastructure (gravel streets, plank sidewalks, water service) for the lots it created by dividing up 110 acres. The lots were snapped up at auctions in 1905, the year the railroad was completed. Hotels, restaurants, a school and two churches all materialized.

The population was 800 when Vegas became incorporated in 1911. By the end of that year, the population had doubled, due to a repair shop for locomotives that created hundreds of new jobs. But the town's fortunes began to decline as automobiles reduced railroad traffic, which contributed to the closing of the maintenance shop. With jobs gone, population decreased, and Vegas almost became a ghost town.

WHAT MADE THE DESERT "BLOOM"?

Two events saved the city, both unfolding in 1931. The Nevada legislature legalized gambling. It didn't have a huge impact at first, but the long-term implications were enormous. (Legalized prostitution didn't hurt, either. Vegas's old red-light district saw plenty of action, including from military men during World War II, before it was shut down.) A second major development reaped immediate benefits for the city: Hoover Dam, a Depression Era venture that's still considered one of the "Seven Wonders of the Industrial World." In 1930, Congress appropriated the funds to build the dam, which would harness the Colorado River's power to provide more electricity, irrigate crops, control flooding and even provide recreation (via the newly formed Lake Mead).

Construction began in 1931 on the project (then also known as Boulder Dam). A consortium of six companies worked together at the site 30 miles southeast of Las Vegas (on the Arizona/Nevada border), using 6.5 million tons of concrete to build a dam 726 feet tall. Workers endured brutal desert temperatures—at one point reaching 130 degrees Fahrenheit. All told, 110 workers died during construction of Hoover Dam. A plaque in their honor reads: "They died to make the desert bloom."

When 20,000 people attended the 1935 dedication ceremony of the dam, overseen by President Roosevelt, Las Vegas got an immense boost in visibility. Word spread about this new gambling oasis in the desert. Tourism began in earnest, and in 1940, the city got another federal boost with the arrival of the Las Vegas Aerial Gunnery School. By 1945, the population had climbed to 17,000. The last act in the creation of the modern-day Sin City was about to begin.

WHEN DID LAS VEGAS BECOME A LAND OF LUXURY?

After a brief campaign in the early 1990s to position Las Vegas as a family-friendly resort town, the city is back to basics, focusing on its unique status as a luxury-minded playground for adults. Developer Steve Wynn, one of the richest men in the world, kick-started a whole new wave of luxury palaces with the $630 million Mirage in 1989. As a symbol of excess, it's hard to top the Bellagio, which cost $1.6 billion to open in 1998 (thanks in part to its artificial lake). It helps people feel like they're not vacationing in the middle of a desert. Add to that the lavish Wynn, Encore, Palazzo and Trump hotels, and the new sprawling CityCenter–which includes the Mandarin Oriental, Aria and Vdara–and you've got more upscale gaming and lodging centered along one road than any other place in the country.

If blackjack and craps aren't your thing, there's always one or two A-list musicians and comedians performing in town, not to mention the bizarre antics of Blue Man Group and the conceptual acrobatics of Cirque du Soleil, which both continue to draw huge audiences year after year. Meanwhile, fashion mavens seek out the latest from Cartier and Chanel, Louis Vuitton and Manolo Blahnik, Barneys New York and Jimmy Choo. In today's Vegas, designer boutiques open with the fanfare of high-profile films or rock tours, accordingly summoning celebrity stars from the film and music industries. In a city dedicated to instant gratification, shopping is theater.

Barely more than a century since the railroad first chugged into this quiet outpost, the utter transformation of Las Vegas from tiny homesteading settlement into luxe metropolis is complete. Though the place might make environmentalists cringe, it's hard not to admire the audacious moxie that turned this city into the most outrageous of American success stories.

WHAT DID THE RAT PACK BRING TO LAS VEGAS?

As the 1950s dawned, one-time teen idol Frank Sinatra was watching his career wane. He needed a boost, just as Las Vegas needed some big-name draws. When the crooner first played the Sands in October 1953, it turned out to be the start of something big: Both entities soon ascended full speed into the American pop-cultural stratosphere.

Sinatra reinvented himself as a serious actor (winning an Oscar in '54 for *From Here to Eternity*) and simultaneously recorded more mature albums under a new record contract. He quickly bought a share of the Sands and

HOW WAS LAS VEGAS TIED TO THE MOB?

Meyer Lansky once called Vegas "a dinky, horrible, little oasis town," but he soon bought into the dream of fellow mobster, Ben "Bugsy" Siegel: to build the greatest casino in the world in that unlikely place. They built the Flamingo on what would famously come to be known as the Strip. It didn't go according to plan: Siegel's original budget of $1.5 million ballooned to three times that, and the "grand" opening on December 26, 1946, was anything but. The casino and hotel lost money hand over fist. An unknown sniper snuffed Siegel in June 1947; the murder—one eyeball was shot right out of his skull—made headlines all over the nation.

Under new mafia management, the Flamingo turned a $4 million dollar profit within a year. The modern era of luxury casinos and resorts had launched, and the mob connections only seemed to add to the burgeoning town's mystique. Frank Sinatra and his Rat Pack only helped grow the town's glamorous aura, though Sinatra had to sell off his casino financial interests in 1963 after the Nevada Gaming Control Board decided that he was too chummy with the mob. By the end of the '60s, when Howard Hughes began snapping up casinos and a TV station, the image of Vegas as a mob-owned town started to shift. Today the influence of organized crime has either significantly waned or been completely eradicated, depending who you talk to.

lured his friends to perform there, too: Dean Martin, Sammy Davis, Jr., Joey Bishop, Peter Lawford—all popular entertainers. They were collectively dubbed "the Rat Pack." (Credit for the name is uncertain: Some say Lauren Bacall came up with it; others credit a gossip columnist who'd been snubbed from a "rat pack" party at Judy Garland's house.) As the pack formed, the famous Strip itself expanded, adding luxury resorts such as the Dunes, Stardust, Riviera and Tropicana.

The Strip became the "It" destination—and Rat Pack gigs the "It" events. Hollywood stars and the general public flocked to Las Vegas to hear the guys sing and ad-lib their way through their immensely popular shows. They made movies together, too, the most famous of which—*Ocean's Eleven*, a 1960 casino-heist meta-comedy—was filmed largely on location at the Sands and the Riviera in pre-dawn hours, after the hard-drinking stars finished their nightly gigs.

The Rat Pack's influence reached beyond showbiz. Sammy Davis, Jr.'s presence helped lead to equality for minorities in Las Vegas. The city had embraced Jim Crow policies, thanks in part to Bugsy Siegel's decision in the '40s to forbid African-Americans access to the Flamingo. Black performers could play the Strip, but they had to enter through stage doors and weren't permitted to sleep in those same hotels where they performed. A few entertainers with enough star clout, like Davis and Harry Belafonte, refused to tolerate such treatment. Davis broke a barrier in 1955 by performing for an integrated audience. His association with the Rat Pack only bolstered his bargaining power, helping to turn the tide of public opinion while local NAACP activists worked behind the scenes with city officials and mobsters. When segregation ended in Las Vegas in 1960, in true Rat Pack fashion, Martin and Davis got a good joke out of it: Martin carried Davis onstage in his arms and said, "Ladies and gentlemen, I want to thank the NAACP for this award."

WHEN DID BUILDING DEMOLITION BECOME A SPECTATOR SPORT?

Vegas has always been a peculiar place with a culture all its own. In the 1950s, after the government created a nuclear test site some 65 miles away, residents and tourists alike would dine atop tall buildings so they could watch mushroom clouds erupt across the Mojave Desert. (That pastime continued until 1963, when the tests went underground.) Today, the bizarre spectacle of choice is certainly more benign, yet some scientists still raise questions about its safety: watching big-name resorts get demolished.

Since 1993, when the Dunes Hotel came crashing down upon itself thanks to some professional dynamite deployment, a surprising number of buildings have toppled: Landmark, Sands, Hacienda, Aladdin, Desert Inn and the list goes on. The motivation is always the same: to make way for the bigger and better.

Controlled demolition companies have made quite a name for themselves in Las Vegas, perfecting the art of the implosion, where a series of planned explosive charges cause a building to crumple in upon itself. It took just 10 seconds in March 2007 to level the Stardust, a 32-story hotel casino that was the Strip's biggest when it was completed in 1958. Several months later, the New Frontier, a hotel-casino from 1942 that hosted Elvis Presley's Vegas debut, also collapsed under its own obsolesce.

Very few events go without fanfare in Las Vegas and demolition is no different. A property's new owners typically plan implosion-viewing parties for invited guests, and spectators gather on the street, eager to watch the spectacle. In an effort to keep crowds to a minimum, the demolitions are usually planned for the pre-dawn hours of the morning—yet, in something of a mixed message, they're sometimes accompanied by fireworks.

All that crashing debris naturally creates a huge dust cloud and a sudden, serious downturn in air quality in the immediate vicinity. If the winds quickly change, the cloud can head directly for the onlookers—which happened when the Stardust came down. Warnings from some scientists to entirely avoid the possibility of such respiratory irritation go unheeded by many. The lure of watching Vegas eat itself is just too tempting. And county officials say the bad air dissipates within several hours—another good reason to set off the explosions in the middle of the night. By morning, it's just another day on the Strip.

BELLAGIO BOTANICAL GARDENS

WHAT HAPPENS IN VEGAS

There's no place like it in the world. This city of half a million people, carved out of an unforgiving desert landscape and fueled by hedonism, may seem to exist purely for one purpose: entertainment. And while Vegas delivers diversions in abundance, it's also home to a thriving arts community, a solid college scene (thanks to the University of Nevada, Las Vegas) and a smattering of industry, from interior design to energy. Still, most people come to Las Vegas to let loose, whether that takes place at a casino or one of the city's many theaters, upscale restaurants, spas or luxury hotels. Here is a snapshot of Sin City.

WHAT ARE POPULAR CASINO GAMES?

While Las Vegas offers shows, food, shopping and luxury accommodations, there's no getting around the fact that it was built—and continues to thrive—on games of chance. And while the urban legend that casinos pipe in oxygen to keep gamblers energized has never been proven, many do pump in air fresheners in to help create positive vibes.

Casino table games include blackjack, baccarat, craps, roulette, pai gow tiles and poker—and not just one kind of poker. There's Pai Gow poker, Let It Ride poker, Three Card poker, Crazy 4 poker and, of course, the ubiquitous Texas Hold 'Em. Slot machines have a home in every casino—in case you missed the deafening ding emanating from each entrance. Then there are the sports and race books, where gamblers can bet on everything from boxing to cricket. Don't worry if you're unfamiliar with the ins and outs of craps or roulette; many casinos offer free table game lessons on weekday mornings—card counting not included.

HOW OVER-THE-TOP IS LAS VEGAS?

Saying everything is big in Las Vegas is an understatement; try ridiculously huge—and we're not only talking about size (although that counts, too). For instance, there's not just a Canyon Ranch SpaClub; there's the largest Canyon Ranch SpaClub in the world (at the Venetian). If the Wynn has a Ferrari dealership and a Manolo Blahnik store, then the Palazzo has to offer a Lamborghini dealership and a Jimmy Choo store. The Palms has a basketball half-court in one of its suites. And, of course, if it's not the pyramids (at the Luxor), then it's the Eiffel Tower (at Paris) or a roller coaster flying by the Statue of Liberty's outreached arm (at New York New York).

WHAT ELSE IS THERE TO DO BESIDES GAMBLING?

With all the money flowing in and around the casinos, it's no wonder that Las Vegas has figured out new and innovative ways for guests to spend any cash they collect. Spas, shopping and world-class entertainers tempt the money right out of your pocket. From full-day facials and body treatments to quick fixer-uppers before a night out to morning-after remedies, relaxation and rejuvenation have become big business in Vegas. Retail therapy is no different. Where else can you take a gondola ride through a tony Italian-inspired mall? Or visit Oscar de la Renta's first boutique fashion store in the U.S.? And the shows. Comedy, music and magic dominate the evening agenda—when you're not at the tables, that is.

If you had something more active in mind, why not take it outdoors? It's not everywhere that you can enjoy more than 300 sunny days a year.

WYNN GOLF COURSE

Las Vegas offers dozens of golf courses to keep even the most avid duffer occupied. Those looking for more of an adrenaline rush will find it behind the wheel in a NASCAR Winston Cup stock car at the Richard Petty Driving Experience at the Las Vegas Motor Speedway, or atop the Stratosphere Tower, where you can be catapulted straight into the air on the Big Shot ride.

IS THE FOOD REALLY THAT GOOD IN LAS VEGAS?

Las Vegas has become one of the top food cities in the country and now boasts more master sommeliers than any other city in America. Some of the famous chefs who have opened restaurants in Vegas include Joël Robuchon and Tom Colicchio at the MGM Grand, Kerry Simon at the Palms and Luxor, Alain Ducasse at THEhotel at Mandalay Bay, Thomas Keller at the Venetian, Michael Mina at the Bellagio, Daniel Boulud at Wynn, Charlie Palmer at the Four Seasons and Mandalay Bay, and Wolfgang Puck, who has restaurants at Caesars, Mandalay Bay, MGM Grand, the Venetian and,

SHOULD YOU PACK A SWIMSUIT?

The dry desert heat in Las Vegas takes some getting used to. So does the scene at the hotel pools. (Let's just say this isn't your neighborhood YMCA.) From the understated elegance of the Four Seasons pool, with its cooling Evian spritz delivered by courteous attendants, to the three-story water slide whisking you through a shark tank at the Golden Nugget, pools and pool parties in Las Vegas have become an art form. Hotels with bigger pool complexes often offer "adults-only" or "European-style" pools among their options. Cabanas at some of the higher-end hotels can run as much as $1,000 a day (with food and drink). If you decide to partake, you'll need to dress the part, so make sure you bring that swim suit and those designer shades—which you can pick up at the Shoppes at the Palazzo, naturally.

most recently, the Palazzo (Emeril Lagasse also has restaurants at the latter three). The new CityCenter corrals nearly 30 more restaurants into the already packed dining scene, backed by heavy hitters such as Pierre Gagnaire, Julian Serrano and Sirio Maccioni. The list goes on and on. Luckily, the 99-cent shrimp cocktail is still available at the Golden Gate Hotel & Casino downtown.

IS THERE ANYTHING NATURAL LEFT IN LAS VEGAS?

If you can see past the neon aura of the Strip, you'll notice that the city is a hub for natural wonders as well. Red Rock Canyon, which offers a number of scenic hikes through its 400-milion-year-old sea bed, is 25 minutes away from the Strip (and even closer to the resorts located in West Las Vegas). Hoover Dam and Lake Mead are east of the city, which means swimming, water skiing, scuba diving and fishing could be in the cards if you're up for the drive. Or make a day of it with a short trip to the Grand Canyon (Arizona), Death Valley (California) or Zion National Park (Utah). Anything is possible in Las Vegas—for a price.

BARNEYS NEW YORK

GONDOLA RIDES AT THE VENETIAN

SIGHTS BEYOND THE SLOTS

The first thing you'll see as your plane touches down at McCarran International Airport is a skyline that's an amalgam of international whimsy, from the Eiffel Tower to the Luxor pyramid to Excalibur castle and everything in between. This fantasyland prides itself on being the ultimate escape—and encourages visitors to interpret that in any way they'd like. The goal of each casino resort is simple: To keep visitors happy and satisfied for as long as humanly possible, 24 hours a day. That translates, in part, into the over-the-top free attractions for which Las Vegas is known, from the erupting volcano at the Mirage to the dazzling water show at Bellagio. As the casinos see it, the less you invest in sightseeing, the more money you'll have for gaming.

If it's your first trip to the city, you'll likely spend most of your time on Las Vegas Boulevard, also known as the Strip. Though Las Vegas' reputation is first and foremost based on gambling, in recent years shopping, dining, spa-ing and clubbing have been vying to oust blackjack as the primary diversion. The constant reinvention of Las Vegas is a way of keeping the visitors streaming in. In the mid 1990s, the city's marketing gurus briefly pushed Sin City as a family-friendly destination, but that quickly gave way to a return to the city's roots as a casino mecca, albeit a much more luxurious one with over-the-top dining, attractions and hotel rooms as the main diversions up and down the Strip.

Of course, not all entertainment is located on that four-mile stretch of boulevard. Las Vegas is also home to Red Rock Canyon National Conservation Area, which is the fifth most popular place in the United States for rock climbing. And there's the Atomic Testing Museum, which delves into Nevada's unique role in the Cold War.

Come to Las Vegas prepared to have the time of your life, but keep in mind that you're visiting the Mojave Desert. That means it's blazing hot in the summer months, as temperatures top 100 degrees Fahrenheit from June to September. If the weather gets to be too much, you can always stay—you guessed it—inside at the gaming tables.

THE STRIP

Few would consider the Strip a traditional neighborhood, but that's not to say that it doesn't have its own neighborhood charms. Paris' Left Bank district wouldn't be complete without the Eiffel Tower; Midtown Manhattan would see a lot fewer tourists without the Empire State Building; and Giza—well, it wouldn't be much without the Pyramids. The Strip offers all of these iconic mainstays and more in a single five-mile stretch. Nowhere else in the country do you have such eclectic opportunities to shop, dine and play. The Strip keeps reinventing itself, and while you can still find small boutiques hawking 2-for-$10 T-shirts and $9.99 all-you-can-eat buffets, today's version veers toward sophisticated fun at hotels like Encore and MGM's Skylofts.

THE ADVENTUREDOME
Circus Circus, 2880 Las Vegas Blvd. S., North Strip, 866-456-8894; www.adventuredome.com

The Adventuredome is the largest indoor amusement park in the United States. The operative word is, of course, "indoor"; it offers rides and respite from the desert's brutal summer heat. With 25 rides and attractions, there are options for kids of all ages and heights. Canyon Blaster, the world's only

WHAT ARE THE BEST FREE SHOWS ON THE STRIP?

Sirens of TI: The pyrotechnics alone will have you awed. The beautiful sirens, buff pirates and sinking ship are an added bonus.

Fountains of Bellagio: This larger-than-life aquatic display is quintessential Vegas. Perfectly choreographed to the music and against the backdrop of the desert night sky (and majestic Bellagio hotel), the fountains come alive.

The Volcano (The Mirage): More eruptive than ever, the newly revamped Volcano brings music and nature together in an explosion of fireballs and steaming lava.

indoor double-loop, double-corkscrew coaster, is one of the most popular thrill rides. Other options include Chaos, which whirls you into oblivion, and the Inverter, with its extreme G-force action. What the rides lack in white-knuckle-gripping terror, they make up for with variety and volume.
Admission: $4-$7 per ride. All-day passes adults $24.95, children 33"-47" tall $14.95. Summer: 10 a.m.-midnight; school year: Monday-Thursday 11 a.m.-6 p.m., Friday-Saturday 10 a.m.-midnight, Sunday 10 a.m.-9 p.m.

BELLAGIO CONSERVATORY & BOTANICAL GARDENS
Bellagio Las Vegas, 3600 Las Vegas Blvd. S., Center Strip, 888-987-6667; www.bellagio.com
Picture an organic art museum, where the displays are made of flowers, shrubs, plants and trees, and change with the seasons. The Bellagio Conservatory and Botanical Gardens does just that, and it's even more beautiful than it sounds. The 13,500-square-foot palatial setting, located across from the resort's lobby, is home to five alternating displays throughout the year, with themes that include the holidays, Chinese New Year, spring, summer and fall. Each season manages to outdo the last. In winter, you might find reindeers made of whole pecans, giant greeting cards comprising thousands of flowers and a 21-foot wreath built from pinecones. Come spring, a whole new world awaits with a live butterfly garden, leaping fountains and butterfly-shaped topiaries. On average, each display consists of 40 trees, 1,500 shrubs and 10,000 blooming plants. Considering that the hotel spends $8 million annually on the Conservatory, this free attraction is a jackpot all around.
Daily 24 hours. Closed for five weeks a year, as the displays are changed.

BODIES...THE EXHIBITION
Luxor, 3900 Las Vegas Blvd. S., South Strip, 800-288-1000; www.bodiestheexhibition.com
This show is something between art, science and just plain macabre. BODIES...The Exhibition is just what it sounds like: human cadavers displayed for all to see. The polymer-preserved bodies, each with its dermis removed, demonstrate everything from the muscular to the vascular systems of the body, so you can see just what you and your muscles look like from the inside when you're, say, playing baseball or throwing darts. Partial-body specimens show what a smoker's lung looks like compared to a healthy lung (try buying a pack of cigarettes after seeing that), and what kind of damage over-eating can do to your organs. The exhibition is educational, but it has raised some controversy since its inception because the bodies were acquired from the

THE EIFFEL TOWER EXPERIENCE

Chinese police (visit the website if you're curious).
Admission: adults $31, seniors $29, children 4-12 $23. Daily 10 a.m.-10 p.m.

BONANZA "THE WORLD'S LARGEST GIFT SHOP"
2440 Las Vegas Blvd. S., North Strip, 702-385-7359;
www.worldslargestgiftshop.com

The self-proclaimed "world's largest gift shop" has far more than the typical tourist knickknacks you'd expect. You'll find fuzzy dice (just begging for a rearview mirror to call their own) and miniature, lighted "Welcome to Fabulous Las Vegas" signs, but there's also an impressive array of bachelor and bachelorette gag gifts, and even a sombrero-wearing dog that sings "La Bamba" when activated. Located at the corner of Las Vegas Boulevard and Sahara Avenue, this 40,000-square-foot space is a Sin City staple even locals frequent. It's the go-to spot for anyone in need of a new nunzilla wind-up doll or "Polly the Insulting Parrot."
Daily 8 a.m.-midnight.

THE EIFFEL TOWER EXPERIENCE
Paris Las Vegas, 3655 Las Vegas Blvd. S., Center Strip, 877-603-4386;
www.parislasvegas.com

Las Vegas is a city obsessed with replication—and we're not talking carbon copies and model airplanes. Though the Eiffel Tower at Paris Las Vegas is half the size of the original at 460 feet, the view from the top is equally stunning. A dizzying windowed elevator ride takes guests up nearly 50 floors to the open-air observation deck, which allows for 360-degree views of Las Vegas. It's intimate up here, and gets packed with tourists on the weekends. If you can get to the border of the deck facing west, you're in for perhaps the best view of the Fountains of Bellagio water show in town. Avoid tripping over men down on one knee. This is a popular spot for marriage proposals.
Admission daily from 9:30 a.m.-7:15 p.m.: adults $10, seniors and children

JUBILEE! BACKSTAGE TOUR

$7, children under 5 free. Admission daily from 7:30 p.m.-12:30 a.m.: adults $15, seniors and children $10. Daily 9:30-12:30 a.m., weather permitting.

FOUNTAINS OF BELLAGIO
Bellagio Las Vegas, 3600 Las Vegas Blvd. S., Center Strip, 888-987-6667; www.bellagio.com

Romance is anything but watered down at Lake Bellagio, as water, music and light meld together in an aquatic ballet. The water echoes human motion seen in dance, swaying while spraying more than 460 feet into the air. The jets' moves are perfectly choreographed to music, with scores from Broadway, the classics and more. If you can't snag a prime place along the Lake Bellagio railing, head to Paris, located across the street from Bellagio, for an equally stellar view. Or book a veranda table inside the Bellagio at Olives restaurant, have a glass of wine (and some delicious freshly made pasta), and enjoy multiple shows throughout your meal. It's one of the most mesmerizing sights in Vegas and, since it's free, you're saving up blackjack dollars every time you watch.

Performances take place every 30 minutes Monday-Friday 3-8 p.m., Saturday-Sunday noon-8 p.m. After 8 p.m. daily, performances are every 15 minutes until midnight.

GONDOLA RIDES
The Venetian Resort Hotel Casino, 3355 Las Vegas Blvd. S., Center Strip, 877-883-6423; www.venetian.com

Who needs the murky waterways of Venice when you can take a gondola ride through the pristine, chlorinated canals of the Venetian Resort Hotel Casino? Choose the indoor canal or the outdoor one, and float in a gondola modeled after the real deal. Of course, rather than floating under historic bridges and sidewalk cafes, you'll be floating past stores like Banana Republic and Ann Taylor. Don't let that detract from the romantic lilt of your gondolier's serenades. The ride takes you through The Grand Canal Shoppes, which cover 500,000 feet of retail space and restaurants—not that you have much

buying power from the confines of your romantic vessel.
Admission: adults and children $16, children 2 and under free. Sunday-Thursday 10 a.m.-11 p.m., Friday-Saturday 10 a.m.-midnight.

IMPERIAL PALACE AUTO COLLECTION
Imperial Palace, 3535 Las Vegas Blvd. S., Center Strip, 702-794-3174;
www.autocollections.com
We all know money and nice cars go hand-in-hand. So it makes sense that Imperial Palace houses one of the largest collections of classic cars in the world. The Auto Collection includes more than $100 million in inventory, and over 250 cars of all varieties—muscle, classic, historic and more. From Johnny Carson's 1939 Chrysler Royal Sedan to the 1957 Jaguar XKSS valued at more than $7 million, the vintage variety is endless. Buy, sell or just stroll through the 125,000-square-foot showroom at your leisure. It's certainly something to keep in mind as you double down or go all in.
Admission: adults $8.95, seniors and children under 12 $5, children under 3 free. Daily 10 a.m.-6 p.m.

JUBILEE! BACKSTAGE TOUR
Bally's, 3645 Las Vegas Blvd. S., Center Strip, 800-237-7469;
www.harrahs.com
There's a lot more to being a showgirl than having a knockout body. It takes stamina, style and an incredibly strong neck to hoist up those headdresses. Peek into the showgirl's world with the *Donn Arden's Jubilee!* backstage tour. A showgirl leads you across the stage, around the set and through the costume room, sharing fun facts about the current production. Did you know that the heaviest headdress weighs 35 pounds? Or, that there is a minimum of nine costume changes for each person throughout the show, and that five different kinds of feathers are used? As more and more traditional showgirl-themed shows are replaced by Cirque du Soleil and other large-scale productions, this is your chance to check out a Vegas icon, before it hits the road for good.
Admission: adults and children over 13 $15. Monday, Wednesday and Saturday 11 a.m.

LAKE OF DREAMS
Wynn Las Vegas, 3131 Las Vegas Blvd. S., Center Strip, 877-321-9966;
www.wynnlasvegas.com
No multi-star hotel on Las Vegas Boulevard is worth its weight without a manmade lake, and the one at Wynn is particularly special. Surrounded by a 120-foot-tall artificial mountain that shields it from Las Vegas Boulevard, the Lake of Dreams breathes an air of exclusivity, just like the rest of Wynn resort. But the lake's true purpose is to wow onlookers throughout the evening, as it plays host to a variety of surreal shows: statues of men and women arise from the water, light and music spring to life, and there's even a giant

FOUNTAINS AT THE BELLAGIO

WHAT'S THE BEST WAY TO SEE LAS VEGAS IN ONE DAY?

The Strip, a.k.a. Las Vegas Boulevard, is the engine that keeps Las Vegas chugging along, and it's a requisite if you have limited time in town. The four-mile street takes you around the world in a matter of hours. See a miniaturized version of New York City, catch views from Paris' most recognized landmark, and travel gondolier-style through the Italian renaissance.

Regardless of where you're staying, it's easiest to begin at one end of the Strip and make your way from there. Cabs are nearly as common as slot machines on Las Vegas Boulevard, so you'll have no trouble finding one (though you may have to go to a hotel entrance to get one to stop). For a cheaper option—albeit pricey as public transportation goes—the high-tech (driverless) monorail can get you through the Strip in less than 15 minutes.

Start at **Mandalay Bay Resort and Casino** and head north, taking the indoor walkway to **Luxor**. While you're there, enjoy a morning poker lesson before hopping on the monorail to **Excalibur**, which puts you Strip-central in no time. From here, pick and choose the casinos that appeal to you. High stakes gamblers will enjoy the enormous and extravagant mega-resorts such as **The Venetian Resort Hotel Casino**, **Caesars Palace** and **Wynn Las Vegas** (and the perks that accompany such invited guests). Whereas the smaller casinos, like **O'Sheas** *(3555 Las Vegas Blvd. S., South Strip, 702-697-2711; www.osheaslasvegas.com)* and **Slots-A-Fun** *(2890 Las Vegas Blvd. S., South Strip, 702-734-0410)* tend to have better payouts and lower minimums. Once you've gotten your gambling fix—and unfortunately come to understand that the house always wins—it's time for some exceptional people gawking. Where else can you watch showgirls mingle with card sharks, and bachelorettes dance the night away in little more than lingerie? For a bit of aromatic pleasure, meander through the **Conservatory and Botanical Gardens at Bellagio** or entice your inner child as you browse the perfectly polished **Ferrari-Maserati** collection at **Wynn Las Vegas**. Depending on what you're in the mood for, there are, of course, a slew of big-name restaurants to choose from for dinner. Cap off your Vegas day with a **Cirque du Soleil** show; with so many to choose from, you're unlikely to go wrong, but our vote goes to **O** at **Bellagio Las Vegas**. If you've got anything left by midnight, the tables are always open.

LION HABITAT

inflatable frog whose mouth moves in sync with Louis Armstrong's *What a Wonderful World*. For the best view of the show, make a reservation on the patio at SW Steakhouse or Daniel Boulud Brasserie, since everyone knows inflatable frogs are best seen on a full stomach, following a bottle of wine. The free shows begin after dark and occur approximately every half hour. *Daily 7 p.m.-12:30 a.m., times vary seasonally.*

LION HABITAT
MGM Grand Hotel & Casino, 3799 Las Vegas Blvd. S., South Strip, 877-880-0880; www.mgmgrand.com
Superstitious folks may choose to toss their chips at MGM Grand, and it's not because the dealers are better or the drinks are more potent. It's because of the lions. An Asian good-luck symbol, lions have made a home at MGM Grand for years, frolicking in their own expansive habitat, just a few feet from the slots. The multi-level dwelling hosts a handful of lions, and even a translucent tunnel that makes you feel as though you're in with the beasts. Before your inner animal advocate gets upset, know that the lions only spend "shifts" in the habitat. When they're not here, lying amid the waterfalls and foliage, they live on an 8.5-acre ranch nearby. Because they're in the habitat for such a limited time, trainers engage them in play or feed them, keeping them on their paws.
Daily 11 a.m.-7 p.m.

THE MIDWAY AT CIRCUS CIRCUS
Circus Circus, 2880 Las Vegas Blvd. S., North Strip, 800-634-3450; www.circuscircus.com
Located across the casino from the Adventuredome, the Midway and Arcade has games for kids, ranging from ski ball to frog toss and more. Clowns, jugglers, acrobats, trapeze artists and other performers put on impressive shows (considering they're free) on a stage by the Midway. If your head isn't spinning yet from the carnival games, hop into the Horse-A-Round bar. The revolving carousel-of-a-bar enamored Hunter S. Thompson

POOL AT THE GOLDEN NUGGET LAS VEGAS

WHAT'S THE BEST WAY TO SEE LAS VEGAS IN THREE DAYS?

Once you've taken in the internationally inspired architectural creations of the Strip (as warped as they may seem), it's time to learn how it all came to be. Rent a car and head out to **Hoover Dam**, a structure responsible for supplying several states with water. The Hoover Dam actually has more masonry mass than the Egyptian pyramids. Plus, the views are spectacular. It's built into a canyon and traps the water from the Colorado River, converting much of it to electricity. Take the Dam Tour, and enter the belly of the beast, 500 feet below ground, where you'll learn about the history and impact of this engineering marvel. Following the tour, take a drive around **Lake Mead**, which is a natural side effect of the dam. It's not an ideal place for lounging (the shores are rocky at best) but it offers some great hiking trails. We recommend the Historic Railroad Trail, which leads you on an old train route through five tunnels, with excellent lake views. Las Vegas is more outdoorsy than you'd think, and it's worth prying yourself away from the blackjack tables to see why.

You've walked the Strip and fed your curiosity at Hoover Dam. Now it's time to head Downtown. Just a short cab ride from the north end of the Strip, the downtown area shows you where it all began. Give a little back to the Las Vegas economy and try a few hands of $5 blackjack at the **Golden Nugget Las Vegas**—every time you gamble here your money goes, in part, toward helping local schools. Admire the light shows that play on the Fremont Street Experience canopy before stopping into the **Golden Gate Casino** *(1 Fremont St., Downtown, 702-385-1906, 800-426-1906; www. goldengatecasino.com)* for its famous 99-cent shrimp cocktail (famous for the price, and tastes pretty good considering). Wash it all down at **The Griffin** *(511 Fremont St., Downtown, 702-382-0577)*, a bar on east Fremont Street with an oddly alluring dungeon feel and a fabulous jukebox. Make your way back to your hotel in time for the sunrise—and grab yourself an Irish coffee before starting the cycle all over again. You'll have time to sleep when you go home.

PENSKE-WYNN FERRARI/MASERATI LAS VEGAS

in *Fear and Loathing in Las Vegas*, and judging from its surreal Midway backdrop, it's easy to see why. While Horse-A-Round keeps your body moving physically, the amount of mental spinning is up to you.
Daily 11 a.m.-midnight.

PENSKE-WYNN FERRARI/MASERATI LAS VEGAS
Wynn Las Vegas, 3131 Las Vegas Blvd. S., Center Strip, 702-770-2000; www.penskewynn.com
Before you go all in with your latest jackpot, swing by Wynn to consider taking home a Ferrari from the only factory-authorized dealership in Nevada. It's actually a wise investment—these are some of the few cars that actually increase in value. That is, if you're patient enough to weather the three- to five-year waiting list. There's a $10 fee to enter and nab a look at the vehicles, which can cost more than $400,000 each. The 10,000 square-foot showroom carries an average of 35 new and used luxury vehicles. And for those who can't afford the wheels, there are plenty of auto-branded trinkets to bring home.
Admission: $10. Monday-Saturday 9 a.m.-6 p.m.

THE ROLLER COASTER
New York-New York, 3790 Las Vegas Blvd. S., South Strip, 800-689-1797; www.nynyhotelcasino.com
If you're going to ride one coaster in Las Vegas, it should be the roller coaster at New York-New York. Zip through the faux New York skyline, past

---

WHAT IS THE MOST EUROPEAN ATTRACTION IN LAS VEGAS?
Gondola Rides (The Venetian Resort Hotel Casino): Choose the indoor canal or the outdoor one, and float in a gondola modeled after the real deal.

IS THERE SUCH A THING AS FAMILY-FRIENDLY IN LAS VEGAS?

We know what you're thinking: Casinos, pricey hotel rooms and "European" pools don't exactly scream kid-friendly holiday. But Las Vegas has something for everyone, and that includes the four-feet and under set.

❶ Start your day at the north end of the Strip at **Stratosphere**. With three depth-defying rides to pick from (Insanity, the Ride, which involves a mechanical arm extending over the edge of the Stratosphere tower and spinning at a force of three Gs, is our personal favorite), the kids will have plenty to get them revved up. For those less inclined to hang 1,000 feet above the cement, visit the observation deck instead. As the tallest free-standing observation tower in the U.S., it offers quite a view of the Strip.

❷ Afterward, stroll south on the Strip for a block until you arrive at **Circus Circus**. If the kids haven't had enough of the thrill rides, they're sure to be sated by **The Adventuredome**. America's largest indoor theme park, including the world's only indoor double-loop roller coaster, lets you escape the desert heat while the kids enjoy the rides. Circus Circus also offers free circus performances daily, and kids are invited onstage to learn a trick or two of their own.

❸ Before they run off and join the circus, snatch up the family and head south to **the Mirage**. Though you may have to pass through the dinging casino, it's worth it to catch a glimpse of the enormous, 20,000-gallon saltwater aquarium behind the front desk in the lobby. Then make your way outside to Siegfried & Roy's **Secret Garden and Dolphin Habitat** to get face-to-face with lions, white tigers, leopards and bottlenose dolphins. Trainers are on hand to answer questions and show off their new litter of white tiger cubs.

❹ By now, you and your entourage have undoubtedly worked up an appetite. **Spago** at **The Forum Shops at Caesars** (right next door to the Mirage) is a good bet for the whole family. It's not the least expensive option, but the food is exceptional and the family-friendly atmosphere means the eye-rolls when a drink spills or a fork is dropped will be at a minimum. Spago has a children's menu with all the favorites including grilled cheese and chicken fingers; meanwhile, you can nosh on crisp calamari and lamb chorizo pizza with goat cheese.

❺ Cross Las Vegas Boulevard and enter **Harrah's Las Vegas** in time for the **Mac King Comedy Show** *(702-369-5222; www.harrahslasvegas.com)*. As one of the only daytime magic shows in Las Vegas, Mac King's routine provides the perfect mid-afternoon respite. Quirky jokes and visual tricks are Mac King's specialty, though his ridiculous plaid suits run a close second.

❻ After the show, saunter back across the Strip to **Bellagio Las Vegas**. You can head inside if you'd like, but the real action is right in front of you—on Lake Bellagio. The **Fountains of Bellagio** sprout into gravity-defying action with choreographed aquatic numbers set to music against the backdrop of one of Las Vegas's most picturesque hotels. The kids will be amazed by the sheer power of the fountains, which at times shoot upwards of 460 feet.

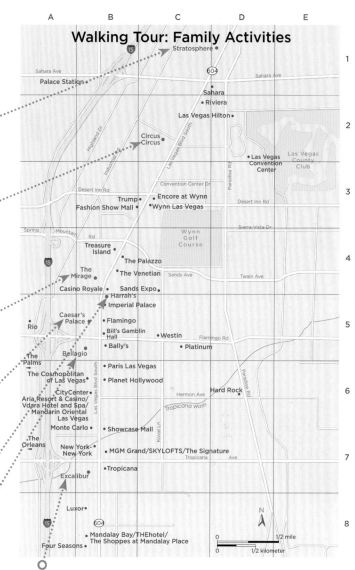

Walking Tour: Family Activities

A B C D E

Stratosphere

Sahara Ave

Palace Station

604 Sahara Ave

Sahara

Riviera

Las Vegas Hilton

Highland Dr

Industrial Rd

Circus Circus

Las Vegas Blvd South

Paradise Rd

Las Vegas Convention Center

Las Vegas County Club

Convention Center Dr

Desert Inn Rd

Trump

Encore at Wynn

Desert Inn Rd

Fashion Show Mall

Wynn Las Vegas

Spring Mountain Rd

Sierra Vista Dr

Treasure Island

Wynn Golf Course

15

The Palazzo

The Mirage

The Venetian

Sands Ave

Twain Ave

Casino Royale

Sands Expo

Harrah's

Imperial Palace

Caesar's Palace

Flamingo

Rio

Bill's Gamblin Hall

Westin

Flamingo Rd

The Palms

Bellagio

Bally's

Platinum

Las Vegas Blvd South

The Cosmopolitan of Las Vegas

Paris Las Vegas

Planet Hollywood

CityCenter

Harmon Ave

Hard Rock

Paradise Rd

Aria Resort & Casino/ Vdara Hotel and Spa/ Mandarin Oriental Las Vegas

Tropicana Wash

The Orleans

Monte Carlo

Showcase Mall

Koval Ln

New York-New York

MGM Grand/SKYLOFTS/The Signature

Tropicana Ave

Excalibur

Tropicana

Luxor

604

N

Mandalay Bay/THEhotel/ The Shoppes at Mandalay Place

Four Seasons

0   1/2 mile
0   1/2 kilometer

❼ Finish the day at the south end of the Strip with a fantastical trip to **Excalibur** *(3850 Las Vegas Blvd. S., South Strip, 702-597-7777; www. excalibur.com)*. This fairytale hotel casino, replete with a moat, drawbridge and gleaming white turrets, is pure fantasy. It doesn't get more family-friendly than the Tournament of Kings.

THE SHARK REEF AQUARIUM

the Statue of Liberty, while admiring the view of Las Vegas Boulevard from 200 feet up. With barrel rolls, a loop and multiple heart-wrenching drops at speeds nearing 70 miles per hour, this coaster is good old nail-biting fun. For those who are afraid of heights (and speed), New York-New York's Coney Island Emporium allows you to keep your feet on the ground and still relish in the flavor of the Big Apple with 12,000 square feet of games and carnival-style entertainment.

Admission: $14. Sunday-Thursday 11 a.m.-11 p.m., Friday-Saturday 10:30 a.m.-midnight; Coney Island Emporium: Sunday-Thursday 8 a.m.-midnight, Friday-Saturday 8 a.m.-2 a.m.

SECRET GARDEN AND DOLPHIN HABITAT
The Mirage, 3400 Las Vegas Blvd. S., Center Strip, 800-374-9000; www.miragehabitat.com

The cats here hold magical secrets behind their eerie blue eyes—literally. These are the white tigers that once performed in Siegfried and Roy's magic show, prior to the incident in which their brother, Montecore, nearly killed magician and trainer Roy Horn in 2003. Though they're no longer disappearing and reappearing on stage, the cats lead a pretty luxurious life, surrounded by exotic plants and waterfalls and other felines, such as snow leopards, lions, golden tigers and black panthers. Following the cats, make your way over to the nearby Dolphin Habitat. It's home to six Atlantic bottlenose dolphins, whom you'll spot leaping, "walking" on water, swimming and doing whatever it is that dolphins do. Because it's primarily a research facility, the Dolphin Habitat doesn't host regular "shows," but the trainers interact with the creatures throughout the day for the public to see. To get even more up-close, inquire about the Trainer for a Day program. Visitors can suit up and rub dorsal fins with some of the earth's smartest creatures.

Admission: adults $15, children 4-12 $10, children 3 and under free. Monday-Friday 11 a.m.-6:30 p.m., Saturday-Sunday 10 a.m.-6:30 p.m.

SHARK REEF AQUARIUM

Mandalay Bay, 3950 Las Vegas Blvd. S., South Strip, 877-632-7800; www.sharkreef.com

Pardon the pun, but this attraction carries a serious bite. Mandalay Bay's stunning aquarium holds more than 2,000 animals, including a variety of sharks, giant sting rays, piranha, golden crocodiles and its newest addition, an 87-pound, 7-foot-long Komodo dragon. With 1.6 million gallons of water, the cool, cavernous shark reef is a quiet yet thrilling escape from the buzzing of the slots. Be sure to swing by the sting ray petting pool before settling in for an underwater aquatic ballet, as floor-to-ceiling glass walls show sea turtles, sharks and a variety of fish frolicking about in their impressive Vegas digs. Part of the floor is glass, too, allowing an eerie view of the sharks as they swim below.

Admission: adults $16.95, children under 12 $10.95, children 4 and under free. Sunday-Thursday 10 a.m.-8 p.m., Friday-Saturday 10 a.m.-10 p.m.

SHOWCASE MALL

3785 Las Vegas Blvd. S., Center Strip

The words "Showcase Mall" should be code for sugar kingdom. Kids love the place as it boasts a slew of family-friendly activities. (There are a few shops, too, but "Mall" is a bit of an exaggeration.) At M&M's World *(702-736-7611)* you'll find every color of M&M imaginable—purple, gray, black, pink, turquoise. Head to World of Coca-Cola *(702-270-5952)* for a refreshing fizzy drink made by an old-fashioned soda jerk as you browse the Coca-Cola memorabilia. Once the kids are fully buzzed on sugar, head upstairs to GameWorks *(702-432-4263)* and let them play video games to their hearts' content. When they start crashing, the United Artists movie theater *(702-225-4828)* provides the perfect respite (and relief from the desert sun thanks to constantly cranked air conditioning).

Store hours vary. M&M's World: Sunday-Thursday 9 a.m.-11 p.m., Friday-Saturday 9 a.m.-midnight. World of Coca-Cola: Daily 10 a.m.-11 p.m. GameWorks: Sunday-Thursday 10 a.m.-midnight, Friday-Saturday 10 a.m.-1 a.m.

SIRENS OF TI

Treasure Island, 3300 Las Vegas Blvd. South, Center Strip, 702-894-7111, 800-288-7206; www.treasureisland.com

Stand your ground early for the Sirens of TI show, because it fills up quickly. This battle between buff young pirates and barely clad sirens takes place in the lake in front of TI (formerly called Treasure Island, and once with a family-friendly pirate show), on Las Vegas Boulevard. There are powerful pyrotechnics, amazing acrobatics and nearly 12 minutes of dialogue. Back in the days of Odysseus, Sirens were best seen, not heard, and that adage

TITANIC: THE ARTIFACT EXHIBITION

hasn't changed, but the visual charade is entertaining nevertheless. Spoiler alert: The sinking of the ship at the end of the melee makes it worth the wait (and maybe even the banter).
Daily 7 p.m., 8:30 p.m. and 10 p.m.

STRATOSPHERE RIDES
The Stratosphere, 2000 Las Vegas Blvd. S., North Strip, 800-998-6937; www.stratospherehotel.com
The screams carry for miles from the top of the Stratosphere, as riders dangle, shoot and blast over Las Vegas Boulevard, nearly 900 feet up. The Big Shot propels passengers up at 45 miles per hour, losing their stomachs and then catching them as they fall back down. X-Scream is like a giant teeter-totter that shoots passengers off the edge of the Stratosphere. And Insanity, the Ride is a giant arm that twirls riders off the edge of the tower, spinning at three Gs. For those who are less inclined to heighten their heart rates, an enclosed 109th-floor observation deck gives a tremendous view of the Las Vegas Valley—and the horrified faces of riders as they're hurled over the edge.
Tower tickets: adults $15.95, seniors and hotel guests $12, children $10. Rides are $12-$13. Tower/ride packages are available. Sunday-Thursday 10-1 a.m., Friday-Saturday and holidays 10-2 a.m.

TITANIC: THE ARTIFACT EXHIBITION
Luxor, 3900 Las Vegas Blvd. S., South Strip, 800-288-1000; www.titanictix.com
This exhibit gives colorful insight into the 1912 tragedy, boasting an extensive collection of artifacts discovered two and a half miles under the sea, including snippets from the last night's dinner menu, luggage, floor tiles and other items salvaged from "the ship of dreams." The 25,000-square-foot exhibit even features a piece of the Titanic's hull and a full-scale replica of the grand staircase. We know the photo op will be tempting, but just try

and keep your inner Leonardo DiCaprio to yourself.
Admission: adults $27, seniors $25, children 4-12 $20, children 3 and under free. Daily 10 a.m.-10 p.m.

THE VOLCANO
The Mirage, 3400 Las Vegas Blvd. S., Center Strip, 800-374-9000; www.mirage.com
For nearly two decades, The Volcano at the Mirage burbled and spewed its innards onto the surrounding lake thanks to some fancy lighting and special effects. It went dormant in February 2007, but after a complete renovation by WET Design, the company responsible for creating the Fountains of Bellagio, the Volcano is erupting yet again, this time with music to match. Thanks to the combined efforts of Grateful Dead drummer Mickey Hart and Indian tabla virtuoso Zakir Hussain, the new Volcano impresses Strip passersby with an exclusive soundtrack to match the erupting rhythms, soaring fireballs and fiery lava.
Daily 7 p.m., 8 p.m., 9 p.m., 10 p.m. and 11 p.m.

OFF-STRIP

The illustrious Strip has grown crowded in recent years, even with the star-studded demolitions, forcing developers to look beyond Las Vegas Boulevard. Big-name hotels like Hard Rock Hotel and Casino, Trump International Hotel Las Vegas and Palms Casino Resort have drawn visitors off the Strip and expanded the tourist center of Las Vegas. So if you're looking to avoid the crowds or go off the beaten path without traveling too far, try some of these off-Strip destinations.

THE ATOMIC TESTING MUSEUM
755 E. Flamingo Road, Off-Strip, 702-794-5161;
www.atomictestingmuseum.org
Few states have as explosive a history as Nevada does. The Atomic Testing Museum, in association with the Smithsonian Institute, educates you about the Nevada Test Site, which is a piece of land the size of Rhode Island that witnessed the bulk of American nuclear tests from 1951 to 1992, only 65 miles from Las Vegas. Get a better understanding of the nuclear world through simulations, artifacts, films and a glimpse into what it was like to work at the test site, as told by the former employees. Be sure to stop by the gift shop to see the assortment of nuclear-themed gifts—including an Albert Einstein action figure.
Admission: adults $12, seniors, military, students, Nevada residents and youth 7-17 $9, children 6 and under free. Monday-Saturday 10 a.m.-5 p.m., Sunday noon-5 p.m.

THE ROLLER COASTER

PINBALL HALL OF FAME
1610 E. Tropicana Ave., Off-Strip; www.pinballmuseum.org

Sin City's "most unique" museum award goes to the Pinball Hall of Fame, a 10,000-square-foot warehouse packed with loads of bleeping, beeping, pinging interaction. The museum holds the world's largest collection of pinball machines dating as far back as the 1950s. Test your reflexes on machines from the Bride of Pinbot to The Family Guy—some even have antique wood rails. Most games only cost a quarter or two, and all proceeds are donated to the Salvation Army. The more you play, the more pinball pays—as if you needed a reason to go another round.

Sunday-Thursday 11 a.m.-11 p.m., Friday-Saturday 11 a.m.-midnight.

SPRINGS PRESERVE
333 S. Valley View Blvd., Off-Strip, 702-822-7700;
www.springspreserve.org

The Mojave Desert isn't all browns and grays. At the Springs Preserve, it's actually green—in more ways than one. This 180-acre historic preservation project is located just a couple of miles from the Strip, and embraces the concept of sustainability—a positive step in a city known for its frequent building implosions. Without these historic springs, Las Vegas wouldn't be what it is today. Originally, this central spot in the valley was the water source for residents and travelers. The springs dried up in 1962, but the Las Vegas Valley Water District has re-created them. The $250 million project

---

WHAT ARE THE BEST SPOTS FOR OUTDOOR RECREATION?

Red Rock Canyon*:* Hiking, biking, horseback riding and rock climbing are at your fingertips in this desert playland.

Springs Preserve: Come to see the value of water in the desert at this eco-friendly oasis. Stay for a bite at Wolfgang Puck's restaurant; it's delicious.

hosts a variety of LEED-certified buildings that includes museums, galleries and interactive displays such as a flash flood, an actual fossil digging area, animal exhibits and more. With eight acres of gardens, miles of walking paths, a play area for kids, an amphitheater and even a Wolfgang Puck restaurant (and you thought all the good grub was on the Strip), the Springs Preserve celebrates the history and culture of Southern Nevada, while also keeping its sights on the future.

Special exhibits: adults $18.95, student and seniors $17.05, children $10.95, children under 5 free. Daily 10 a.m.-6 p.m.

VEGAS INDOOR SKYDIVING
200 Convention Center Drive, Off-Strip, 877-545-8093;
www.vegasindoorskydiving.com

This indoor simulation skydiving gig is not for the faint of heart. First, you watch a video and sign a lengthy disclaimer. Then you step into a one-piece jumpsuit, put on your flight goggles and enter the chamber. Once inside an instructor works with you as you lie, facedown, on what feels like metal fencing. Then they start the DC-3 propeller, and it makes enough wind (up to 120 mph) for you to float. So if the thought of jumping from an airplane is too terrifying to stomach, you can still experience the (simulated) thrill of freefall at this unique attraction.

First flight $75, second flight on same day $40. Minimum weight to fly is 40 pounds. Daily 9:45 a.m.-8 p.m.

DOWNTOWN

The area that once represented the heart of Las Vegas is now often regarded as an afterthought. When visitors come to Sin City in search of the authentic "Vegas Experience," Downtown is rarely on the docket. Only 10 to 15 minutes from the Strip, this local neighborhood trades luxury hotels for a more vintage vibe (and more affordable gambling options). Nevertheless, the powers that be are still trying to turn Downtown into a first-string destination for cash-carrying tourists. The Fremont Street Experience leads the way with a canopy made of millions of LED lights and a themed light show to match. Many independent bars dot the area, including The Beauty Bar and Hogs & Heifers. All in all, Downtown offers casinos with lower minimums, more casual dining options and one of the largest gold nuggets in the world, weighing in at 61 pounds.

FREMONT STREET EXPERIENCE
425 Fremont St., Downtown, 702-678-5777;
www.vegasexperience.com

The Fremont Street Experience light canopy typifies vintage Las Vegas. Located downtown, the production spans five football fields and a whole host of historic casinos and neon signs. Despite the live music and street-fair atmosphere on the ground, the real action is in the sky. Six times nightly, the canopy springs into a vibrant show, as 12 million lights draw all eyes up. Music ranging from classic rock to classic Vegas blasts from surrounding speakers, and is choreographed to match the illumination. One of the best spots to watch is at Gold Diggers, the second-story nightclub at the Golden Nugget. Their patio is directly under the canopy, affording great views of the show, and the tourists swigging beer from football-shaped containers.

Show hours vary. See website for details.

THE NEON MUSEUM
509 E. McWilliams Ave., Downtown, 702-387-6366;
www.neonmuseum.org

It's referred to as the Boneyard for a reason. The Neon Museum holds the vestiges of vintage Vegas. This is where the history comes to rest—that which avoided implosion, that is. The signs and architecture date back to the 1940s, and include relics such as The Golden Nugget sign. The most recent addition is La Concha, a shell-shaped building designed by Paul Revere Williams that was saved from demolition and painstakingly moved here. While restoration of the historic mid-century modern building continues, tours of the museum are by appointment only and must be made at least one day in advance.

Admission: $15 minimum donation. Tours: by appointment.

THE TANK
The Golden Nugget, 129 E. Fremont St., Downtown, 800-634-3454;
www.goldennugget.com

This should be as close as you'll ever come to swimming with the fishes. The $30 million tank at the Golden Nugget is a 200,000-gallon aquarium full of sharks, sting rays and fish—and a three-story, translucent waterslide goes right through the center of it. The Tank is located smack-dab in the middle of the hotel's swimming pool, so even non-sliders can go head-to-head with the sharks, swimming loops around the Tank and making faces at the toothsome fin-flappers. Those who get their fill of sharks from Discovery Channel's *Shark Week* can lounge in the partially submerged chaises that line the pool.

Admission: adults $20, children under 11 $15, children under 2 free. Hotel guests free. Daily 10 a.m.-8 p.m.

SUBURBS

Though they lie little more than 20 minutes from the Strip and Downtown, the Las Vegas suburbs are literally a world away. You won't find any grand canals or Eiffel Tower replicas here. Instead, it's all well-planned communities with cobblestone streets, dog-friendly parks and that good old-fashioned Pleasantville feel. Summerlin sits to the north of the Strip and draws locals for its famed shopping on Charleston Boulevard. You'll come up short if you're on the hunt for a Maserati dealership or Barneys outlet, but those in need of a new swimsuit or a chaffing dish are in luck. Red Rock Canyon is in Summerlin, supplying the neighborhood with a myriad of hiking and biking trails and other outdoor activities.

To the south, the district of Henderson is a friendly neighborhood that appears as if it were plucked straight out of old Americana, with the quaint shopping and dining options to match. Lake Las Vegas draws more

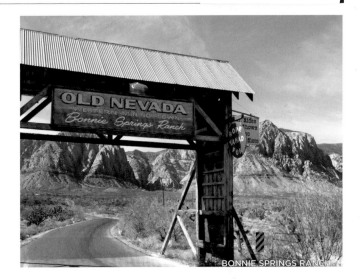
BONNIE SPRINGS RANCH

tourists than its suburban counterparts due to the plethora of luxury resorts, including the Green Valley Ranch Resort, Spa and Casino, which has opened alongside the 320-acre man-made lake. If you're craving a relaxing getaway or an escape from the crowds on the Strip, Lake Las Vegas may be just the place for you.

BONNIE SPRINGS OLD NEVADA
1 Gunfighter Lane, Blue Diamond, 702-875-4191;
www.bonniesprings.com
Gunfights break out in the streets and public hangings are common in Bonnie Springs, a replica of an 1880s mining town, where the spirit of the Old West is still kicking. Located just outside of Red Rock Canyon, about 25 miles from Las Vegas, this 115-acre ranch is a wild spot for the family, with a petting zoo, miniature train, stage coaches and even a cemetery. Wander the shops, check out the shows and enjoy a "Bonnie burger" at the restaurant or a beer at the saloon. The circular fire pit is the perfect spot for a mug of hot chocolate in the wintertime—it does occasionally get cold in the desert.
Admission: $20 per car (up to six people). Summer: Wednesday-Sunday 10:30 a.m.-6 p.m. Winter: Wednesday-Friday 11 a.m.-5 p.m., Saturday-Sunday 10:30-5 p.m.

RED ROCK CANYON NATIONAL CONSERVATION AREA
SR 159, 702-515-5350, Summerlin; www.redrockcanyonlv.org
Grab that karabiner and head to Red Rock Canyon National Conservation Area. Located just 17 miles from the Las Vegas Strip, Red Rock Canyon is a popular spot for rock climbing, but it's also a naturalist's heaven with nearly 200,000 acres, and miles and miles of hiking and biking trails complemented by waterfalls, springs, wild burros, creosote bushes, pinion pine trees and more. The canyon is one of the world's largest wind-deposited formations, and is part of the Navajo Formation, created nearly 200 million years ago. A 13-mile paved scenic road circles through Red Rock, with

stops and lookout points marked along the way, so even the car-dependent can feel at one with nature.

Admission: $7 per car, $3 per motorcycle. Park: Daily 6 a.m.-7 p.m. Hours vary seasonally; call for details. Visitor center: Daily 8 a.m.-4:30 p.m.

WYNN ESPLANADE

DESIGNERS IN THE DESERT

Upscale shopping has found a niche in Las Vegas, and it's all within walking distance of the Strip. Deluxe, marble-floored shopping complexes filled with high-end retailers have become as common along the Strip as the sounds of slot machines and the flash of neon lights. The haute spots here can be compared to those found in Paris, London or New York, with wares ranging from simple to unbelievable. Pick up a trinket from Tiffany & Co. or set your sights on the rare cars at the Ferrari-Maserati dealership inside Wynn Las Vegas. If you can dream it, you can probably purchase it in Las Vegas.

THE STRIP

BELLAGIO LAS VEGAS
Bellagio Las Vegas, 3600 Las Vegas Blvd. S., Center Strip, 702-693-7111; www.bellagiolasvegas.com
Overlooking the Bellagio lake where the famed fountain show blasts off throughout the day, Via Bellagio offers a wide selection of luxury shopping options. When you seek out the roster here—Bottega Veneta, Christian Dior, Prada, Giorgio Armani, Gucci, Tiffany & Co., Yves Saint Laurent, Chanel and Fendi—you can pretty much guarantee that dropping your winnings won't be hard to do. After browsing the shops of Via Bellagio, head to the Via Fiore shops outlining the Conservatory and Botanical Gardens. For luminous artwork, Chihuly offers paintings and original glass blown by artist Dale Chihuly, who created the glass chandelier in the hotel's lobby. Or put a bit of beauty in your yard with a decorative gift from the Giardini Garden Store. If you can't resist some hotel gear, visit Essentials, which sells Bellagio-themed clothing, accessories and gifts. Not only can you pick up the typical tourist T-shirt, but there are hand towels and other household items to remember your travels.
Daily 10 a.m.-midnight. Essentials is open 24 hours a day, daily.

CRYSTALS RETAIL AND ENTERTAINMENT
3720 Las Vegas Blvd., S., Center Strip, 866-754-2489; www.crystalsatcitycenter.com
The gorgeous Crystals shopping center—designed to look like an outdoor park—within CityCenter is devoted to high-end retailers including Louis Vuitton, Roberto Cavalli, Lanvin, Cartier and Prada, as well as new-to-Las Vegas outposts of Paul Smith, Tom Ford and Miu Miu. An impressive wooden tree house structure at the center of the complex contains the concierge desk on the lower level and a dining terrace for Mastro's Ocean Club above. Other restaurants include Wolfgang Puck Pizzeria & Cucina, the pan-Asian Social House and Beso, a dazzling venue from actress Eva Longoria Parker and celebrity chef Todd English. Eve Nightclub is located on the second floor of the restaurant. The Gallery showcases work by renowned artist Dale Chihuly.
Sunday-Thursday 10 a.m.-11 p.m., Friday-Saturday 10 a.m.-midnight.

ENCORE ESPLANADE
Encore Las Vegas, 3121 Las Vegas Blvd. S., Center Strip, 702-770-8000; www.encorelasvegas.com
Sure, the Encore Esplanade is a thoroughfare, taking you from Wynn Las Vegas to Encore Las Vegas and vice versa. But what a thoroughfare it is. The sprawling indoor boulevard exudes class with latticed archways,

FASHION SHOW

elaborate chandeliers and verdant greenery. The boutiques aren't shabby either. Encore Esplanade has all the luxury of its sophisticated neighbor with a touch more edge. Case in point: Chanel or Hermès will have you ready for the high-rollers room, while Rock & Republic and Shades will get you decked to hit the clubs afterwards—convenient since Vegas's hottest club, XS, is located in the Esplanade. If you can't get enough of the Wynn lifestyle, stop by Homestore, an interiors store featuring many of the items used to decorate the hotel.
Sunday-Thursday 10 a.m.-11 p.m., Friday-Saturday 10 a.m.-midnight.

FASHION SHOW
3200 Las Vegas Blvd. S., North Strip, 702-784-7000; www.thefashionshow.com
One of the first malls on the Strip to feature high-end retailers, the Fashion Show underwent a multimillion-dollar expansion in 2002 to keep up with its neighbors. And we're not talking typical upgrades here. An 80-foot-long runway and stage were built right down the center of the two-story mall to host live fashion shows, and it's already been put to use during press conferences by Mayor Oscar Goodman, flanked by his usual entourage of showgirls, and for local charity fundraisers. You can rent it out for private events and have the guest of honor rise from below the floor on a sunken podium (really). But it's the shopping that attracts fashionistas from around the world. The nearly two million-square-foot mall has six anchor stores: Neiman Marcus, Saks Fifth Avenue, Macy's, Dillard's, Nordstrom and Bloomingdale's Home. Other shopping-mall standbys include J. Crew, Banana Republic, Lacoste and Gap. A massive food court boasts everything from pizza to Mediterranean food, as well as the usual Wendy's and KFC. These may not be the pick of high-rolling foodies, but they'll keep you satiated through your shopping spree. For a classier (and quieter) alternative, try the Nordstrom Marketplace Café.
Monday-Saturday 10 a.m.-9 p.m., Sunday 11 a.m.-7 p.m.

THE GRAND CANAL SHOPPES AT THE VENETIAN

THE FORUM SHOPS AT CAESARS PALACE
Caesars Palace, 3500 Las Vegas Blvd. S., Center Strip, 702-893-4800;
www.caesarspalace.com

The cobblestone faux-Roman streets that intersect inside Caesars' Forum
Shops carry travelers from around the world to such retail meccas as Harry
Winston, Baccarat, Gucci, Louis Vuitton, Versace and Jimmy Choo. This is
one of the more upscale malls in the Las Vegas valley, but calling it a mall
is not giving it all its due. Aside from shopping at this tony spot, there's the
entertainment. The free Atlantis Show brings Roman gods and a simple
story to life with animatronic "actors" that spring to action every hour. A
Festival Fountain show also entertains guests; but don't miss the restaurants. Although there is much to choose from in Vegas, many stars still go
back to their favorites at the Forum Shops. Singer Mariah Carey makes
sure to stop in at Spago every time she is in Sin City—she loves the food
so much, she has her favorite pasta dishes delivered to her hotel room, and
has twice reserved the back room for a post-show feast. The Palm, BOA
Steakhouse and Joe's Seafood, Prime Steak & Stone Crab are a few of the
many fine-food finds scattered throughout this 636,000-square-foot mall. A
winding circular escalator carries shoppers from the marbled first floor to
the top third floor (parading you past all the window displays), where you will
find some of the best views of the Strip at Sushi Roku.
Sunday-Thursday 10 a.m.-11 p.m., Friday-Saturday 10 a.m.-midnight.

THE GRAND CANAL SHOPPES AT THE VENETIAN
The Venetian Resort Hotel Casino, 3377 Las Vegas Blvd. S., Center
Strip, 702-414-4500; www.venetian.com

This elegant space sings of Italy: It boasts painted frescos, polished marble,
gondoliers and, of course, exceptional shopping. Aside from the luxury
retailers you'll find at other shopping destinations such as Venetzia and
Movado, there is also a nice array of independent boutiques. History buffs
can have their pick of authentic Spanish galleons, coins and other finds at
Ancient Creations; delicate, hand-blown Venetian glass sits pretty at Ripa

de Monti; handmade Venetian masks and period pieces await you at Il Prato, and Ca'd'Oro is the place to go for exquisite jewelry. A winding indoor canal below the cobblestoned walkways links the shops together, and if you've always dreamed of having a gondolier steer you from storefront to storefront, now's the time to make it a reality, as rides with singing gondoliers are available. Throughout St. Mark's Square–the center of the Grand Canal Shoppes–actors, musicians and strolling singers entertain guests, and living statues come to life. If cash is tight after one too many rounds on the roulette wheel, the Grand Lux Café offers solid comfort food at affordable prices. Or if you want to splurge, try Canaletto in St. Mark's Square. *Sunday-Thursday 10 a.m.-11 p.m., Friday-Saturday 10 a.m.-midnight.*

LE BOULEVARD SHOPS
Paris Las Vegas, 3655 Las Vegas Blvd. S., Center Strip, 702-946-7000; www.parislasvegas.com
They've tried very hard to give an authentic feel to Le Boulevard, and they've nearly pulled it off. Stroll through the cobbled streets and take in the French-style shops that line this shopping center and you might feel like you are in the City of Lights, albeit in miniature. Small in comparison to other hotel shopping areas along the Strip, Le Boulevard is impressive for its attention to detail. From Les Enfants children's shop, where you can pick up soft little shirts and stuffed toys, to the Parisian décor store Les Eléments, Le Boulevard is drenched in decadent French culture. Grab an imported cheese and pair it with a fine wine from La Cave. If you are walking the Strip from casino to casino, duck into Le Boulevard to get from Paris to Bally's inside. It's a nice diversion, even if you aren't a Francophile.
Hours vary; walkway is open 24 hours.

MIRACLE MILE SHOPS
Planet Hollywood Resort & Casino, 3663 Las Vegas Blvd. S., Center Strip, 888-800-8284; www.miraclemileshopslv.com
Recently redesigned with a contemporary flair, this meandering mall is filled with 170 stores, including French Connection, Ann Taylor Loft, Bebe and Lucky Brand Jeans. You'll notice many shoppers with Alpaca Imports shopping bags, from an odd little store filled with the softest alpaca (a cousin of the llama) sweaters and slippers, as well as sheepskin rugs, car seat covers and home décor from around the world. Catch the free entertainment at small podiums around the mall, or at the V Theater in the middle of the mall, while you sip a coffee or eat gelato from the Aromi d'Italia. A favorite attraction for families is the live indoor rainstorm near Merchants' Harbor. Thunder, lightning and a light rain that turns torrential create a dramatic effect as you pass. If you're hungry, you won't find the usual food court choices here. Instead

WHERE ARE THE CITY'S BEST BARGAINS?

Before hotels added luxe boutiques to their lobbies and designer malls became a mainstay, Las Vegas was known for its deals and steals. Now you have to dodge a designer window display just to reach your room. There is some relief: Two high-end outlet malls bookend the famous Strip, so you're never far from a designer handbag or shoes at a deep discount. This way, you can go home with goods and still have something left over for the slots.

LAS VEGAS OUTLET CENTER
7400 Las Vegas Blvd. S., South Strip, 702-896-5599;
www.lasvegasoutletcenter.com

This enclosed mall was the first true outlet mall on the Strip, luring tourists from the high-end shops to the tail end of the Boulevard. Offering deep discounts at more than 130 stores, including Adidas, DKNY, Converse, ECCO, Kenneth Cole, Coach, Fossil, Bose, Nike, Reebok, Tommy Hilfiger and more, you can take home serious steals at up to 65 percent off. Try to avoid visiting on the weekends, when tourists descend by the busload. Also, eat before you come. There's a basic food court to please those with a penchant for fried foods, but save your money for the tastier stuff at your hotel.
Monday-Saturday 10 a.m.-9 p.m., Sunday 10 a.m.-8 p.m.

LAS VEGAS PREMIUM OUTLETS
875 S. Grand Central Parkway, Off-Strip, 702-474-7500;
www.premiumoutlets.com

Stroll the wide sidewalks at this sister to the Outlet Center and take advantage of discounts at stores such as Coach, Lacoste, A|X Armani Exchange, Dolce & Gabbana, Catherine Malandrino and more. Burberry always has a nice selection of accessories, including hats, headbands and scarves with the signature plaid pattern. Check the clearance area in the back for some truly good finds. On Tuesday there is a 50 Plus Shoppers special, giving anyone older than 50 an extra 10 percent off. Monthly sales are also listed on the website, so check before you drop in. When you get hungry, bypass all the usual suspects at the food court and head straight to Makino, a sprawling sushi buffet.
Monday-Saturday 10 a.m.-9 p.m., Sunday 10 a.m.-8 p.m.

they've concentrated on restaurants such as Pampas Churrascaria Brazilian Grille or Sin City Brewing Co. If you just want a quick bite, you can pop into La Salsa Cantina, Sbarro pizza or the fun, frenzied Cheeseburger Las Vegas. *Sunday-Thursday 10 a.m.-11 p.m., Friday-Saturday 10 a.m.-midnight.*

THE SHOPPES AT THE PALAZZO
The Palazzo Resort Hotel Casino, 3325 Las Vegas Blvd. S., Center Strip, 702-607-7777; www.palazzolasvegas.com

One of the newest shopping complexes on the Strip, the Shoppes at the Palazzo houses the first Barneys New York in Vegas. At 85,000 square feet, it's a destination unto itself, complete with its own valet and entrance on the Strip. If that's not enough to lure you in, there are also boutiques by Christian Louboutin, Catherine Malandrino, Diane von Furstenberg and Michael Kors. If you find yourself parched after all that hanger-lifting, swing by the Double Helix Bar for some wine; there are more than 50 wines by the

THE SHOPPES AT THE PALAZZO

glass to choose from. Or down a few tasty bites at Emeril's Table 10 before hopping back on the shopping circuit.

Sunday-Thursday 10 a.m.-11 p.m., Friday-Saturday 10 a.m.-midnight.

TOWN SQUARE
6605 Las Vegas Blvd. S., South Strip, 702-269-5000;
www.townsquarelasvegas.com

Designed to look like a quaint Italian village, Town Square is lined with cobbled avenues that wind through this stunning shopping, dining and entertainment mecca. The open air space, located at the corner of Sunset Road and Las Vegas Boulevard, is home to numerous shops, including Steve Madden, BCBG Max Azria, Robb & Stucky furniture and H&M (which is the one of the few places to find inexpensive fashion in this tony town). You could spend an entire day here and not get bored. Free shows in the park in the middle of Town Square are family-friendly and concerts are held in the evening. Aside from the eclectic mix of retail and restaurants, there's also an 18-screen movie theater, a sprawling children's park, a picnic area and restaurants. Recently, Brio Tuscan Grille opened inside Town Square, as well as California Pizza Kitchen and the Blue Martini bar. (There's usually a one- or two-hour wait to get into the Blue Martini on weekends after 10 p.m., so don't show up too famished.)

Sunday 11 a.m.-8 p.m., Monday-Thursday 10 a.m.-9 p.m., Friday-Saturday 10 a.m.-10 p.m., with bars and restaurants open later.

WHAT ARE THE TOP SHOPPING COMPLEXES ON THE STRIP?
The Forum Shops at Caesars Palace: The complex alone is worth a visit. Toss in the bling of Harry Winston and the classic style of Christian Dior and you have reason to spend the whole day.

Fashion Show: Housing all of the retail staples, you're sure to find an outfit for every occasion here, and a place to flaunt it (on the 80-foot catwalk inside).

WHAT ARE THE BEST STORES FOR WOMEN'S CLOTHING?

Barneys New York (The Shoppes at the Palazzo): With so many designer labels in one place, the options are endless. The valet can help you load your choices into your car or taxi.

Tory Burch (The Shoppes at the Palazzo): Chic apparel and must-have accessories from this young designer have found their niche in Vegas, where you can never have too much sparkle and bling.

WHAT IS THE BEST STORE FOR GIFTS?

Homestore (Encore Esplanade): If you can't bring the whole family to the hotel, why not bring the hotel to the whole family? This eclectic interiors store at the Encore Esplanade is packed with exclusive Wynn and Encore furnishings and accessories.

WHAT IS THE BEST PLACE TO SPLURGE?

Vertu (Wynn Las Vegas Esplanade): Say goodbye to that aging flip-phone. It's time for an upgrade and Vertu has the best hand-crafted phones in the world, and a price tag to match.

WYNN LAS VEGAS ESPLANADE

Wynn Las Vegas, 3131 Las Vegas Blvd. S., Center Strip, 702-770-7000, 888-320-7123; www.wynnlasvegas.com

Since opening in 2005, Wynn has added even more luxury to its list of high-end boutiques. Some of the most exclusive names in haute couture have found a home in Wynn's elegant Esplanade. Owner Steve Wynn first brought high-end shops to Las Vegas when he opened the Bellagio more than a decade ago, and he's continued that trend in his eponymous luxe resort. Shops include Oscar de la Renta, Alexander McQueen, Manolo Blahnik, as well as Vertu, the luxury-phone creator that starlets covet (at up to $20,000 each). For $10 you can wheel around the Ferrari-Maserati dealership to check out some of the most expensive cars in the country. Louis Vuitton makes sure to stock the latest designs of its handbags here, and a walk through Cartier offers an impressive sight of diamonds and jewelry design that you won't soon forget. Even if you're not in Vegas to shop, the Wynn Esplanade is worth the trip for its beauty. Skylights bathe shoppers in soft, natural light in this high-ceilinged posh palace, and stained-glass accents round out the experience. Can't make it down to the Esplanade? The powers that be have thought of that, too, offering a complimentary personal shopping service for guests of Wynn Las Vegas.

Sunday-Thursday 10 a.m.-11 p.m., Friday-Saturday 10 a.m.-midnight.

DOWNTOWN AND OFF-STRIP

Las Vegas may be known for many things, but there's one secret spot that eludes visitors: The plethora of antiques available in what is quickly becoming known as Antique Row. Hollywood scouts often knock on the doors of the shops along Antique Row looking for props from certain eras to lend legitimacy to period sets. You'll find both mini-malls as well as quaint homes-turned-shops along a five-mile stretch in and around Charleston Boulevard. You can pick up fur stoles or add to your collection of ashtrays. You'll also find pieces from imploded legendary hotels like the Dunes and the Sands.

TOWN SQUARE

THE ATTIC
1018 S. Main St., Downtown, 702-388-4088; www.atticvintage.com
You may have seen the credit card ads and other glimpses in glossy magazines of this self-proclaimed world's largest vintage clothing store. With its '60s retro décor and multi-tiered main room stuffed with feathers, fedoras and full suits from the past, you could spend hours playing dress-up and trying on new personas for your Vegas vacation. The clerks are very helpful in throwing together a cool look.
Tuesday-Saturday 10 a.m.-6 p.m.

MAIN STREET ANTIQUES, ART & COLLECTIBLES
500 S. Main St., Downtown, 702-382-1882;
www.mainstreetantiqueslv.com
This cavernous string of buildings connects collectibles in a dizzying selection that you can't imagine. Antique hunters from around the world

---

WHICH STORES HAVE THE BEST SHOES?
In Step (Encore Esplanade): If you can see past the Swarovski crystal-covered couch, you'll find your feet in good company with shoes from designers such as Galliano, Chloé and Nicholas Kirkwood.

Jimmy Choo (The Forum Shops): It's nearly impossible to leave empty handed after seeing the collection of stylish stilettos on offer here.

WHICH ARE THE BEST MALLS FOR WINDOW SHOPPING?
The Forum Shops at Caesars Palace: The winding spiral escalators whisk you up three stories, passing an endless slue of luxury stores.

Via Bellagio (Bellagio Las Vegas): With the fountains of Bellagio as a backdrop, the window displays at Fendi, Prada and Yves Saint Laurent are all the more enticing.

stop by regularly to check out the latest from more than 40 dealers who dabble in vintage Vegas. We picked up a 1950s-era ebony puzzle box with ivory detail for $20. The box unfolds to reveal two trays with grooves for cigarettes. Furniture, obscure odds and ends, pottery, slot signage and much more make for an interesting afternoon wandering through the past. The store ships worldwide, so you don't have to worry about paying the airlines an extra bag fee if you find something you just can't pass up. Don't be afraid to haggle, either; vendors expect nothing less. You can get quite a deal from tired sellers who want to move items.

Tuesday-Sunday 10 a.m.-6 p.m.

NOT JUST ANTIQUES MART

1422 Western Ave., Off-Strip, 702-384-4922;
www.notjustantiquesmart.com

You can grab a nice little lunch and a piece from the past at this charming mart. Small in comparison to some of the others, this 12,000-square-foot mall is home to dozens of dealers who specialize in everything from gaming memorabilia to period furniture and glassware. Every item has a story, and the vendors are more than happy to tell you if they know the history of a particular piece. If you're a new collector or want to start, this is the place to get your feet wet as the pool of knowledge here is huge. A tea-room gallery upstairs takes reservations for high tea parties, perfect for mothers and daughters, family reunions or a bachelorette breather before or after a night on the town. Located in the Arts District just off Charleston Boulevard, you can ask for directions to the latest art installations or gallery shows within walking distance of the antique mart.

Monday-Saturday 10:30 a.m.-5:30 p.m., Sunday noon-5 p.m. First Friday of every month open until 10 p.m.

THE SPA AT WYNN LAS VEGAS

TABLE GAMES

Late night revelry, smoky casinos and haute cuisine indulgences are hardly the stuff of peaceful contemplation. Still, beyond Las Vegas' electric chaos, cucumber water-plied guests regularly take the plunge (into Jacuzzi tubs) and belly up to the tables (massage, that is). In fact, spa culture has recently become nearly as integral to the Las Vegas experience as gambling itself. In a town where newer, bigger and better is key to livelihood, already lavish spas constantly update their cutting-edge retreats and often offer discounts to locals (so always ask, if you qualify). While older accommodations and boutique hotels tend to offer more intimate relaxation experiences (still sizeable by average standards), the Strip's newer additions—some of the world's largest hotels—boast enormous versions. At all these hot urban oases, whether on the Strip or in a destination like Henderson or Summerlin, the newest pampering trends catch on quickly.

STAR-RATED SPAS

★★★THE BATHHOUSE
THEhotel at Mandalay Bay Resort & Casino, 3950 Las Vegas Blvd. S., South Strip, 877-632-9636; www.mandalaybay.com

The Bathhouse makes its home inside Mandalay Bay's boutique sidekick THEhotel, giving the spa a very intimate feel (by Vegas standards, at least). Designed with simple stripped-down European aesthetics in mind, the imposing slate-gray walls throughout the space have an almost-industrial, gallery-like vibe. Luxuriating in the Jacuzzi pool, for instance, you feel almost as if you've sneaked into a heated museum fountain. Even the Jacuzzi warnings look artistic and cool, printed on the wall in an interesting typeface. Every once in a while, though, a bright, geometric-patterned pillow or flower arrangement offers a pop of color. Crème brûlée body treatments and hot spiced rum stone massages demonstrate a propensity towards intermingling the senses (taste, smell and touch). If you need to look bikini-ready upon arrival, treatments like the Cell-U-Less Herbal Wrap offer a boost.

★★★★CANYON RANCH SPACLUB
The Palazzo Resort Hotel Casino/The Venetian Resort Hotel Casino, 3355 Las Vegas Blvd. S., Center Strip, 877-220-2688; www.canyonranchspaclub.com

The newly renovated and expanded Canyon Ranch SpaClub—at 134,000 square feet—is enormous. In fact, as you wander past the impressive Palazzo into the Venetian and toward the neutral-toned spa (festooned with raw organic design elements like bamboo) you'll enter the biggest spa in North America (with more than 100 treatment rooms). Canyon Ranch's wellness reputation—as the foremost pioneer of modern day ultra-luxury health resorts—precedes the Sin City addition (the first Canyon Ranch opened in 1979 in Tucson, Arizona). And it has unveiled something exclusive and brand new: The Aquavana pre-treatment plunging experience allows guests to move between invigorating spaces such as a Wave Dream, Salt Chamber, Igloo, Rasul mud room and Snow Cabin, in addition to the usual steam and sauna. No appointment is necessary, as long as you buy a day pass to the spa ($35 or less per pass if purchased for several days). Not for cynics are new-age signatures like Vibrational Therapy, which

THE SPA AT TRUMP

combines crystal sounding bowls, essential oils, Chakra stone placements, acupoints and negative ionization of the Cavitosonic chamber to balance the body's energy fields. A Yamuna Hands-On Treatment, in which muscles are massaged with a special ball, may offer more tangible satisfaction. And while the fitness center is an afterthought at many spas, Canyon Ranch SpaClub offers holistic wellness programs. The multi-colored climbing wall is also the spa's aesthetic centerpiece, so be aware that if you scale it you might attract some attention.

★★★QUA BATHS & SPA
Caesars Palace, 3570 Las Vegas Blvd. S., Center Strip, 866-782-0655; www.caesarspalace.com

Mile-high ceilings and lavish azure décor—mimicking an underwater world—welcome you to Qua Baths & Spa at Caesars Palace. After slipping on your robe, stroll around the corner to the sizeable relaxation lounge. If you're thirsty, head to the Tea Room, where an herbal sommelier will find the perfect concoction to ease you into a mellow mood before your treatment. Signature experiences like the Hawaiian Lomi Lomi and Chakra Balancing—with aromatherapy oil dripped onto the third eye (that's "forehead" to you) and energetic stones arranged on your back—may seem a bit far-fetched but are actually very relaxing. "Social spa-ing" is also a priority here and

---

WHICH SPAS HAVE THE BEST MASSAGES?

The Spa at Mandarin Oriental, Las Vegas: The signature Oriental Harmony involves two therapists working together and concludes with a simultaneous head and foot massage.

The Spa at Wynn Las Vegas: All the massages here are exceptional (as are the masseuses), but the custom massage lets you get a rubdown right where you need it most.

THE SPA AT ENCORE LAS VEGAS

shared amenities truly deliver: Three Roman baths (separate pools ranging in temperature from 76° to 104°) sit poised atop polished stone steps and are surrounded by opalescent walls, just waiting for a group to soak and chit-chat. But a favorite is the amazing Arctic Ice Room (best used as cooling relief after a sauna and/or a Laconium steam), where a water and moisturizer mix, posing as snow, falls upon heated seats and floors—a truly refreshing winter wonderland.

★★★★★THE SPA AT ENCORE LAS VEGAS
Encore Las Vegas, 3121 Las Vegas Blvd. S., Center Strip, 702-693-7472; www.encorelasvegas.com

The wow-factor is certainly in play at this ritzy rejuvenation center. Taking pointers from the Spa at Wynn, Encore carries the Asian theme further with glowing gold lanterns, life-size Buddhas and blossoming orchids. The expansive reception area looks like the lobby of a luxury hotel rather than a sterile spa environment (with plenty of pillow-laden couches for lounging), while the locker rooms are unusually bright and airy. The separate men's and women's spaces are sprawling in size, with large saunas and steam rooms, as well as just about any amenity you might need to refresh post-treatment. But it's not just about the décor; technology plays a part as well. State-of-the-art waterfall showers use digital screens to let you control water temperature, water pressure from the six shower heads, and mood lighting, and the personal lockers don't require keys. A transformation ritual might be just what you need after a long losing battle in the casino. Try the Lavender Stone Ritual, which incorporates lavender and sea salt to calm frayed nerves, or the Vitamin Infusion Facial, giving your system a boost of vitamins and collagen to heal damaged skin. The onsite salon offers everything from manicures and pedicures to cuts and colors, as well as a full menu of traditional barbershop services. You can also buy a day pass and enjoy all of the outrageous amenities of the spa without a treatment. It may be the best $30 you spend in Vegas.

WHICH SPA HAS THE MOST UNIQUE TREATMENT?

Spa Bellagio Las Vegas: Born again takes on a new meaning after experiencing the Watsu treatment, a massage performed while you float in a private pool, which is said to mirror the birth experience.

WHICH SPAS HAVE THE BEST SALONS?

The Spa at Encore Las Vegas: Where else can you get a view of the Strip from your pedicure chair? Settle in and experience superior salon services at this attractive spot.

Kim Vo Salon (The Mirage): What happens in Vegas stays in Vegas, including that grown-out haircut you arrived with. One visit to this celebrity colorist and you'll be good as new.

★★★★THE SPA AT THE FOUR SEASONS HOTEL LAS VEGAS

Four Seasons Hotel Las Vegas, 3960 Las Vegas Blvd. S., South Strip, 702-632-5000; www.fourseasons.com/lasvegas

You'd never know you were in Sin City at The Spa at The Four Seasons Hotel Las Vegas, as there's no casino and, hence, no stroll—on the road to relaxation—through intentionally disorienting chaos. Once you wander into the hotel's tasteful lobby, a representative immediately leads you to your destination. The Spa's subdued décor is seamless. This intimate refuge swathed in mild tones is on the smaller side, so personal attention (in concert with The Four Seasons' usual impeccable service) is a plus. Shuffling to the Zen lounge in one of the city's plushest robes, you sip cucumber water or herbal tea and nibble on an array of treats from dried fruit to pastries. Don't be surprised by the smell of fresh-baked goods either; fresh doughnuts are served in the lobby café, and sinful mini-chocolate muffins are omnipresent in the spa (finally, snacks you actually want to eat). The Spa's services are some of the most effective and clinical of the Vegas bunch, so you're asked to fill out a health information form at onset. Opt for a unique results-oriented facial like the signature Vitality of the Glaciers, an anti-aging RNA, DNA and collagen treatment that jump starts your cellular metabolism. Think you liked hot rocks on your back? You'll leave the new Everlasting Flower Stone facial, with poppy seed exfoliation, hibiscus extract and rhodochrosite rocks, feeling relaxed.

★★★★★THE SPA AT MANDARIN ORIENTAL, LAS VEGAS

Mandarin Oriental Las Vegas, 3752 Las Vegas Blvd. S. Center Strip, 888-881-9530; www.mandarinoriental.com/lasvegas

Located within the serene Mandarin Oriental, this spa is luxuriously designed with dark woods and exotic Shanghai undertones, making it a welcome respite from the bustle of the Strip immediately below. Guests are greeted with tea and a cool towel before being whisked away to the elegantly appointed locker rooms and relaxation area. Be sure to budget enough time to take full advantage of the steam room, dry sauna, vitality pool and Laconium room. An ice fountain and experience showers provide luxurious means to cool down. The relaxation lounge is inviting, with plush chairs and panoramic views of the Strip, and heated Tepidarium chairs to soothe aching muscles. Each guest receives their own attractive souvenir amenities kit with razor, toothbrush and other necessities. Many of the

CANYON RANCH SPACLUB

massage rooms are designed with couples in mind. While a variety of treatments are offered, the highlight may just be the Chinese Foot spa, which offers authentic and luxurious foot massages. Be sure to take a dip in one of the outdoor pools located just outside the spa area with incredible views of the Strip.

★★★THE SPA AT RED ROCK
Red Rock Casino, Resort & Spa, 11011 West Charleston. Summerlin. 866-767-7773; www.redrocklasvegas.com
As Red Rock is situated closer to a national park than the Strip, spa services extend outside their casino-adjacent digs and into the great outdoors. "Adventure Spa" activities include horseback riding and rock climbing, as well as location-specific experiences like rafting down the Colorado River and hiking to natural hot springs. Inside, mosaic pebble fountains, a bright red relaxation area with a faux snakeskin centerpiece and a chocolate and turquoise color scheme lend a "boutique" feel to the ultra-modern (yet-retro '60s/mod-style) spa. If you're up for something different, try the Ashiatsu massage, where a masseuse actually suspends from the ceiling to walk on your back, or the radiance facial, which uses a cinnamon enzyme peel and active protein enzymes to improve skin's elasticity.

★★★★THE SPA AT TRUMP
Trump International Hotel Las Vegas, 2000 Fashion Show Drive, Off-Strip, 702-797-7878; www.trumplasvegashotel.com
The Spa at Trump International Hotel is among Vegas' most intimate and, of course, swankiest refuges. A spa attaché guides you through 11,000 square feet of Rain Shower and eucalyptus steam-laden space to help discern your signature intention: Calm, Balance, Purify, Heal or Revitalize. Special gemstone-infused oil massages are meant to heal internally and externally. To get event-ready, try the Dermal Quench: hydration with oxygen and hyaluronic serum delivered with hyperbaric pressure for extra absorption. Or, for long-lasting benefits, sample the Dermalucent with LED skin rejuvenation;

or a hotel-exclusive Ultimate Kate facial (combining both of the above and a foot massage). Late-night partiers flock to the Morning-After Eye Cure to refresh before starting the cycle again. Of course, The Donald wouldn't open a spa without some kind of service for luscious locks, so try an Espresso Yourself hair treatment for damage control.

★★★★★THE SPA AT WYNN LAS VEGAS
Wynn Las Vegas, 3131 Las Vegas Blvd. S., Center Strip, 702-770-3900; www.wynnlasvegas.com

No need to feel a pang of guilt as you pass exercise bikes between treatments. At The Spa at Wynn, the fitness center sits outside the pampering area, unlike at many other spas. The décor is plush, and the waiting room—adorned with a large "fire and ice" fireplace—is comfortable and relaxing. You could lounge here on one of the ultra-comfortable couches sipping herbal tea and flipping through magazines for hours post-treatment. The lovely Jacuzzi room harkens to a mermaid's lair, with its lily pad-covered walls inset with stones, Deluge showers that simulate waterfalls, and a central soaking bath. Exotic Asian- and Middle Eastern-inspired treatments are signatures here, but the real attraction is the ultra-indulgent, 80-minute Stone Ritual, a soothing full-body massage using heated stones to melt the knots in overworked muscles. Other treatments include Thai massage, shiatsu, and facials that will do everything from boost the collagen in your visage to impart a glow to tired, dull skin. Male estheticians are plentiful here, so make sure to specify if you have a gender preference. If the views in your room at Wynn are too difficult to pull yourself away from (and at night, they are alluring, no matter which direction your room faces), you can opt to have a massage performed in the privacy of your own retreat. Manicures and pedicures at the onsite salon are performed in comfortable chairs cordoned off by curtains that provide extra privacy. An army of black-clad, top-notch stylists are on hand to offer cuts, coloring and even makeup application, which makes the salon a favorite for visiting brides and their bridal parties celebrating their big day.

★★★★SPA BELLAGIO LAS VEGAS
Bellagio Las Vegas, 3600 Las Vegas Blvd. S., Center Strip, 888-987-6667; www.bellagio.com

Bellagio's spa is a well-oiled machine, albeit a large machine that runs well thanks to the efficiency of its technology-aided staff, who don headsets to subtly communicate with each other as they whisk you into the spa. Once checked in at the second story spa (having wandered past the full-service salon, enormous manicure/pedicure area and a gentlemen's "Barber Shop"), disrobe and re-robe in the large changing area, then head to the coed waiting area. (At last, you can sit with your significant other before a couple's treatment.) The designers adorned the space with spectacular natural elements like wall-mounted orchid installations complete with waterfalls; enormous terra cotta pots; and backlit jade inlaid in fossilized sandstone floors. An extensive menu offers options from the luscious Deep Coconut Surrender massage, which features warm coconut milk drizzled on your back amidst hot stones, to more experimental treatments like spinal realignment essential oil Raindrop Therapy. But the mosaic Watsu massage is the spa's major claim to fame: In a large, steamy, sea blue- and green-tiled private space, submerged in 94-degree water, you experience a Zen Shiatsu-technique massage, which some say mirrors the experience of being born.

★★★★SPA MIO
The M Resort Spa & Casino Las Vegas, 12300 Las Vegas Blvd. S., Off-Strip, 702-797-1800; www.themresort.com
Natural wood and exposed brick, eucalyptus-scented air and the soothing sound of grasshoppers as you step off the elevators are just a few of the defining elements of Sin City's newest oasis. The 23,000-square-foot space has all the usual amenities—sauna, steam room, Jacuzzi—but it's the organic slant that draws the biggest buzz. The 50-minute Organic facial incorporates organic orchard fruits like papaya and apricots to nourish and hydrate the skin. The 80-minute Wild Flower and Earth wrap starts with a vigorous exfoliation before the body is painted with a blend of mineral-rich mud from the Atlas Mountains (apparently, it's an old beauty secret from Morocco) and your choice of essential oils. The fitness center boasts some of the best desert views in Vegas through its floor-to-ceiling windows, making even a workout an organic experience.

OTHER SPAS

AQUAE SULIS SPA
JW Marriott Las Vegas Resort & Spa, 221 N. Rampart Blvd., Summerlin, 702-869-7807; www.jwlasvegasresort.com
Deeply invested in the healing powers of water, Aquae Sulis Spa at JW Marriott in locally beloved Summerlin—20 minutes from the Strip—is modeled after a Roman temple. In addition to sampling refreshing hot and

THE MIRAGE SPA

cold plunges, linger in a six-chamber Hydro-circuit pool in the outdoor gardens (complete with waterfalls), a signature pre-treatment experience. Aquae Sulis' services target the spirit, as well as the body; the Cranial Sacral massage redirects your body's flow of energy by way of your head, while the spiritual Reiki releases anxiety and regenerates the body. Otherwise, nourish your skin with tasty treats in topical and aromatherapy forms; as the menu includes Chocolate Delight, Cucumber Melon, Chamomile, Wine and Coffee Break scrubs.

THE MIRAGE SPA AND KIM VŌ SALON
The Mirage, 3400 Las Vegas Blvd. S., Center Strip, 702-791-7472; www.mirage.com

If you find sitting in the shade of a tree peaceful, but think Vegas' palms and intense heat leave something to be desired, The Mirage Spa may be the retreat for you. A "Birch Garden" and indoor arbor welcomes guests to the urban escape, while modern details such as bamboo stalks produce a warm, Zen-like atmosphere. Microfiber sheets in the treatment rooms are one of the claims to fame, along with high-end products from Eminence Organic skin care, and results-oriented facial add-ons (meant to mimic medi-spa treatments without the injections) like glycolic, lip and eye treatments. The Kim Vo Salon, helmed by the Beverly Hills colorist, is also a draw, with a separate men's barbershop for those who want a traditional trim.

PARIS SPA BY MANDARA
Paris Las Vegas, 3655 Las Vegas Blvd. S., Center Strip, 702-946-4366; www.parislasvegas.com

Inside the spa's spacious relaxation room on the hotel's second floor, muted tones are accented with purple pillows, and Jacuzzi tubs are slightly overshadowed by huge, brightly colored wall murals of recreated Matisse masterpieces. Since the French are known for their sustaining beauty secrets, opt for European-inspired anti-aging treatments such as the Ionithermie Cellulite Reduction Treatment; the Paris for Lovers couples experience with scrubs, massages, pastries and room service in a special Jacuzzi suite; or La Thérapie HydraLift Facial, which uses galvanic frequencies to deliver hydrating oxygen into the skin.

PLANET HOLLYWOOD SPA BY MANDARA
Planet Hollywood Resort & Casino, 3667 Las Vegas Blvd. S., Center Strip, 702-785-5772; www.planethollywoodresort.com
With its frenetic energy inside and out, Planet Hollywood might be one of the least likely spots for a mellow retreat. Nonetheless, a recent makeover turned this Moroccan-style spa into a Balinese retreat. Lanterns, intricately patterned tiles and candles welcome you in the reception area, and a sizeable retail space tempts you to browse. The spa menu, also recently revised along Asian themes, is extremely thorough, including advanced Elemis treatments like Pro-Collagen Quartz and Tri-Enzyme Resurfacing facials. But the signature slice of heaven is the Mandara Four-hand Massage; it's performed by two therapists, combining Hawaiian Lomi Lomi and Swedish practices, and will leave you feeling relaxed for days.

SPA AT ARIA
Aria Resort and Casino, 3730 Las Vegas Blvd., Center Strip, 702-590-9600; www.arialasvegas.com
The sleek and modern Spa at Aria brings nature in Aji stone, water gardens, and natural light to create a sense of warmth, calmness, and tranquility. Besides a slew of fantastic treatments, the spa offers unique relaxation rooms. The salt room is a breath of fresh air—the salty air will leave your skin looking completely refreshed and you'll be breathing easier afterward. The heated-stone ganbanyjoku beds are another highlight—the warm beds are said to accelerate your metabolism, soothe your muscles and eliminate toxins. If nothing else, they are incredibly relaxing. Unique treatments include the Thai Poultice Massage, which soothes muscles with warm traditional poultices infused with lemongrass, ginger, and prai extract.
In the Harmonic Body Buff, therapists use Clarisonic brushes to cleanse and smooth your skin's surface using salt, sugar or gommage.

THE SPA AT GREEN VALLEY RANCH
Green Valley Ranch Resort, Spa and Casino, 2300 Paseo Verde Parkway, Henderson, 702-617-7777; www.greenvalleyranchresort.com
Despite being under the same ownership as the Red Rock Casino Resort, The Spa at Green Valley Ranch Resort has a more eclectic, breezy vibe. The hipster "Pond" pool area offers a clubby atmosphere, complete with open-air cabanas topped with bold red-and-yellow-patterned banquets and gauzy white curtains. In the spa, natural, barely there tones and raw organic elements—including pools of water—adorn the walls. Specialty

---

WHICH SPAS ARE BEST FOR GROUPS?
Canyon Ranch SpaClub: With more than 100 treatment rooms, there is enough space for everyone to be pampered SpaClub style.

Qua Baths & Spa: The more the merrier in these Roman Baths, where "social spa-ing" is a celebrated practice. Business meetings and family retreats have never been so enjoyable.

WELL SPA

treatments skew sweet and tropical, and include Paradise Papaya, featuring pineapple-papaya products and live protein enzymes; Orange Oasis scrub and massage with orange blossom for damaged skin, and the Hydra Quench Cocoon.

SPA MOULAY
Loews Lake Las Vegas Resort, 101 Montelago Blvd., Henderson, 702-567-6049; www.loewshotels.com
Lake Las Vegas was created so that visitors could feel transported to exotic places of their choosing without going far. At Spa Moulay, go Moroccan with ethnic-inspired treatments (often with authentic ingredients) such as the Moulay Buff with couscous sugar scrub, Moroccan Clay Wrap and Moroccan Salt Glow with imported oils. Though the indoor treatment rooms are beautifully adorned with rich-crimson-and-forest-green-patterned throws, intricate lanterns and other carefully chosen themed-décor accents, the outdoor experience offers whimsical spaces in true seclusion (surrounded by lush foliage). Even outdoor yoga classes seem like a heavenly undertaking (assuming it's not the dead of summer). Every need has been considered (there's even a Mini Moulay Little Spa Day for you and a child under 12 years old—perfect for that mother-daughter getaway weekend).

VDARA HEALTH & BEAUTY
Vdara Hotel & Spa, 2600 W. Harmon Ave., Center Strip, 702-590-2474; www.vdara.com
Vdara Hotel & Spa—one of the newest hotels on the strip within the CityCenter complex—offers this beautiful 18,000 square-foot spa. With two levels, a full service salon, fitness center, sauna, eucalyptus steam room, hot plunges and a champagne bar, you might never want to leave. As you enter the serene spa's reception area on the second floor, you'll be greeted by a lovely waterfall. Enjoy a glass of champagne and browse the boutique before following the waterfall upstairs to the waiting room and treatment

rooms on the third floor. Light wood floors and a clean color palette of white, sea foam green, light blue, brown and light pink with candles and flowers all around sets the mood, particularly in the relaxation and meditation area with its comfortable chaise lounge. The spa is dedicated to environmental responsibility, using and offering green paraben-free products, including a vegan nail treatment line, and brands such as Aveda, Red Flower and Peter Thomas Roth. Treatments cover all bases from an espresso mud body scrub to the couples massage, anti-inflammatory muscle repair massage, and tea tree acne treatment facial. The fitness center offers a range of equipment along with classes such as yoga and strength training. And don't forget about the gorgeous pool outside; rent one of the Spa Cabanas (decked out with a television, ceiling fans, hand sinks, a refrigerator with water and fresh fruit, and private seating and plunge pools) and enjoy a lavish treatment outside.

WELL SPA
The Platinum Hotel and Spa, 211 East Flamingo Road, Off-Strip, 702-636-2424; www.theplatinumhotel.com
More demure than most of its Las Vegas counterparts, the WELL Spa offers a truly private experience, as it's possible to go through an entire pampering session without seeing another guest. Maybe that's because it's less well known, but regardless, it's a great perk. Bells and whistles are less obvious at this hotel, which sits only five minutes off the Strip, but feels miles away from the famous street's ostentatious displays. The pretty pool area is adorned with burgundy, burnt ember and yellow striped pillows and is gorgeous for evening cocktails or a dip. The seasonal treatment menu is always evolving, but alongside the standards is the notable Well Spa Cure—a scrub, shower, slather and scalp massage with antioxidant-rich pomegranate.

THE PALAZZO LAS VEGAS RESORT HOTEL AND CASINO

DESERT DREAMING

Living large in Las Vegas is no tall order, especially since the city contains more over-the-top luxury hotels than anywhere else in the country. Enormous, multi-level hotel suites, bathrooms with soaking spa tubs spacious enough to fit five, and personal attachés eager to fluff your pillow, reset your iPod or unpack your suitcase are all within easy reach. The Las Vegas mentality of constantly upping the ante has resulted in some incredible properties lining the Strip. Even standard rooms seem to trump your average hotel room.

But Sin City isn't just a playground for the privileged. Last-minute hotel deals run rampant, allowing anyone to have a taste of the good life. There are also plenty of smaller, often older hotels that pack in the charm of vintage Vegas. No matter where you stay, you're sure to experience a level of glamour that you can't find anywhere else.

THE STRIP

★★★BALLY'S LAS VEGAS
3645 Las Vegas Blvd. S., Center Strip, 877-603-4390;
www.ballyslasvegas.com

If Vegas conjures images of showgirls then look to Bally's, which offers the quintessential showgirl sensation, *Donn Arden's Jubilee!* Like the show, Bally's epitomizes classic Vegas with its center-Strip location and traditional-style guest rooms. The beige-on-beige décor can feel a bit dated, but the rooms are comfortable and the floor-to-ceiling windows provide nice views of the Strip. The North Tower rooms have been renovated more recently, so be sure to specify when you book. Eight tennis courts (illuminated for night play) and access to two nearby golf courses motivates those who thought they'd spend all their time at the pool (which isn't a bad plan B, especially if you secure one of the cabanas). Movie buffs may remember Bally's as the spot where the Flying Elvis' skydivers landed in the film *Honeymoon in Vegas*.

2,814 rooms. Restaurant, bar. Tennis. Fitness center. Pool. Spa. Business center. $151-250

★★★★BELLAGIO LAS VEGAS
3600 Las Vegas Blvd. South, Center Strip, 888-987-6667;
www.bellagio.com

With its world-class art offerings—from the Chihuly glass sculpture over-looking the lobby to the masterpieces gracing the walls of The Bellagio Gallery of Fine Art—the Bellagio continues to hail as the class act of the Strip. Water is the element of choice here, with the magical Fountains of Bellagio, Cirque du Soleil's awe-inspiring water-themed performance *O*, and five beautifully manicured courtyard pool areas. The guest rooms continue the aquatic adventure with Italian marble deep-soaking tubs and glass-enclosed showers. Flat-screen TVs, a fully stocked minibar and electronic drapes round out the contemporary décor. For those looking to raise the stakes, the Bellagio Tower suites flaunt deep, dark wood furnishings, extra-spacious floor plans and a striking panoramic view of the city.

3,933 rooms. Restaurant, bar. Fitness center. Pool. Spa. Business center. $251-350

BELLAGIO LAS VEGAS

★★★CAESARS PALACE
3570 Las Vegas Blvd. S., Center Strip, 702-731-7110, 866-227-5938;
www.caesarspalace.com

With a name like Caesars, you'd expect a bit of Roman excess—but that's an understatement, considering the Palace's 85 acres, 26 restaurants, five (soon to be six) towers and eight pools, including one for swim-up blackjack. Your only problem will be deciding where to go first. The original circular casino is still popular and offers a 14,000-square-foot poker room and a Pussycat Dolls-themed area with go-go dancers performing in bronze cages. No matter which of the towers you retreat to, your room is guaranteed to give a lesson in tasteful opulence with plush linens, modern décor, LCD TVs (including one embedded in the bathroom mirror) and oversized walk-in showers with dual rain showerheads. A sixth tower, the Octavius, was in the works at press time and is expected to feature 665 new guest rooms that include the latest in amenities. Until then, the Augustus Tower has the newest and most up-to-date rooms, with views of the newly renovated Garden of the Gods pool complex or the Strip.

3,400 rooms. Restaurant, bar. Fitness center. Pool. Spa. Business center. $151-250

★★★★ENCORE LAS VEGAS
3121 Las Vegas Blvd. S., Center Strip, 888-320-7125, 702-770-8000;
www.encorelasvegas.com

The newest resort in Steve Wynn's luxury Vegas repertoire, Encore delivers the same exceptional service and class as its flagship property with more of a boutique vibe. The casual elegance of the décor is both playful and intimate, from the vibrant red chandeliers in the casino to the alluring golden buddha in the spa to the signature butterfly motif fluttering throughout the property (said to portend good luck). Guest suites are awash in neutrals, reds and blacks, and have floor-to-ceiling windows with views of the Strip, swiveling flat-screen TVs, and limestone and marble baths. With five restaurants onsite, your taste buds will want for nothing. An evening at Sinatra

ENCORE LAS VEGAS

will have you crooning between bites of house-made pasta, while Botero is sure to have you seeing food as a higher art form. The spa gets top billing in Las Vegas with 37 treatment rooms in which to enjoy a transformation ritual or fusion massage. And if the tables have been good to you, leaving you money to burn, book a VIP table at XS or Surrender, two of Vegas' hottest nightclubs. The Encore Beach Club features a three-tiered swimming pool, luxurious cabanas and bungalows.

1,767 rooms. Restaurant, bar. Fitness center. Pool. Spa. Business center. $351 and up

★★★★FOUR SEASONS HOTEL LAS VEGAS
3960 Las Vegas Blvd. S., South Strip, 702-632-5000;
www.fourseasons.com

Tranquility isn't a word often used to describe the Las Vegas Strip, but it can be found at the Four Seasons. Located on floors 35 through 39 of the Mandalay Bay resort, this non-gaming hotel has its own entrance, restaurants and a pool with attendants at the ready to provide the requisite Evian spritz, fresh fruit and chilled water. They'll even provide you with a swimsuit to keep in case you hadn't planned on taking a dip during your trip. The elegance of the hotel extends to the guest rooms, which start at 500 square feet of luxury with down duvets and pillows, floor-to-ceiling windows overlooking the city and twice-daily housekeeping service. If this sybaritic lifestyle ever gets stale, Mandalay Bay's 135,000-square-foot casino is downstairs, and then it's back upstairs to your tranquil quarters.

424 rooms. Restaurant, bar. Fitness center. Pool. Spa. Business center. Pets accepted. $351 and up

★★★HARRAH'S LAS VEGAS
3475 Las Vegas Blvd. S., Center Strip, 800-214-9110;
www.harrahs.com

Bill Harrah opened his first bingo parlor in Reno in 1937, but never lived to see his eponymous hotel-casino open in the middle of the Las Vegas Strip (it would have been a long wait; Harrah's opened as a replacement for the Holiday Casino in 1992). The rooms are pretty much what you'd expect from a hotel built in the early nineties (muted colors, standard-issue furniture) but they're spacious and clean, and some even have Nintendo (just don't expect Wiis). The most updated rooms are in the Mardi Gras Tower, but even these are frill-free. The Carnaval theme (think Rio pre-Lent) spills out onto the street, where the outdoor Carnaval Court Bar & Grill offers a stage with live bands, a busy bar featuring "flair" bartenders and blackjack tables (on weekends).

2,640 rooms. Restaurant, bar. Fitness center. Pool. Spa. Business center. $61-150

★★★LUXOR
3900 Las Vegas Blvd. S., South Strip, 702-262-4444; www.luxor.com
Boasting the world's brightest beam of light, the Luxor's famous pyramid shape has become synonymous with the Strip. The hotel's 30 stories are serviced by "inclinators" that run at a 39-degree angle in each corner of the pyramid. The décor is contemporary and simple with warm colors, Egyptian-themed bedspreads and work spaces—just watch your head when you're near the window (that slanted wall will get you every time). The rooms in the twin 22-story towers are larger and offer better views of the city lights with floor-to-ceiling (non-slanted) windows. Luxor jumped on the Cirque bandwagon when they opened the Cirque du Soleil show featuring magician Criss Angel, *Believe*. The LAX Nightclub is one of the sultriest spots on the Strip.

4,400 rooms. Restaurant bar. Fitness center. Pool. Spa. Business center. $61-150

★★★MANDALAY BAY RESORT & CASINO
3950 Las Vegas Blvd. S., South Strip, 702-632-7777;
www.mandalaybay.com
From the 14-foot-high salt-water aquarium in the lobby to the 11-acre Mandalay Bay Beach, which includes 2,700 tons of real sand, waves and a lazy river, this hotel offers more than most Las Vegas resorts for non-gamblers. Families traveling with kids are big business for Mandalay Bay, but the hotel covers the adult playground concept, too, with THEhotel at Mandalay Bay, a boutique-style hotel-within-a-hotel that has a separate entrance, check-in and spa. Space isn't an issue at this mega-resort, which almost feels like a small city—a city with its own 135,000-square-foot casino, 1.7 million-square-foot convention center and 12,000-seat event

---

WHICH HOTELS ARE BEST FOR A LIVELY SCENE?
Hard Rock Hotel & Casino Las Vegas: Thanks to an ever-expanding club scene, Hard Rock has earned itself the title as the spot for rock-and-roll celebs and their entourages. The hotel's newer nightspot, Wasted Space, brings live bands in on the action as well as DJs.

Palms Casino Resort: Between the Playboy Club and the Hugh Hefner Sky Villa Suite, which includes a rooftop cantilevered Jacuzzi pool, huge living room and round rotating bed, this resort claims the city's most raucous atmosphere.

center that hosts everything from boxing to Beyoncé concerts. The guest rooms recently got a facelift and now are outfitted in classic neutral tones, chic modern furnishings and enormous marble baths. You can even pick your room—maybe an unobstructed Strip view, or one with a spa tub, or perhaps a room with a "playpen couch" that allows for face-to-face seating. *4,328 rooms. Restaurant, bar. Fitness center. Pool. Spa. Business center. $151-250*

★★★★MANDARIN ORIENTAL LAS VEGAS
3752 Las Vegas Blvd. S., Center Strip, 702-590-8888;
www.mandarinoriental.com/lasvegas
The smallest of the new CityCenter hotels, this 47-story, non-gaming hotel delivers the same sophisticated elegance and top-notch service that its namesake properties have been providing for years. Spacious guest rooms include floor-to-ceiling windows and state-of-the-art entertainment systems. The 27,000-square-foot spa includes 17 treatment rooms with seven couples suites, as well as a fitness center with yoga and Pilates studios. If you'd rather get your exercise outdoors, try one of the hotel's two lap pools before grabbing lunch at the café or one of the premier restaurants onsite, including Twist, the first U.S. restaurant by chef Pierre Gagnaire. *392 rooms. Restaurant, bar. Fitness center. Pool. Spa. Business center. $351 and up*

★★★MGM GRAND HOTEL & CASINO
3799 Las Vegas Blvd. S., South Strip, 702-891-7777;
www.mgmgrand.com
With more than 5,000 hotel rooms in four 30-story towers, 170,000-square-feet of casino space and a 6.6-acre pool complex, the MGM takes the "Grand" in its name seriously. Even the entrance looms large with its icon, a 45-foot-tall, 100,000-pound bronze lion (the largest bronze statue in the country), greeting guests from atop a 25-foot pedestal. Guest rooms vary based on the tower, but all include comfortable pillow-top mattresses, oversized bathrooms with marble vanities and work spaces. Rooms in the West Wing have been recently renovated and up the ante with Bose Wave radios, sleek modern furnishings and flat-screen TVs in the bathrooms. It's nearly impossible to choose from more than a dozen signature restaurants

---

WHAT ARE THE BEST NON-GAMING HOTELS?
Mandarin Oriental, Las Vegas: This outpost of the luxurious Mandarin Oriental hotels offers the same quiet luxury as the other locations, in the heart of Las Vegas.

The Signature at MGM Grand: Everything is at your fingertips at this hotel within a hotel. The guest suites are enormous, and the private fitness center and pool area for Signature guests only ensure that you won't be fighting for a treadmill or a chaise lounge. And when you get the urge to double down, you're only steps away from one of Vegas' largest casinos.

Trump International Hotel Las Vegas: The Donald knows a thing or two about living large, which is exactly what you'll experience upon checking into this golden highrise. An attentive attaché meets your every need, from unpacking your bags to arranging an in-room feast.

MANDARIN ORIENTAL LAS VEGAS

onsite, but Joël Robuchon should be at the top of any foodie's list. The Cirque du Soliel show, KÀ, is a must-see.

5,044 rooms. Restaurant, bar. Pool. Fitness center. Spa. Business center. $151-250

★★★THE MIRAGE

3400 Las Vegas Blvd. S., Center Strip, 702-791-7111; www.mirage.com

The theme of the Mirage is that of a South Seas oasis dropped into the middle of the desert. As part of the tropical feel, Siegfried & Roy's Secret Garden and Dolphin Habitat features tigers, panthers, leopards and bottle-nose dolphins (which you can swim with for a price). The Mirage's tropical theme continues at the pool complex where verdant gardens mix with freeform lagoons and a cascading waterfall. The poolside chaises are func-tional, but during the busy season, you'll be lucky to find an empty one. The "Bare" pool, where bikini tops are optional and an ID is required, is a more comfortable choice, if you're not shy (and willing to pay). When booking, ask for a deluxe or Tower deluxe room, as these recently underwent a $90 million renovation and now feature pillow-top mattresses, down comforters and LCD TVs, not to mention impressive views of the mountains, the Strip or the pool.

3,044 rooms. Restaurant, bar. Fitness center. Pool. Spa. Business center. $61-150

★★★MONTE CARLO RESORT & CASINO

3770 Las Vegas Blvd. S., South Strip, 702-730-7777; www.montecarlo.com

As the name suggests, Monte Carlo is all about the feeling of the Riviera. Water takes center stage with a 21,000-square-foot pool, waterfalls, a lazy river and wave pool. When the desert sun gets the best of you, retreat to one of the private cabanas, complete with a flat-screen TV, radio, phone and refrigerator. The Lido-like atmosphere carries into the monochromatic guest rooms with cherry wood furniture and Italian marble baths. For a more spacious experience, upgrade to a Monaco suite and enjoy a clean, modern design with black chrome and shades of gray, dark brown and white—essentially what you'd expect if you were to spend your holiday in Monte Carlo. Restaurant offerings include the BRAND Steakhouse, and for the all-night crowd, there's a 24-hour Starbucks in the lobby. The recently opened Hotel 32 occupies the top floor of the Monte Carlo and offers VIP airport transport service and sleek suites stocked with high-def TVs and iPod docking stations.

2,992 rooms. Restaurant, bar. Fitness center. Pool. Spa. Business center. $151-250

★★★NEW YORK-NEW YORK
3790 Las Vegas Blvd. S., South Strip, 702-740-6969;
www.nynyhotelcasino.com

Only in Las Vegas can the Big Apple be so accessible. Best known for its checker-cab roller coaster, New York-New York whirls guests through the city's most recognizable monuments, including the Empire State Building and the Statue of Liberty, in a matter of minutes. Guest rooms are given appropriate names like Park Avenue and Broadway Deluxe, which offers nearly 450 square feet of space and includes marble counter tops and a glass tub enclosure. When space is available, you can upgrade to a spa suite for a nominal fee. Entertainment options run the gamut from dueling pianos at the Bar at Times Square to Cirque du Soleil's show *Zumanity* to rockin' DJs at the ROK Vegas nightclub.

2,024 rooms. Restaurant, bar. Fitness center. Pool. Spa. Business center. $151-250

★★★★THE PALAZZO LAS VEGAS RESORT HOTEL CASINO
3325 Las Vegas Blvd. S., Center Strip, 702-607-7777;
www.palazzolasvegas.com

This sister property of the Venetian opened in December 2007 at an estimated cost of $1.9 billion. The guest rooms in the 50-story tower start at 720 square feet and are decorated in a contemporary Italian style complete with remote-controlled Roman shades and curtains to block out that searing desert sun. The rooms also offer Egyptian linens from Anichini and have been reviewed by a feng shui master for proper energy flow (always good to have before hitting the slots). The swank Shoppes at Palazzo has

WYNN LAS VEGAS

more than 50 stores, including an 85,000-square-foot Barneys New York, with the New York vibe continuing in the Broadway musical *Jersey Boys* at the Palazzo Theater. Celebrity chefs such as Mario Batali, Wolfgang Puck, and Emeril Lagasse have all opened signature restaurants here, bringing with them a hip crowd of hungry, happy revelers.

3,066 rooms. Restaurant, bar. Fitness center. Pool. Spa. Business center. $251-350

★★★PARIS LAS VEGAS
3655 Las Vegas Blvd. S., Center Strip, 702-946-7000;
www.parislasvegas.com

With a half scale version of the Eiffel Tower (built using Gustav Eiffel's original drawings) dotting the skyline, Paris Las Vegas offers a Vegas version of the City of Lights. Francophiles will be either entranced or dismayed (the bar at the sports book is called Le Bar du Sport). The 34-floor tower is modeled after Paris's Hotel de Ville (the city hall) and features guest rooms ranging from 750 to 4,180 square feet in size and decorated using European-style furniture and fabrics in warm colors. The 85,000-square-foot casino is surrounded by Paris street scenes and features a ceiling painted to emulate the city's sky. At 100 feet up, the Eiffel Tower Restaurant offers skyline views of the Strip, while the street-side Mon Ami Gabi supplies a great vantage point for the Fountains of Bellagio.

2,916 rooms. Restaurant, bar. Fitness center. Pool. Spa. Business center. $151-250

★★★PLANET HOLLYWOOD RESORT & CASINO
3667 Las Vegas Blvd. S., Center Strip, 702-785-5555;
www.planethollywoodresort.com

Previously the Aladdin, this Sheraton-managed hotel brings a little Hollywood to Sin City. Focused on the cult of celebrity, there is plenty of movie memorabilia to go around in the rooms decorated in shades of yellow, purple, red,

THE SIGNATURE AT MGM GRAND

black and white. Three acres of gaming include the Playing Field race and sports book. Restaurants include Koi (a paparazzi favorite in Los Angeles) and the Strip House from New York. A newly constructed all-suites luxury tower opened in 2010, which features studios, and one- and two-bedroom suites with kitchenettes, floor-to-ceiling windows and spa tubs. The hotel often hosts movie premieres and is home to the popular Peepshow. Head to the Pleasure Pool for a party atmosphere.

2,600 rooms. Restaurant, bar. Fitness center. Pool. Spa. $151-250

★★★★THE SIGNATURE AT MGM GRAND LAS VEGAS
145 E. Harmon Ave., South Strip, 877-612-2121;
www.signaturemgmgrand.com

Luxury properties have been popping up along the Las Vegas Strip for years, so it should come as no surprise that one of Sin City's biggest players has an über-luxe offering all its own. The Signature at MGM Grand consists of three separate towers that are connected to the MGM Grand via indoor walkway. The all-suite hotel has no casino and a no-smoking policy to ensure a relaxing getaway atmosphere for its guests. Whether you book a junior suite or a very large two-bedroom, you'll be treated to a deluxe king-sized bed, 300-count Anichini cotton sheets, a marble and granite bathroom with dual sinks and a spa tub, a kitchenette with Sub-Zero stainless steel appliances and wireless Internet throughout. But the perks go beyond the guest rooms; a 24-hour concierge is there to attend to your every request, private fitness centers for Signature guests only are outfitted with state-of-the-art equipment, and each tower boasts its own private pool with cabanas and cocktail service, so you'll never be vying for that last chaise lounge. There's also a cafe for breakfast and lunch, a cocktail lounge which serves food and a Starbucks. From the moment you enter through the grand private entrance, you'll be whisked away to a pleasantly quiet experience.

1,728 rooms. Restaurant, bar. Fitness center. Pool. Business center. $251-350

WHICH HOTELS ARE BEST FOR A QUIET ESCAPE?

Four Seasons Hotel Las Vegas: Perched atop Mandalay Bay Resort and Casino, this luxury hotel delivers as much Las Vegas as you want. A private pool and entrance allow you to avoid the temptations of the slots. And if you change your mind, the card sharks are waiting right downstairs.

Green Valley Ranch Resort, Spa and Casino: The Beach and The Pond are reason enough to come to this Mediterranean desert oasis. Both pool areas will have you utterly relaxed in no time. If you need an extra boost, try the palatial spa for a scrub and a rubdown.

Mandarin Oriental, Las Vegas: This serene, luxurious choice is located right in the middle of the action but is non-gaming. The soaring 23-story lobby of is a zen of Oriental calm.

Trump International Hotel Las Vegas: You'll have little reason to leave your room with a custom-stocked refrigerator and a jet-steam bathtub. Of course, if there is something you need, your personal attaché will be more than happy to get it for you.

The Venetian (Venezia Tower): You'd never know you were in the desert after a visit to the Venezia pool garden courtyard. Plants and flowers surround both pools and hot tubs. Guest suites lining the pool area are equally verdant with elaborate trellises concealing private terraces and balconies.

★★★★★SKYLOFTS AT MGM GRAND
3799 Las Vegas Blvd. S., South Strip, 877-711-7117;
www.skyloftsmgmgrand.com

With thousands of guests streaming through the doors of the MGM Grand each day, it can be hard to get personalized attention, which is why the clever people at MGM created Skylofts, an ultra-luxury, stylish boutique hotel within the hotel. Occupying the top two floors of the MGM Grand, Skylofts is the brainchild of designer Tony Chi, and evokes an urban loft with modern furniture, steam rooms, flat-screen TVs in the bathrooms and custom Bang & Olufsen entertainment systems. A 24-hour butler is at your beck and call, offering everything from lifts from the airport in a custom Maybach limousine to custom chef-prepared gourmet room service to movies on demand. Check-in takes place in the privacy of your own room (rather than in line at the MGM below), a luxury that in Las Vegas is worth its weight in casino chips.
51 rooms. Fitness center. Spa. Business center. $351 and up

★★★THEHOTEL AT MANDALAY BAY
3950 Las Vegas Blvd. S., South Strip, 702-632-7777, 877-632-7800;
www.mandalaybay.com

THEhotel's odd naming convention is just about its only showy, Vegas-style gimmick. This all-suite boutique hotel located within the Mandalay Bay is all about class. Its slicker-than-thou décor (minimalist with Art Deco touches and a Mid-Century Modern aesthetic) seems to have been plucked from the pages of a magazine, and the sizable suites (they start at 725 square feet) feature elegant marble and granite bathrooms, down comforters and 42-inch flat-screen TVs, and stunning views of the Strip and the Las Vegas valley mountains. The clientele isn't far behind, either—you can find young and sophisticated types cutting through the gleaming black-and-white

FOUR SEASONS HOTEL LAS VEGAS

WHICH HOTELS HAVE THE BEST SUITES?

Encore Las Vegas: Expect luxe amenities such as plush beds, ample Desert Bambu bath products and in-room minibars. Unlike the open floor plan of Encore's sibling, Wynn Las Vegas, the living and sleeping areas of each suite are separated by a wall and a clever swiveling 42-inch flat-screen TV.

Four Seasons Hotel Las Vegas: It's impossible to overlook the scenic beauty of Las Vegas when staying in one of these panoramic suites. The Sunrise/Sunset Suite boasts three banks of windows offering views of the Strip, the mountains beyond and the surrounding desert, and that's just from the living room.

The Palazzo Las Vegas Resort Hotel Casino: Few things feel more regal than walking into a double-door Italian marble foyer. And that's just the entryway. At more than 1,200 square feet, each Palazzo Siena Suite blends Italian opulence and modern amenities like flat-screen HDTVs and remote-controlled Roman shades and curtains.

Skylofts at MGM Grand: You'd never know you were in Las Vegas, at least as long as you stayed in your room—which is quite possible considering the smallest Skyloft rings in at 1,440 square feet and comes with a personal 24-hour butler, steam shower, in-room espresso machine and cutting edge stereo sound system.

Tower Suites at Encore Las Vegas: This exceptional hotel within a hotel delivers the utmost in luxury. A private entrance and registration lounge lets you bypass the mayhem of the casino floor before being whisked up to your modern and cosmopolitan suite with custom artwork and high-tech amenities.

Tower Suites at Wynn Las Vegas: The exclusivity that typifies the Tower Suites experience carries to the guest rooms in the form of a private access elevator, wall-to-wall and floor-to-ceiling windows with automatic black-out shades and one of the largest bathrooms on the Strip. If this doesn't sound swank enough, the Parlor Suite offers 1,280 square feet of opulence with views of the famed 18th hole, walk-in closets and a mahogany-and-granite wet bar for mixing that perfect martini.

PALMS CASINO RESORT

lobby to get to their suite or to Mix, a scenester's dream of a restaurant outfitted in stark white and a canopy of hanging glass globes. It's gorgeous enough to make you forget about any grammatical gambits.

1,117 rooms. Spa. Fitness center. Restaurant, bar. $251-350

★★★★★TOWER SUITES AT ENCORE LAS VEGAS
3121 Las Vegas Blvd. S., Center Strip, 888-320-7125, 702-770-8000; www.encorelasvegas.com

Taking its cues from its flagship property (and next door neighbor), Tower Suites at Wynn Las Vegas, this exceptional hotel within a hotel delivers the utmost in luxury, making you feel more at home than ever—assuming your home includes panoramic views of the Strip and a flat-screen TV in the bathroom. A private entrance and registration lounge lets you bypass the mayhem of the casino floor before being whisked up to your hotel room. Suites are cosmopolitan and modern with neutral and black tones, signature Encore artwork, and high-tech features such as one-touch climate controls and wireless office equipment. Access to a private pool reserved for Tower Suites guests guarantees that you'll always find an empty chaise lounge with your name on it. Restaurants run by celebrity chefs, an electric club scene and ritzy shopping options on The Esplanade round out the Encore experience.

267 rooms. Restaurant, bar. Fitness center. Pool. Spa. Business center. $351 and up

★★★★★TOWER SUITES AT WYNN LAS VEGAS
3131 Las Vegas Blvd. S., Center Strip, 877-321-9966, 702-770-7000; www.wynnlasvegas.com

Located within Wynn Las Vegas, the luxurious Tower Suites offers not only the ultimate in intimate hotel experiences, but also the amenities to round out the perfect stay (think fine cuisine, high-end shops, an exclusive golf club, a Ferrari dealership). Guests of the Tower Suites enter from the south gate entrance, which means no walking through a casino floor or fighting

CAESARS PALACE

WHICH HOTELS ARE MOST CLASSIC LAS VEGAS?

Bellagio Las Vegas: Few images are as iconic to Las Vegas as the dancing water displays of the Bellagio Fountains. Whether you catch the majestic fountain show from atop the Eiffel Tower, a square of sidewalk on the Strip or in a scene on the silver screen, you know you're in Sin City.

Caesars Palace: A major presence on the Strip for nearly five decades, this gleaming white structure still draws crowds to its original circular casino. Though the casino may seem dark in comparison to many of the newer gaming spots, Caesars will forever have history on its side.

MGM Grand Hotel & Casino: When it opened in 1993, the MGM Grand was the largest hotel in the world. Though it has surrendered that title, its illuminated green exterior remains synonymous with the Strip. It doesn't hurt that it still has the city's biggest casino.

THE VENETIAN RESORT HOTEL CASINO

crowds to get to check-in. Instead, you're greeted by an army of smiling Wynn employees standing at attention to take care of your every desire. Additional amenities include a personal shopper, an exclusive restaurant and a private pool with personal cabanas outfitted with ceiling fans, lounge chairs, mini-bars and flat-screen TVs. Guest rooms have the feel of residential apartments and feature wall-to-wall and floor-to-ceiling windows; automatic drapery and lighting controls; the pillow-top Wynn Dream Bed featuring 100 percent Egyptian cotton linens with a 310 thread count; and enormous bathrooms with soaking tubs, glass-enclosed showers and nightlights under his and her sinks.

608 rooms. Restaurant. Fitness center. Pool. Spa. Business center. $351 and up

★★★TREASURE ISLAND (TI)
3300 Las Vegas Blvd. S., Center Strip, 702-894-7111;
www.treasureisland.com

While visitors to Treasure Island—now called simply TI—won't find any real pirates here, they will find a unique band of pirates frolicking about the front entrance every 90 minutes from 7 to 11:30 p.m. The free nightly show has been transformed from its earlier, more family-friendly incarnation into the more adult-themed *Sirens of TI*, but the swordplay and pyrotechnics are still cool for all ages. The guest rooms have all been renovated to include floor-to-ceiling windows, marble bathrooms and pillow-top beds. A new nightclub from designer Christian Audigier features rhinestone-encrusted skulls and an outdoor terrace facing the Siren show in case you don't want to fight the crowds that gather on the Strip. The hotel's tropical pool provides cabanas and the TI Party Tub, an over-sized hot tub that can hold up to 25 people.

2,885 rooms. Restaurant, bar. Fitness center. Pool. Spa. Business center. $151-250

ARIA RESORT & CASINO

★★★TROPICANA LAS VEGAS
3801 Las Vegas Blvd. S., South Strip, 702-739-2222;
www.tropicanalv.com

An affordable alternative to neighboring hotels MGM Grand and New York-New York, the Tropicana delivers a prime location and brand-new upgrades. All the rooms were revamped in 2010. The Paradise Tower features 42-inch flatscreen televisions and warm colors, while the Island Tower has a tropical vibe with original artwork from Latin artists. Nikki Beach, the popular Miami beach club, is scheduled to open in the spring. The Vegas location will feature a restaurant, swim-up blackjack, sand volleyball courts, a private island in the center of the pool and outdoor concert space. For the novice gambler, the casino offers instruction (in case you want to brush up on your craps skills) and a casual, less-stressful environment in which to learn how to play—not to mention lower minimums.

1,876 rooms. Restaurant, bar. Fitness center. Pool. Spa. Business center. $61-150

★★★★THE VENETIAN RESORT HOTEL CASINO
3355 Las Vegas Blvd. S., Center Strip, 702-414-1000;
www.venetian.com

Built on the former site of the historic Sands Hotel in the center of the Las Vegas Strip, the Venetian takes the idea of a mega-resort to a new level. The Italy-themed property features two towers comprising more than 4,000 suites, more than 2.25 million square feet of meeting space, 80-some-odd stores in its Grand Canal Shoppes, and 20 restaurants from celebrated chefs such as Thomas Keller, Wolfgang Puck and Emeril Lagasse. The newest suites are found in the Venezia Tower, which has a separate check-in area and offers access to the private Venezia Garden Pool Deck. But the best part? The bathrooms. Nearly a third of the size of the room itself, each bathroom includes a Roman tub with a separate glass-enclosed shower, marble countertops and intricate gold detailing. Additional amenities include a private work area with fax/printer/copier, dual-line telephone, wireless Internet

access and flat-screen TVs in both the bedroom and living room.
4,027 rooms. Restaurant, bar. Fitness center. Pool. Spa. Business center. $151-250

★★★★WYNN LAS VEGAS
3131 Las Vegas Blvd. S., Center Strip, 877-321-9966, 702-770-7000; www.wynnlasvegas.com
In his most personal resort to date, Steve Wynn has put his name, voice and signature on just about everything you could think of—including an 18-hole golf course attached to the back of the resort, designed by Tom Fazio and Wynn himself. Wynn's penchant for fusing nature, art and luxury is also on display, with flowers and trees, waterfalls and lagoons scattered about the property along with original fine art draping the walls. Resort rooms average 640-square-feet in space (nearly twice as large as standard Vegas hotel rooms) and, like the more expensive rooms in the Tower Suites, include wall-to-wall and floor-to-ceiling windows, the pillow-top Wynn Dream Bed (covered in 100 percent Egyptian Cotton and 300-plus-thread-count sheets) and Desert Bambu bath amenities. Entertainment includes the unique show *Le Rêve* ("the Dream") and the Blush Boutique Nightclub overlooking the casino, while shopaholics will enjoy window shopping along the Wynn Esplanade, which includes a Manolo Blahnik boutique and a Ferrari-Maserati dealership.
2,063 rooms. Restaurant, bar. Fitness center. Pool. Spa. Business center. Golf. $251-350

JUST OPENED
ARIA RESORT & CASINO
3730 Las Vegas Blvd. S., Center Strip, 866-359-7757; www.arialasvegas.com
With more than 4,000 guest rooms and suites, Aria is Vegas' latest mega resort. Everything is big at Aria, from the three-story lobby to the gargantuan 215,000-square-foot pool area. Guest rooms offer modern décor and one-touch technology, controlling everything from the curtains to the room temperature. Entertainment options are equally enticing, from Haze Nightclub to The Gold Lounge. The casino incorporates natural sunlight into

BELLAGIO LAS VEGAS

WHICH HOTELS HAVE THE MOST RELAXING POOLS?

Bellagio Las Vegas: This hotel is a class act all the way, right down to its five beautifully manicured, Mediterranean-themed courtyard pool areas. Grab a private cabana and order a mint-kissed, berry-infused Bellagio mojito from the Pool Bar. Or bypass the tipple altogether and arrange for a poolside massage, a one-way ticket to utter relaxation.

Four Seasons Hotel Las Vegas: This stately pool—framed by neoclassical-inspired columns—may not be the largest on the Vegas Strip, but that's because it's the biggest around on service. Pool attendants are always at the ready to provide the requisite Evian spritz, fresh fruit and chilled water. The hotel even offers disposable swimsuits for those guests who forget theirs.

Green Valley Ranch Resort, Spa and Casino: Think modern Mediterranean instead of Italian villa—the meticulously manicured pool grounds at Green Valley are decked out in white and light blue hues and sprinkled with infinity-edge dipping pools and stylishly simple private cabanas. Not only that, but there are two areas: The Beach (with actual sand), and The Pond, a sleek, semi-enclosed pool area near the bar.

The M Resort Spa & Casino Las Vegas: It pays to be a VIP at M Resort, especially on the Villaggio Del Sol pool deck where private cabanas and day beds are stocked with iHome docking stations, flat-screen TVs, private hot tubs and sun decks, Evian misters and refreshing cucumber chilled towels. If you're looking to avoid the kids, try Daydream, the city's newest contender in the adult pool scene.

Red Rock Casino, Resort & Spa: With its suburban locale, Red Rock can afford to spread out, claiming three acres of space for the pools, including 19 private cabanas and the Sand Bar offering the requisite tropical drinks—umbrellas included.

Wynn Las Vegas: If ever there was an oasis in the desert, this multi-pool area adorned with Mediterranean-style trellises is it. Cool off in one of the two free-form swimming pools, gamble at the European-style bathing pool or reserve a cabana for more privacy.

The Venetian Resort Hotel Casino: While most guests are distracted by the Venetian's gondolas, we make for the resort's other water-bound attraction: its two massive pools. For the ultimate in relaxation, soak at the lounge pool or simply sit back on your lounge chair, order a cocktail or something to nibble on from Wolfgang Puck's RIVA restaurant and take in the rays.

THE PALAZZO LAS VEGAS RESORT HOTEL CASINO

its design, and includes exclusive high-limit salons for VIP guests. Cirque du Soleil's newest theatrical sensation based on the life of Elvis Presley, *Viva Elvis*, has been playing here to rave reviews by Elvis fans.

4,004 rooms. Restaurant, bar. Fitness center. Pool. Spa. Business center. Casino. $251-350

ARIA SKYSUITES
3730 Las Vegas Blvd. S., Center Strip, 866-359-7757;
www.arialasvegas.com

Part of the Aria Resort and Casino in the massive CityCenter complex, the Aria Sky Suites are an ultra-exclusive experience. A limousine picks you up at the airport and whisks you to the private lobby, where drinks and hors d'oeuvres await upon check-in. (Bonus: Snacks as well as coffee, soda and libations are complimentary in the lobby throughout your stay. Who said free drinks were only for the gambling set?) Whether you choose a one- or two-bedroom suite or penthouse, or an expansive Sky Villa, the contemporary design won't disappoint—nor will the view. Electronic controls satisfy your every whim, from closing the shades for an early morning bedtime or afternoon nap to summoning the butler to draw a bath. Although you feel far removed from the Aria Casino and CityCenter offerings, they are only a quick elevator ride away. That is, if you ever desire to roam from your luxury confines.

312 rooms. Restaurant, bar. Fitness center. Pool. Spa. Casino. $351 and up.

FLAMINGO LAS VEGAS
3555 Las Vegas Blvd. S., Center Strip, 702-733-3111, 800-732-2111;
www.flamingolasvegas.com

The Flamingo was Bugsy Siegel's dream project realized when it opened in 1946 and according to legend, the name comes from the long legs of his showgirl girlfriend, not the bird itself. Still, six-foot flamingos flank the European-style "GO" pool, while the newly renovated Flamingo Go Rooms

TRUMP INTERNATIONAL HOTEL LAS VEGAS

feature retro furnishings that include white vinyl headboards and splashes of Flamingo pink throughout the space—those looking for a more subdued experience might be more comfortable in the less colorful deluxe rooms. Go rooms have also been updated with the latest in high-tech devices, such as iPod docking stations, flat-screen HDTVs and motorized drapes. Be sure to check out one of the shows in the Flamingo Showroom which have included such comedians as George Wallace and Vinnie Favorito, as well as popular acts including Donny and Marie.

3,545 rooms. Restaurant, bar. Fitness center. Tennis. Pool. Spa. Business center. $151-250

VDARA HOTEL & SPA
2600 W. Harmon Ave., Center Strip, 866-745-7767; www.vdara.com
Guest suites with open-floor plans, custom-designed artwork and a champagne bar in the spa are just a few of the details that set this new non-gaming CityCenter property apart from the rest on the Strip. As one of the major players in the massive CityCenter venture, this all-suite hotel is modern and luxurious in design (the brainchild of famed architect Rafael Vinoly) with large picture windows and frameless glass-enclosed showers in each of the guest rooms. The Vdara Pool and Lounge, occupying space above the entrance to the hotel, is reserved for guests only and offers made-to-order cocktails and semi-private plunge pools alongside spa cabanas.

1,495 rooms. Restaurant, bar. Fitness center. Pool. Spa. Business center. $251-350

THE COSMOPOLITAN OF LAS VEGAS
3700 Las Vegas Blvd., Center Strip, 702-698-7000;
www.cosmopolitanlasvegas.com
The only hotel to open on the Las Vegas strip in 2010, this newly constructed, gleaming glass and steel hotel and casino will bring another 2,995 rooms to

the city. Part of Marriott's new Autograph Collection of independent hotels, the Cosmopolitan has studios and one-bedroom suites that are stocked with just-released technology (flat-screen TVs, entertainment systems, technology control panels) and spacious bathrooms with Japanese soaking tubs. The resort's arrival brings a chance for another roster of star chefs to open their first-ever Vegas restaurants, from Costas Spiliadis (with a Sin City branch of his New York-based Estiatorio Milos) to Scott Conant (Scarpetta). Joining the lineup is José Andrés, who will open tapas bar Jaleo and Mexican-Chinese concept China Poblano, and Los Angeles-based chef David Myers with his French brasserie concept Comme Ça. Pools have become big business in Vegas, and Cosmopolitan's gambit includes three, one of which, the Boulevard Pool, is the only to overlook the Strip. Rounding out the offerings at the resort are a spacious casino, a spa and a nightclub overseen by the Tao Group.

2,995 rooms. Restaurant, bar. Fitness center. Spa. Pool. $251-350

OFF-STRIP

★★HARD ROCK HOTEL & CASINO LAS VEGAS
4455 Paradise Road, Off-Strip, 702-693-5000, 800-473-7625; www.hardrockhotel.com

If you've never jammed on air guitar in your basement, the charms of The Rock may be lost on you. This rock 'n' roll-themed hotel is awash in memorabilia, but it's the rockers themselves (plus actors, models and sports stars) who really pull in the crowds. A center for stag parties, the Hard Rock attracts a 20-something set that's eager to hang out at the Tahitian-style pool wearing as little as possible. The standard guest rooms offer Bose stereo systems, plasma TVs, lots of plush linens and French doors that open onto either a pool or a mountain view. The 1,300-square-foot Celebrity Suite features a lounge area with a wet bar and a pool table, while the Penthouse ups the ante even more by adding a single-lane automated bowling alley and a mosaic hot tub with a view of the Strip.The new HRH Tower Suites offers private check in, a spa, new custom suites and restaurants of its own.

1,493 rooms. Restaurant, bar. Fitness center. Pool. Spa. Business center. $151-250

★★★LAS VEGAS HILTON
3000 Paradise Road, Off-Strip, 702-732-5111; www.lvhilton.com

The place where Elvis Presley broke concert attendance records, and where Barry Manilow played for years most recently, the Hilton has a long

---

WHAT ARE THE MOST LUXURIOUS HOTELS?

Tower Suites at Encore Las Vegas: A private entrance, intimate atmosphere and exceptional service give this majestic resort an exclusive feel. It doesn't hurt that Steve Wynn had his seemingly magical hand in everything from the casino décor to the world-class cuisine to the elite retail offerings in The Esplanade.

Tower Suites at Wynn Las Vegas: Revolutionizing the concept of casual luxury on the Strip, the Tower Suites are sumptuous and beautiful. Suites are spacious and comfortable, and customer service is impeccable. Even the late night casino pit bosses wear a friendly smile.

LIQUID AT ARIA

WHICH HOTELS HAVE THE MOST LIVELY POOLS?

Encore Beach Club: Get a taste for Vegas nightlife during the day at this multi-tiered pool club decorated in vibrant red, just like chic the resort. Daybeds feature private safes and cabanas have flat-screen televisions and refrigerators. Eight bungalows have private infinity pools. Spend the afternoon floating on one of the large lily pads, playing blackjack or watching people dance around the shower poles.

Encore Las Vegas: By day, the colorful butterfly mosaics decorating the pool floor, the uber-soft chaise lounges and surrounding flower gardens exude the elegance and beauty synonymous with Wynn. By night, the pool area turns more sultry as it becomes a playground for the hotel's hottest club, XS. Don't bother wearing a swimsuit to the club, however—XS only allows shallow wading.

Hard Rock Hotel & Casino La Vegas: The door may read Hard Rock Hotel, but by the pool area, it is pure essence of Tahiti. The complex, which is kitted out with tiki-style cabanas, lush vegetation and meandering pools and trails, takes the heat off the desert sun and an unlucky streak at the casino. But if you're ready to hit the tables again, there's no need to head back indoors—this pool area has swim-up blackjack at the Poolside palapa.

Liquid at Aria: This swank pool area includes private cabanas and a 50-seat restaurant. Relax on one of the large daybeds as you listen to the DJ spin. Avoid the cover by showing up for lunch—the fish tacos and mojitos are delicious.

Mandalay Bay Resort & Casino: It's not really a pool so much as the Caribbean transported to Nevada: the 11-acre Mandalay Bay's Sand-and-Surf Beach is home to three pools, various whirlpools, 2,700 tons of real sand, waves and a lazy river. The area is lots of fun for the kids, but it can be just as fun for adults, especially if you rent one of the cabanas or pool beds in the sophisticated Moorea Beach Club.

Tao Beach: This exclusive pool party at the Venetian is always a scene. Flanked by a large buddha, just as the indoor club is, the pool is filed with fun-seekers looking to soak up the sun while cooling off with alcoholic popcicles or specialty-made cocktails.

Wet Republic: Celebrities are alway hosting parties—everyone from Kim Kardashian to Sean "Diddy" Combs—at this always-hopping pool at the MGM Grand. The pool offers bottle service and pitchers of specialty cocktails.

FOUR SEASONS HOTEL LAS VEGAS

history on the Strip. Sports fans should enjoy the Hilton's Race and Sports SuperBook, which is considered one of the best in town for those who love putting bets down on everything from ponies to pugilists. The guest rooms have been recently renovated with a neutral color scheme, contemporary furnishings and new beds. If you can, upgrade to a premium room, which has high-end linens and plasma TVs. Business travelers no longer have to worry about walking in the heat in their suits thanks to the addition of a skybridge connecting the hotel to the Las Vegas Convention Center.

2,957 rooms. Restaurant, bar. Fitness center. Tennis. Pool. Spa. Business center. $151-250

★★★LAS VEGAS MARRIOTT SUITES
325 Convention Center Drive, Off-Strip, 702-650-2000; www.marriott.com
A smoke-free non-gambling hotel set directly across from the Las Vegas Convention Center, the Las Vegas Marriott Suites offers a convenient location for those attending a conference. The adjacent Monorail Station affords easy access to several stops along the Strip for those who simply can't resist throwing down a few chips between meetings. Some of the newly renovated guest rooms have separate living and sleeping areas, while all offer work stations with high-speed Internet access, cotton-rich linens and custom duvets. Essentially, this is a very pleasant stay for those who want to be in Vegas without really being in Vegas.

278 rooms. Restaurant, bar. Fitness center. Pool. Business center. $61-150

★★★★THE M RESORT SPA & CASINO LAS VEGAS
12300 Las Vegas Blvd. S., Off-Strip, 702-797-1000;
www.themresort.com
The newest addition to Henderson, the M Resort provides a refreshing alternative to typical Vegas. Instead of the constant dinging of slot machines and flashing of neon signs, the M Resort is a study in natural light, trickling waterfalls and the subtle scent of eucalyptus, which is filtrated through the

MGM GRAND HOTEL & CASINO

hotel. Lest you forget you're in Las Vegas, guest rooms offer views of the Strip through floor-to-ceiling windows, as well as Bose sound systems, flat-screen TVs and marble vanities. The sprawling 100,000-square-foot Villaggio Del Sole Pool and Entertainment Piazza includes two pools, cabanas, an outdoor cocktail lounge and a stage for live music performances. Nine onsite restaurants and bars ensure that you're well fed throughout your stay. *390 rooms. Restaurant, bar. Business center. Fitness center. Pool. Spa. $61-150*

★★★PALMS CASINO RESORT
4321 W. Flamingo Road, Off-Strip, 702-942-7777, 866-942-7777;
www.palms.com

Home to Bravo's *Celebrity Poker Showdown*, the Palms is known for its Hollywood-hip credentials and its themed "fantasy" suites. Sports fans will enjoy the Hardwood Suite, which has its own basketball court, or Kingpin Suite, which offers two regulation bowling lanes. The Palms has also revived the classic Playboy Club, which includes a lounge and gaming venues and Playboy Bunnies wearing both vintage and updated Roberto Cavalli-designed attire. It's the closest thing you can get to a Sunset Strip hotel in Las Vegas, and it hits home with the 30-something hipster crowd. The three-acre pool complex features an air-conditioned gaming area and a catwalk for swimsuit shows. The Palms Place tower has 599 condominium suites (many of which are available to rent as hotel rooms) and is attached to the Palms by the SkyTube, an elevated, enclosed moving walkway (to avoid that oppressive desert heat).
1,359 rooms. Restaurant, bar. Fitness center. Pool. Spa. Business center. $151-250

★★★THE PLATINUM HOTEL & SPA
211 E. Flamingo Road, Off-Strip, 702-365-5000, 877-211-9211;
www.theplatinumhotel.com

With no gaming and a no-smoking policy throughout the hotel, the sleek

Platinum would seem almost anti-Vegas. But that doesn't mean it isn't hip. The guest rooms, which run between 900 and 2,200 square feet, are all residential-style suites and include living rooms, gourmet kitchens, sound systems, double vanities and whirlpool tubs in the bathroom and private balconies offering views of the Strip or the nearby mountains. Chef Jay Watson oversees the restaurant, which is on the fifth floor and adjoins a lounge and pool deck area with outdoor fire pits and cabanas.

255 rooms. Restaurant, bar. Fitness center. Pool. Spa. Business center. $151-250

★★★TRUMP INTERNATIONAL HOTEL LAS VEGAS
2000 Fashion Show Drive, Off-Strip, 702-982-0000, 866-939-8786; www.trumplasvegashotel.com

Trump International Hotel Las Vegas has The Donald's signature panache written all over it—here in the form of the 24-karat gold glass windows that wrap around the 64-story building. Located just off the Strip adjacent to the Fashion Show mall, the non-gaming Trump is another jewel in a neighborhood that also houses Wynn. The elegant condominium suites (available for purchase) feature floor-to-ceiling windows offering panoramic views of the city, custom-designed furnishings in warm earth tones that play off the white duvets, and a luxe marble bathroom with a separate shower and jet-stream tub. Not only is the refrigerator custom-stocked, but each guest is assigned a Trump Attaché to make sure every whim is granted. If you're curious about what fills the Trump table at home, book a table at DJT, a lovely restaurant that offers modern American fare. Otherwise, you can request an in-room chef to prepare a meal in your personal kitchen—which has appliances by Sub-Zero, Wolf and Bosch—and serve them course by course. The Spa at Trump also comes with an attaché, who can customize everything from the infused elixir tonics to the music selections on your iPod.

1,282 rooms. Restaurant, bar. Fitness center. Pool. Spa. Business center. Pets accepted. $251-350

★★★THE WESTIN CASUARINA LAS VEGAS HOTEL CASINO & SPA
160 E. Flamingo Road, Off-Strip, 702-836-5900, 866-716-8132; www.westin.com

The Westin Casuarina offers a relaxing Westin experience just a block from the Strip. For businesspeople or meeting-goers, it's a mile from the Las Vegas Convention Center (in one direction) and the convention complex at Mandalay Bay (in the other), to leave you plenty of time to either relax by the pool or try your luck at the gambling tables before and after your business. The hotel's Heavenly Bed, Heavenly Bath and muted tones in the guest rooms and a Westin Kids Club onsite (in case you brought the kids along) make for a comfortable stay. The 20,000-square-foot casino in the lobby acts as a nice (and not-so-subtle) reminder that you're still in Vegas.

826 rooms. Restaurant, bar. Fitness center. Pool. Spa. Business center. Pets accepted. $151-250

ALSO RECOMMENDED
EMBASSY SUITES LAS VEGAS
4315 Swenson St., Off-Strip, 702-795-2800; www.embassysuites.com

Embassy Suites is all about consistency; if you've stayed at an Embassy Suites in the past, you know what to expect: a free cooked-to-order breakfast, complimentary happy hour and a separate bedroom and sitting

NEW YORK-NEW YORK

WHAT ARE THE BEST THEMED HOTELS?

New York-New York: Why deal with the hassles of Manhattan? New York-New York falls a bit on the kitschy side, but the famed roller coaster provides checkered cab service to all the hot tourist sights including the Empire State Building and the Statue of Liberty—without all of the traffic.

Paris Las Vegas: Judging from all of the wedding proposals that take place at the top of the Eiffel Tower, Paris Las Vegas is as good as the real thing when it comes to stirring up romance. With unparalleled views of the Fountains of Bellagio and the Strip, you're better off saving your euros for the casino.

The Venetian Resort Hotel Casino: Beautiful both outside and in, the Venetian takes its cues from historic Italian architecture and design. The casino is reminiscent of the Doge's Palace, the serenading gondoliers are dressed in authentic garb, and the detailed frescoes in the Great Hall are meticulous renditions of the original works. Add in a cappuccino or a creamy gelato and you might as well be in Italy.

THE M RESORT SPA & CASINO LAS VEGAS

area in each room. This particular Embassy Suites was recently renovated and also offers flat-screen TVs, work spaces with ergonomic chairs, and sleek black and tan décor. The hotel is across from über-hip Hard Rock, the University of Nevada, Las Vegas campus and close to the gay-friendly district nicknamed "the Fruit Loop."

220 rooms. Complimentary breakfast. Restaurant, bar. Fitness center. Pool. Business center. $61-150

RIO ALL-SUITE HOTEL & CASINO
3700 W. Flamingo Road, Off-Strip, 702-777-7777, 866-746-7671; www.riolasvegas.com

Although the Rio has an Off-Strip location that prohibits you from casino-hopping, you'll find there's plenty to keep you occupied here. People-watching takes the top spot on the list, thanks to the hundreds of sunglass-donning, stone-faced players flocking to the World Series of Poker tournaments. Penn & Teller entertain nightly and the Village Seafood Buffet gets high marks—as does the new adults-only pool that is open to the public (but charges a cover) and features DJ Madam Malixa spinning Top 40 and hip hop throughout the day. The guest rooms are all suites and while the décor leaves something to be desired, you'll have plenty of room to spread out with more than 600 square feet of space.

2,522 rooms. Restaurant, bar. Fitness center. Pool. Spa. Business center. $61-150

DOWNTOWN

★★★GOLDEN NUGGET LAS VEGAS
129 E. Fremont St., Downtown, 702-385-7111, 800-846-5336; www.goldennugget.com

More than $160 million has been spent on renovations to the Golden Nugget since it was purchased by the Landry's Restaurants company in 2005, and now the hotel—which originally opened in 1946 and retains its

Gold Rush-kitsch design—is the closest thing to a Strip-style property in the downtown area. The most striking addition is the hotel's Tank pool, which features a 200,000-gallon aquarium filled with sharks—no more dangerous than the poker variety you'll find in the casino—and a 30-foot waterslide that runs right through it. The hotel is made up of four towers. Rooms in the Rush Tower are modern and sophisticated with plenty of space, feather beds, flat-screen televisions and great views. Rooms in the Spa Tower run 1,500 square feet on two levels and offer whirlpool baths, floor-to-ceiling windows, wet bars and even a shoeshine machine. Before getting cozy at the tables, pay a visit to the hotel's "Hand of Faith," a gold nugget found in 1980 with an estimated worth of $425,000 and a weight of 61 pounds, 11 ounces.

2,300 rooms. Restaurant, bar. Fitness center. Pool. Spa. Business center. $61-150

ALSO RECOMMENDED
MAIN STREET STATION CASINO BREWERY & HOTEL
**200 N. Main St., Las Vegas, 702-387-1896, 800-713-8933;
www.mainstreetcasino.com**
The Main Street Station is located, appropriately, on Main Street, where it connects with Fremont at the beginning of the Fremont Street Experience. The hotel has a Victorian theme and is filled with unique artifacts that include Buffalo Bill Cody's private rail car, a fireplace from Scotland's Prestwick Castle and a piece of the Berlin Wall (found in the men's bathroom off the casino floor). Guest rooms have been recently renovated with a few of the same Victorian touches as the casino, including sconces and dark mahogany headboards. The rooms are still basic and can feel cramped, though. Main Street also offers an RV park for anyone who wants to camp out in Sin City come winter.

406 rooms. Restaurant, bar. Pool. $61-150

SUBURBS
★★★GREEN VALLEY RANCH RESORT, SPA AND CASINO
**2300 Paseo Verde Parkway, Henderson, 702-617-7777, 866-782-9487;
www.greenvalleyranchresort.com**
A Mediterranean-style oasis in the middle of the desert, the Green Valley Ranch Resort is situated in Henderson, between the Strip and the Lake Las Vegas resorts. The sprawling property feels more like an estate than a Vegas hotel, with personal touches like one-of-a-kind furnishings, plush sitting areas and textured accents. The casino does have a solid supply of dinging slot machines, but it's all done with a level of class that is rarely found on the Strip. Goose-down pillows, separate tubs and showers, twice-daily housekeeping service, and plush, terry-cloth robes turn guest rooms into refuges. Whether you spend your day at The Beach (with actual sand) or The Pond, you'll be treated to pools that promote excess. Of course, the property would be lost without an equally luxuriant spa that includes tempting treatments and a private lap pool.

495 rooms. Restaurant, bar. Fitness center. Pool. Spa. Business center. $151-250

MANDALAY BAY RESORT & CASINO

★★★JW MARRIOTT LAS VEGAS RESORT & SPA

221 N. Rampart Blvd., Summerlin, 702-869-7777;
www.jwlasvegasresort.com

When the JW Marriott first opened in Summerlin in 1999, it was one of the only hotels in the town, a suburb better known for its golf offerings and proximity to Red Rock Canyon. The resort is only a 20-minute drive from the Strip, but you'll have little reason to stray. The hotel has its own restaurant row with everything from Italian to Asian to Irish, 54 acres of gardens, an 11,000-square-foot pool with a cascading waterfall and a 50,000-square-foot casino (which caters to locals who prefer it to the tourist-trodden gaming rooms on the Strip). If you have yet to realize that square footage is no object here, the 40,000-square-foot spa, 100,000 square feet of function space and nine championship golf courses, including the TPC Las Vegas, should do the trick. The oversized guest rooms range from 560 to 1,950 square feet and offer views of the garden, the Strip or the surrounding mountains. Marble bathrooms with Jacuzzi tubs and separate rain showers, walk-in closets, ceiling fans and triple-sheeted beds make the time spent in your room nearly as enjoyable as that spent outdoors.

548 rooms. Restaurant, bar. Fitness center. Pool. Spa. Business center. $251-350

★★★LOEWS LAKE LAS VEGAS RESORT

101 Montelago Blvd., Henderson, 702-567-6000;
www.loewshotels.com

Golf, kayaking, fishing, hiking and spa treatments? Is this Vegas? Well technically it's Lake Las Vegas, a 320-acre man-made and privately owned lake that is closer to the town of Henderson than to Las Vegas proper (it is 17 miles from the Strip, for those who want to take in a show after all the outdoor recreation). The resort has a Moroccan theme and guest rooms offer amenities that include flat-screen TVs, plush terry robes, Lather bath products and twice-daily maid service. Entertainment in the area includes a concert series in the summer and a floating skating rink (yes, ice skating in the desert) in the nearby MonteLago Village during winter. Duffers will enjoy the Reflection Bay Golf Course and the Falls Golf Course. And, lest the kids and pets feel left out, Loews offers onsite specialty programs for both.

493 rooms. Restaurant, bar. Fitness center. Pool. Spa. Business center. Pets accepted. $151-250

★★★RED ROCK CASINO, RESORT & SPA
11011 W. Charleston, Summerlin, 702-797-7777;
www.redrocklasvegas.com

A favorite among local hipsters, the Red Rock is located in the Summerlin neighborhood, which had been known more for its golf courses and proximity to Red Rock Canyon (hence the name) than its dinging slot machines and thumping nightclubs. That all changed when the Red Rock opened in 2006. Roomy suites provide a respite from the gaming scene, with dark chocolate-brown tones and oversized, overstuffed pillows. Ask for a room facing the canyon for a spectacular sunset view. Grab a drink at the Lucky Bar or throw a few rocks at the 72-lane Red Rock Lanes bowling center. With its suburban locale, Red Rock can afford to spread out, claiming three acres of space for the pools, including 19 private cabanas and the Sand Bar offering refreshing drinks.

814 rooms. Restaurant, bar. Fitness center. Pool. Spa. Business center. $151-250

Suite Retreat.

7,093 Suites

32 Award-Winning Restaurants

201 Spectacular Shoppes

4 Amazing Shows

It's all Inside

THE VENETIAN® | THE PALAZZO®

LAS VEGAS

WELCOME TO
THE VENETIAN® AND THE PALAZZO®

THE BREATHTAKING ACCOMMODATIONS at The Venetian and The Palazzo offer a degree of luxury unavailable anywhere else in Las Vegas. Our suites average 700 square feet – roughly twice the size of most Las Vegas hotel rooms – and each one is designed to be a perfectly appointed retreat. And, for extra special treatment, stay with us at Prestige at The Palazzo, a level above the rest.

The best dining, shopping, and entertainment; all under one extraordinary roof.

EVERY ROOM A SUITE

THE VENETIAN® | THE PALAZZO®

LAS VEGAS

CARNEVINO

TOP TOQUES

You'll be hard-pressed to find a restaurant in Las Vegas that doesn't have a celebrity chef on its roster. The city has burst onto the culinary scene with a slew of elite dining experiences that would give any major metropolitan area a run for its money. Whether you're looking to partake in a four-hour gastronomic adventure at Alessandro Stratta's famed Alex or just grab a few slices of pizza at local favorite Settebello, you're guaranteed a meal that will satisfy the senses.

THE STRIP

★★★★★ALEX

Wynn Las Vegas, 3131 Las Vegas Blvd. S., Center Strip, 702-248-3463; www.wynnlasvegas.com

Perhaps it is the walls lined in mother of pearl and the 22 karat gold sand-casted candelabras at the entrance, or the custom-carved mahogany ceiling and boiserie wood marquetry. Whatever the secret, Alessandro Stratta's namesake restaurant has awed diners and garnered accolades since settling in at Wynn Las Vegas in 2005. The richly appointed dining room is only a hint of the luxury and grandeur that await you on the plate. The cuisine of the French Riviera is what Stratta focuses on, and he executes it with such style and grace you'll think you're in the South of France. You will find entrées such as roasted squab and seared foie gras or olive oil poached kanpachi that concentrate on enhancing natural flavors with subtle touches and aromatic sauces. The seasonal tasting menu, which runs at $185 per person, or $295 if you include wine pairings, travels through seven courses from a tangy heirloom tomato and octopus carpaccio amuse-bouche to a rich Wagyu strip loin with wild mushrooms to a perfectly subtle toasted vanilla custard topped with maple-poached peaches. Service is attentive and pleasant, but not overwhelming. A meal at Alex will certainly be one of those long marathon dining evenings, where you'll likely leave fuzzy from the wine pairings and, above all, pleasantly satiated.

French. Dinner. Closed Sunday-Tuesday. Jacket requested. $86 and up

★★★AQUAKNOX

The Venetian Resort Hotel Casino, 3355 Las Vegas Blvd. S., Center Strip, 702-414-3772; www.venetian.com

Contrary to what you might think, seafood is big business in the desert, especially at places like Aquaknox, which has its own selections flown in daily. The restaurant lets you know from start to finish that they're serious about underwater delicacies, from the lights bathing the whole space in aquatic blue hues to the water cascading down around the bottles in the wine wall. Though the menu varies between Mediterranean and Asian influences, both treatments take full advantage of beautiful seafood sourced from around the world. The signature fish soup, much more than a solution for leftover scraps, is chock full of the choicest lobster, John Dory, mussels and clams in a fragrant and rich tomato saffron broth.

Seafood. Lunch, dinner. $36-85

★★★★AUREOLE

Mandalay Bay Resort & Casino, 3950 Las Vegas Blvd. S., South Strip, 702-632-7401; www.mandalaybay.com

When you come to Aureole, come thirsty. The 42-foot steel and glass wine tower that greets you at the door holds 10,000 bottles of wine and comes

AUREOLE

complete with "Wine Angel Stewards," servers who float on wires to snag your bottle of choice from the towers. Throw in one of the foremost chefs in American contemporary cuisine and a soaring modern interior, and you've got Aureole. But this restaurant isn't all big names and acrobatic wait staff; there's soul in the cooking, too. Charlie Palmer's menu treats fresh-off-the-farm ingredients with elegance and sophistication, evidenced in dishes such as the scallop sandwiches in a crisp potato crust and monkfish osso buco with chanterelles and pork belly stuffed cabbage. A handheld computer gives you access to the expansive wine list, which is sent directly to the aerialists in the tower. It's worth ordering a bottle just to watch the show, which is part Cirque du Soleil, part *Mission: Impossible*.
Contemporary American. Dinner. $86 and up

★★★B&B RISTORANTE
The Venetian Resort Hotel Casino, 3355 Las Vegas Blvd. S., Center Strip, 702-266-9977; www.bandbristorante.com
Celebrity chef Mario Batali's restaurant empire has expanded to Las Vegas with a few new ventures. B&B Ristorante (the other "B" stands for his partner, winemaker Joe Bastianich) is a small space where you might bump elbows with your neighbors, but the coziness adds to the jovial atmosphere. Batali's menu at this spot is simple, rustic Italian with a gourmet edge. The salumi are a must-try—all are made fresh in house by executive chef Zach Allen or cured in house, with the exception of the prosciutto di San Danielle, which is imported from Italy. More adventurous options include a light and airy lamb's brain francobolli. A pasta tasting menu is available for those who can't decide on which dish to order. The wine list, featuring some Bastianich private label bottles, is extensive, especially as far as—you guessed it—Italian wines go.
Italian. Dinner. $36-85

BRADLEY OGDEN

★★★BOUCHON
The Venetian Resort Hotel Casino, 3355 Las Vegas Blvd. S., Center Strip, 702-414-6200; www.bouchonbistro.com

Star chef Thomas Keller has dreamed up his version of a French bistro, and it's appropriately elegant and tasteful, yet completely comfortable (the original is in Napa Valley). The room, designed by Adam Tihany, is spacious and simple, trimmed in dark woods against white walls and brass rails, and feels just like an authentic brasserie. The dress code is Las Vegas chic, meaning that just about anything goes. Men in suits sit next to tourists in jeans and flip-flops, and everyone focuses on the simple flavors of the food. It's not about pretentious, tiny eats at Bouchon; it's about a solid meal of bistro standards, from steak frites to roasted lamb in thyme jus. Every dish comes with pommes frites, which is a good thing, since these French fries are revered as some of the best in Las Vegas. A casual brunch on weekends on the patio overlooking the pool and its sunbathers is a good way to get some fresh desert air.
French bistro. Breakfast, dinner, Saturday-Sunday brunch. $36-85

★★★★BRADLEY OGDEN
Caesars Palace, 3570 Las Vegas Blvd. S., Center Strip, 877-346-4642; www.harrahs.com

Located off the casino floor at Caesars Palace, chef Bradley Ogden's eponymous restaurant, with its décor accented by rich wood, feels a million miles away from the Strip. Ogden is best known for his farm-to-table culinary philosophy, as well as his passion for using organic products from sustainable resources. Though the menu changes seasonally, you can be sure that you're getting the freshest ingredients prepared so that their true flavors shine through. This is definitely an upscale restaurant, but the affable waitstaff makes the experience comfortable, inviting and warm. The menu is an honest reflection of simple American cuisine, so dishes will be ones you recognize. The burger, available at the bar, is often cited as one of the best in Las Vegas. Another mainstay, the twice-baked Maytag blue cheese

Botero: This fun poolside space is visually stunning, the menu is delicious and you won't be able to get enough of desserts such as the ice cream cupcakes and PB & J brioche doughnuts.

LAVO: Palazzo's hottest nightclub is only steps away when dining at this posh spot, so the people-watching is guaranteed to be gossip-worthy. Small dishes to share ensure that you won't be too full to hit the dance floor straight from dinner.

Postrio Bar & Grill: Situated in St. Mark's Square at the Venetian, Postrio gets you in on the action from the patio, as the open space swarms with casual shoppers, passers-by and the occasional juggler.

Tao: The sexy Asian décor puts everyone in a party mood, whether you're grabbing pre-nightclub cocktails or a few maki rolls.

souffle—fluffy, rich and savory—is divine and a necessary indulgence every time you find yourself in this dining room.
Contemporary American. Dinner. $86 and up

★★★CARNEVINO
The Palazzo Las Vegas Resort Hotel Casino, 3325 Las Vegas Blvd. S., Center Strip, 702-789-4141; www.carnevino.com

If you love a good steak and great wine, you'll be happy at chef Mario Batali's Carnevino. While there are Italian dishes on the menu (such as pappardelle with porcini trifolati), made-in-the-Midwest meat is the main attraction. You're guaranteed a good cut, as the steaks are all-natural and free of hormones and antibiotics. The Italian villa-inspired dining room is decked out in dark wood, plump cushions, a marble bar and a big bronze bull, just in case you didn't know it was a steakhouse. Order a bottle from the never-ending wine list and share the slightly charred Florentine porterhouse, which is rubbed with sea salt, pepper and fresh rosemary. This succulent steak is one of the highlights of Mario Batali's menu.
Steak, Italian. Lunch, dinner. 36-85

★★★CRAFTSTEAK
MGM Grand Hotel & Casino, 3799 Las Vegas Blvd. S., South Strip, 702-891-7318; www.craftrestaurant.com

Meat purists will want to sink their teeth into the prime cuts here. Chef Tom Colicchio, who also moonlights as the exacting head judge on Bravo's *Top Chef,* goes by the philosophy that simpler is better. That goes for the dining room, too, which is plainly decorated with wooden tables without tablecloths, bare branches in vases and spare bulbs dangling from the ceiling. When it comes to food, Colicchio refuses to let fancy sauces or complicated preparations take away from the meat. But fewer ingredients don't mean fewer choices: You can have your piece of protein roasted, grilled or braised; you can get cuts from Idaho, New York or Australia; you can opt for corn-fed or grass-fed beef; and you'll have to pick from sizes ranging from six to 32 ounces. A solid option is the Kobe skirt steak. If you're not a meat fan, go for the shellfish sampler, a tempting platter teeming

with fresh chilled lobster salad, Alaskan king crab, oysters and clams. At a back-to-basics restaurant like this, when it comes time for dessert, stick to the classics and get the sinful chocolate soufflé with espresso ice cream doused with caramel sauce.
Steak. Dinner. $86 and up

★★★CUT
The Palazzo Las Vegas Resort Hotel Casino, 3325 Las Vegas Blvd. S., Center Strip, 702-607-6300; www.palazzolasvegas.com
Wolfgang Puck is at it again. This time it is in the form of a steakhouse at the Palazzo that some say is the best place for steak in Las Vegas. The 160-seat metallic dining room manages to feel simultaneously industrial and warm thanks to well-chosen appointments and lamp-lit chandeliers. In the adjacent bar, sample custom cocktails and dishes from the smaller "Rough Cuts" bar menu. The classic steakhouse offerings are given the Puck treatment, including the use of Wagyu and pure Japanese Kobe beef, but innovative dishes such as double thick pork chop atop an apple and nectarine moustarda allow the chef's true talents to shine through. Other hits from the menu include the Indian-spiced Kobe short ribs, slow cooked for eight hours and finished with a purée of curried corn.
Steak. Dinner. $86 and up

★★★DELMONICO STEAKHOUSE
The Venetian Resort Hotel Casino, 3355 Las Vegas Blvd. S., Center Strip, 702-414-1992; www.venetian.com
Celebrity chef Emeril Lagasse is best known for his talent with Creole cuisine, and at Delmonico he brings this influence to the steakhouse concept. The dining room, with its high-backed chairs and padded banquettes, vaulted ceilings and track-lighting, is comfortable enough to enjoy the kind of meal Lagasse can provide. The steaks and chops themselves are standard steakhouse fare, but some options, such as bone-in rib eye or a chateaubriand for two, are carved and presented tableside. Don't overlook the appetizers: a Creole boiled gulf shrimp cocktail with a piquant horseradish sauce will call your taste buds to attention. To wash it all down, there is a spectacular wine list that has garnered many awards for its vast and high-quality selections.
Steak, Creole. Lunch, dinner. $36-85

★★★EMERIL'S
MGM Grand Hotel & Casino, 3799 Las Vegas Blvd. S., South Strip, 702-891-7374; www.mgmgrand.com
The restaurant that started the Emeril Lagasse empire in New Orleans

FIAMMA TRATTORIA

now has a home at MGM Grand. The same spunk that Lagasse exudes on television is present in the fun dining room (complete with a 14-foot wrought-iron fish sculpture to greet you at the entrance), even if its namesake chef isn't always behind the burners. Focused heavily on Creole and Cajun flavors, the menu is both home-style and sophisticated, elevating low-country cuisine. The seafood gumbo is a standout starter, as is the signature New Orleans barbecue shrimp. A hearty lunch requires little more than the seafood pan roast, which is full of fresh seafood, jambalaya and a butter sauce spiked with Emeril's own herb essence.
Seafood, Cajun. Lunch, dinner. $36-85

★★★FIAMMA TRATTORIA
MGM Grand Hotel & Casino, 3799 Las Vegas Blvd. S., South Strip, 702-891-7600; www.mgmgrand.com
This cozy, chic trattoria encourages lingering. Clusters of bamboo form nests of lighting that hang above chocolate banquettes with honey-hued pillows. You'll want to sit near the undulating sculptural wave wall in front of the glass-enclosed, blazing fireplace, a nod to the restaurant's name, which means "flame" in Italian. The menu isn't as contemporary as the décor, but it updates old-school Italian faves. Spaghetti comes with Kobe meatballs, raviolini is stuffed with short ribs and splashed with Barbera wine sauce and sprinkled with pecorino romano, and gnocchi become puffs of lobster instead of potato. If you're not in the mood for pasta, choose entrées like the involtino di coniglio (roasted rabbit leg) or the brasato (Piemontese braised beef short ribs). Be sure to leave room for the Italian desserts. Cheesecake gelato and basil-lime sorbetto give fresh alternatives to the usual flavors, but a real treat is the crochette, crispy amaretti doughnuts that come with a trio of dunking sauces: chocolate ganache, vanilla bean glaze and strawberry jam. If you can't eat another bite, opt for a glass of Italian wine and huddle in front of the beautiful fireplace.
Italian. Dinner. $36-85

JOËL ROBUCHON

★★★JASMINE
Bellagio Las Vegas, 3600 Las Vegas Blvd. S., Center Strip,
702-693-7223; www.bellagio.com

Going out for Chinese has never felt so refined. With a great view of Lake Bellagio, this dining room is regal and elegant with warm pastel tones and glowing chandeliers. Chef Phillip Lo's menu includes traditional Cantonese, Szechwan and Hunan fare as well as nouveau Hong Kong cuisine. Traditional dishes like hot and sour soup are done with panache. The Maine lobster dumplings with a ginger dipping sauce are excellent, as is the caramelized pork tenderloin. Be sure to specify that you'd like a table by the open windows to ensure an uninterrupted view of the famed Bellagio fountains. *Chinese. Dinner. $36-85*

★★★★★JOËL ROBUCHON
MGM Grand Hotel & Casino, 3799 Las Vegas Blvd. S., South Strip,
702-891-7925; www.mgmgrand.com

One of the world's greatest chefs, Joël Robuchon has come to epitomize fine, French cuisine. The intimate dining room is regal, from the black and white tiled entryway to the chandelier in the middle of the room. There is even an indoor patio where a façade of flowing greenery transforms a windowless side room into a classical garden. The 16-course tasting menu will set you back $385, but it's worth it. What makes his food so special is the innovative ways he shows his respect for ingredients. Take Le Caviar Osciètre, one of Robuchon's signature dishes, for example. Elevating the ingredient beyond typical blinis and crème fraîche, he combines thin slices of warm scallops with lime zest, smooth cauliflower cream, avocado and Osetra caviar to create a total sensory explosion of surprisingly complementary textures and flavors. You'd never think to mix these ingredients yourself, but when

WHAT ARE THE BEST STEAKHOUSES?

Craftsteak: Chef Tom Colicchio likes to keep things simple. And when you have such high-quality ingredients, like Kobe skirt steak and Alaskan king crab, it's an easy mantra to follow.

CUT: The industrial décor and low lighting lets all the fanfare fall on the meat itself, which is well deserved with dishes such as slow-cooked Indian-spiced Kobe short ribs.

Carnevino: Organic and all-natural seem to be attached to just about everything these days. But when your steak is free of hormones and antibiotics, as it is at Carnevino, you can truly taste the difference.

Delmonico Steakhouse: It's all about presentation at Emeril's steakhouse. Order the bone-in rib eye or chateaubriand for two and you'll be treated to seeing your meal carved tableside.

Jean Georges Steakhouse: This restaurant stands out by featuring cuts from all over the world, including Japan, Argentina and Uruguay.

SW Steakhouse: The steak is good. But don't neglect the sides, which range from truffled creamed corn to garlic and aged goat cheese.

you bite into his creations, they just make sense. Service is formal and flawless—exactly what you'd expect from a restaurant of this caliber.
French. Dinner. $86 and up

★★★L'ATELIER DE JOËL ROBUCHON
MGM Grand Hotel & Casino, 3799 Las Vegas Blvd. S., South Strip, 702-891-7358; www.mgmgrand.com
It might be safe to call L'Atelier ("workshop" in French) a more casual offering from master chef Joël Robuchon, as a meal here is somewhat more interactive than at the formal Joël Robuchon located right next door. The dining room, decorated in reds and blacks, features an open-air kitchen and counter seating where you can watch chefs prepare your food. No surprise here: The cuisine is all French, and signature dishes include a langoustine fritter with basil pesto and free-range quail stuffed with foie gras. Two tasting menus are available, though you can order à la carte to mix and match your own personal Robuchon experience.
French. Dinner. $36-85

★★★LAVO
The Palazzo Las Vegas Resort Hotel Casino, 3325 Las Vegas Blvd. S., Center Strip, 702-791-1800; www.lavolv.com
Before the party crowd heads upstairs to club LAVO, they gather for dinner and drinks at this first-floor restaurant. Join the party and order up a bunch of dishes to share, such as the Kobe meatballs with whipped fresh ricotta, spagetti carbonara, cacciatore pizza and grilled New York prime strip with garlic gorgonzola butter. You'll want to keep dessert all to yourself; tasty treats include the delectable chocolate bread pudding with silky dulce de leche and vanilla ice cream, or the warm apple crisp, which updates

plain old apple pie with cinnamon ice cream and a bowl made of hazelnut streusel. You'll want to linger in this dining room; the high ceilings with coned chandeliers, low leather booths and tables make it a cozy social spot. If you feel like continuing the evening, make your way to the gorgeous glass-and-wood-screened bridge that leads to the lively nightclub.

Italian. Dinner. $36-85

★★★★LE CIRQUE

Bellagio Las Vegas, 3600 Las Vegas Blvd. S., Center Strip, 702-693-7223; www.bellagio.com

The original Le Cirque in New York City is legendary because the food is spectacular, and because the service, often led by family patriarch Sirio Maccioni himself, is stellar and welcoming. Le Cirque at Bellagio holds to the same principles. Maccioni's sons run the restaurant to the same exacting standards as its East Coast sibling. In the vibrantly colored, circus-tent-like dining room, expertly executed French cuisine is served. Le Cirque's signature dish, the potato-crusted sea bass with a red wine reduction, lives up to its reputation as an outstanding offering. The three-course, $98 prix fixe menu is a smart choice.

French. Dinner. $86 and up

★★★★MICHAEL MINA

Bellagio Las Vegas, 3600 Las Vegas Blvd. S., Center Strip, 702-693-7223; www.bellagio.com

Tucked behind the Bellagio's stunning Conservatory, Michael Mina feels like a nice little secret. The restaurant is the perfect storm of design and cuisine, from its chic décor with floor-to-ceiling blond wood shelves to its innovative menu and equally sleek wine collection. Michael Mina, one of the few restaurants on the Strip that does a vegetarian tasting menu, is well-known for its tasting trios, which feature a singular product presented three different ways, ideal for those who want to expand their palates. Ingredients such as boneless Colorado rack of lamb, American Kobe rib eye and Nantucket Bay scallops get Mina's signature trio treatment. Seafood also factors in heavily on this menu, done primarily in the style of contemporary California cuisine. If you have a soft spot for foie gras, order a dish of whole foie gras, which is carved tableside and proves as savory for the eyes as the taste buds. Mina's signature root beer float, a swimmingly icy blend of sassafras ice cream and root beer sorbet, seals the deal on this American classic.

Contemporary American. Dinner. Closed Wednesday. $86 and up

WHICH RESTAURANTS SERVE THE BEST CONTEMPORARY AMERICAN FOOD?

Auerole: Charlie Palmer's menu treats fresh-off-the-farm ingredients with elegance and sophistication, and there's an excellent wine list to match.

Bradley Ogden: The farm-to-table philosophy and emphasis on organic produce ensure that each and every dish is served at the peak of freshness.

Michael Mina: Mina's signature trios—three different presentations of the same ingredient—keep your taste buds on their toes and your belly pleasantly satiated.

LE CIRQUE

★★★★MIX IN LAS VEGAS
Mandalay Bay Resort and Casino, 3950 Las Vegas Blvd. S., South Strip, 702-632-9500; www.mandalaybay.com

Alain Ducasse's artful restaurant atop THEHotel at Mandalay Bay offers one of the most stunning views of the Strip. Walking into the restaurant is like entering into a modern art museum with its sleek, white décor and enormous chandelier, made of 15,000 hand-blown Murano glass balls. With the glitter of the lights of the Mandalay Bay sign outside the windows and surrounded by the glass bubbles, you'll feel like you've entered a flute of champagne. The chic design of the restaurant is reflected on the plate as well. American cuisine is interpreted using contemporary haute French technique, producing dishes such as lobster salad served with a tangy apple and vegetable mosaique, and surf and turf made with halibut and foie gras rather than the standard lobster and steak.

Contemporary French. Dinner. $86 and up

★★★NOBHILL TAVERN
MGM Grand Hotel & Casino, 3799 Las Vegas Blvd. S., South Strip, 702-891-7337; www.mgmgrand.com

San Francisco chef Michael Mina's Nobhill Tavern is one of the great contemporary American restaurants on the Strip. Many ingredients on the menu are sourced from the Bay Area and all over the country, including poultry and organic produce. Try one of Mina's specialties, such as the San Francisco cioppino with steamed shellfish, tomato broth and basil oil, or chicken and dumplings served with roasted cauliflower, carrots and baby leeks. If you're looking for a bite at the bar, try the cheeseburger sliders or dig into Mina's famous lobster pot pie. Finish with desserts such as a pecan-praline sundae or apple crisp with cinnamon ice cream. The restaurant's design takes its cues from the best Bay City spots, complete with dark wood accents, intimate booths and a soothing, earthy color palette.

Contemporary American. Dinner. $86 and up

CRAFTSTEAK

WHAT ARE THE BEST CELEBRITY CHEF RESTAURANTS?

Alex: Alex gets top billing for hitting it out of the foodie-sphere on every level: lavish décor, congenial service, and most of all, flawless nouveau French cuisine and wine pairings courtesy of chef Alessandro Stratta.

Bartolotta Ristorante di Mare: Book one of the private cabanas around the lagoon and prepare for the pure comfort of chef Paul Bartolotta's authentic Italian dishes.

B&B Ristorante Celebrity chef Mario Batali's restaurant empire includes this cozy spot with a jovial atmosphere. Batali's menu is simple, rustic Italian with a gourmet edge.

Bouchon: Star chef Thomas Keller has dreamed up his version of a French bistro, and it's appropriately elegant and tasteful.

Craftsteak: Chef Tom Colicchio, the exacting head judge on Bravo's *Top Chef,* goes by the philosophy that simpler is better, and it always works.

Joël Robuchon: It's no wonder Robuchon has come to epitomize fine, French cuisine. What makes his food so special is the innovative ways he mixes ingredients to create a total sensory explosion of surprisingly complementary textures and flavors.

Mix in Las Vegas: Alain Ducasse's artful restaurant atop THEhotel offers one of the most impressive views of the Strip. That is, if you can peel your eyes off the dining room's stunning minimalist décor.

Restaurant Guy Savoy: This quiet, cool and sophisticated spot is Guy Savoy's only American venture, and thankfully, you'll get the same quality treatment and meal here that you would at the original Guy Savoy in Paris.

MICHAEL MINA

★★★OLIVES

Bellagio Las Vegas, 3600 Las Vegas Blvd. S., Center Strip, 702-693-7223; www.bellagio.com

Celebrity chef Todd English is best known for his take on rustic Italian and Mediterranean cuisine. His dim and sexy Jeffrey Beers-designed restaurant at the Bellagio overlooks the famed fountains, and features outdoor patio seating for those wanting an even closer look. Like the original Olives in Boston, the menu focuses on the best of his Italian cooking, including brick-oven flatbreads and pastas made in-house. The brick oven roasted chicken with avocado purée and fried polenta is particularly tasty and surprisingly light. This is one of those restaurants that is not only consistent every time you have a meal at the same outpost, but state to state as well. The waitstaff is upbeat and knowledgeable, so they feel like family and strive to help you feel the same way.

Mediterranean. Lunch, dinner. $36-85

★★★THE PALM

The Forum Shops at Caesars Palace, 3500 Las Vegas Blvd. S., Center Strip, 702-732-7256; www.thepalm.com

The Palm has that classic steakhouse vibe and a staff that remembers your name. But you don't have to be a regular to enjoy a meal here. There are no frills, no fancy presentations, just honest-to-goodness solid steakhouse fare, as well as some traditional Italian-American dishes, staying true to the original New York City concept. The veal scallopini with Milanese, piccata or Marsala sauce is consistently wonderful. Of course, if you're more inclined to have a steak, you're in good company. The 32-ounce prime rib for two is fantastic; smaller appetites are well sated with the 9-ounce filet mignon. And since you were always taught to eat your vegetables, a side of creamed spinach balances out the meal.

Steak. Lunch, dinner. $36-85

★★★★PICASSO

Bellagio Las Vegas, 3600 Las Vegas Blvd. S., Center Strip, 702-693-7223; www.bellagio.com

Only in Las Vegas can you sit and eat a full meal among priceless works of art by a legendary artist. Picasso, with its stunning view of the Fountains of Bellagio, is by far one of the most elegant and awe-inspiring dining rooms in the world. And if all the Picassos surrounding you aren't enough, culinary artist Julian Serrano prepares his own masterpieces for you to enjoy. The sublime degustation and prix fixe menus are predominantly French and Spanish influenced, and the wines, with more than 1,500 selections to choose from, are sourced exclusively from European vineyards. The menu changes almost daily based on what's fresh each morning. If you can catch the pan-seared sea scallops with potato mousseline and leeks, you're in for a culinary treat.

French, Spanish. Dinner. Closed Tuesday. $86 and up

★★★POSTRIO BAR & GRILL

The Venetian Resort Hotel Casino, 3377 Las Vegas Blvd. S., Center Strip, 702-796-1110; www.wolfgangpuck.com

Located in St. Mark's Square at the Grand Canal Shoppes at The Venetian, Postrio is a perfect spot to enjoy a casually elegant meal, with some priceless people-watching to boot. The interior of the restaurant is subtle, with intimate booths and soothing colors. Sitting on the faux patio (you're still inside a mall) allows you to watch not only passers-by, but also the entertainment (in the way of jugglers, singers and musicians) that roams around the plaza. Postrio is Wolfgang Puck's blend of American and Mediterranean cuisine, so expect plenty of fresh flavors and ingredients prepared in unexpected ways. Try the lobster club sandwich; it's one of the best on the Strip. For a heartier dish, opt for the kurobuta pork schnitzel with Austrian potatoes. If you're in luck, Puck's famous 13-layer tiramisu with coffee anglaise and chocolate sorbet will be available.

American. Lunch, dinner. $36-85

★★★PRIME STEAKHOUSE
Bellagio Las Vegas, 3600 Las Vegas Blvd. S., Center Strip, 702-693-7223; www.bellagio.com

A concept by celebrity chef and restaurateur Jean-Georges Vongerichten, Prime delivers a true luxury steakhouse experience. From its plush brown and blue décor to the contemporary art hanging on the walls, the room sings decadence. The menu offers standard steakhouse dishes, but it's the detailed presentation that sets it apart from other steak places. Vongerichten is known for the Asian influences and flavors in his dishes, and he continues this theme in dishes such as grilled diver scallops in a soy-yuzu broth, or filet mignon over shishito peppers. The wine list is impressive, featuring the best of the big reds of California. If you forgot to secure a reservation weeks in advance, try your luck on the outdoor terrace, where you can sample tasty appetizers and desserts without calling ahead.
Steakhouse. Dinner. $36-85

★★★★RESTAURANT GUY SAVOY
Caesars Palace, 3570 Las Vegas Blvd. S., Center Strip, 702-731-7385; www.harrahs.com

Located in the Augustus Tower of Caesars Palace, Guy Savoy's only American venture is quiet, cool and sophisticated. Run by Guy's son Franck, you can be assured that you'll get the same quality treatment and meal here that you would at the original Guy Savoy in Paris—minus the Eiffel Tower view. Two tasting menus (one 10-course and one four-course) are available, and both offer Savoy's signature dish of artichoke and black truffle soup, a divine concoction served with toasted mushroom brioche and an earthy truffle butter. For a more casual experience, grab a seat at the Bites & Bubbles bar where you can order smaller tasting portions of the menu as well as fantastic champagnes by the glass.
French. Dinner. Closed Monday-Tuesday. Bar. $86 and up

★★★SEABLUE
MGM Grand Hotel & Casino, 3799 Las Vegas Blvd. S., South Strip, 702-891-3486; www.mgmgrand.com

Delicious seafood is the theme at Seablue, one of two Michael Mina-helmed restaurants at MGM Grand. Watch the chefs in the open-air kitchen from the aquatic-themed dining room, complete with water cascading down the walls. The menu changes with the season, and all the seafood is caught wild and flown in daily. The kitchen draws from traditional Mediterranean cooking techniques, including the use of tagines (Moroccan clay ovens), and simple grilling to make the seafood shine. The Seablue paella is not traditional Spanish paella, but it is loaded with fresh seafood, rabbit, and chorizo and finished with a saffron risotto. One of the biggest hits on the menu is the lobster corndog, a luxurious version that puts the original to shame. Delicate lobster sausage is dipped in batter, fried and served with a pungent but refreshing mustard crème fraîche.

Seafood. Dinner. $86 and up

★★★SHIBUYA
MGM Grand Hotel & Casino, 3799 Las Vegas Blvd. S., South Strip, 702-891-3001; www.mgmgrand.com

MGM Grand's Japanese restaurant is so much more than just a sushi bar. Taking its name from a popular neighborhood in Tokyo, Shibuya features traditional Japanese cuisine executed with contemporary twists and techniques. The interior is chic and almost clubby; the cool physique of the glass cube wall behind the sushi bar at the entrance is balanced by the appearance of natural woods throughout the space. High quality ingredients make for interesting preparations, including the toro tartare, which features gorgeous tuna belly enhanced with achiote oil and made more decadent with the addition of caviar and gold leaf. If you're feeling adventurous, opt for the live Maine lobster served three ways: the tail as sashimi, the claws as tempura and the rest in a silky miso soup. Boasting the only certified sake sommelier in Las Vegas, Shibuya has the Japanese fine dining experience covered from all angles.

Japanese. Dinner. $86 and up

★★★TABLE 10
The Palazzo Las Vegas Resort Hotel Casino, 3327 Las Vegas Blvd. S., Center Strip, 702-607-6363; www.emerils.com

Enter the French Quarter-inspired iron gates of Table 10 to get a taste of Emeril "Bam!" Lagasse's Cajun flavors and his seafood-heavy comfort cuisine. Watch all of the action at the Food Bar, which gives you a glimpse of the chefs manning the grills and flitting about the busy kitchen. Watching them cook will make your stomach rumble, so start off with the traditional gumbo with bits of andouille sausage or the crab trinity, a holy union of snow crab cocktail, lump crab rémoulade and jumbo lump citrus onion salad. Keep the fresh-from-the-ocean theme going with the to-die-for lobster dome, with chunks of Maine lobster, sweet corn, mushrooms, leeks and spinach in truffle-sherry cream sealed in a flaky crust. For dessert, get the white chocolate malassadas, doughnut-like cousins to native-to-New-Orleans beignets, with cinnamon sugar and vanilla bean crème anglaise.

Cajun, American. Lunch, dinner. $36-85

WHAT ARE THE BEST RESTAURANTS FOR SEAFOOD?
Bartolotta Ristorante di Mare: Fresh seafood is flown in regularly straight from Italy and prepared in authentic dishes that let the true flavors of the fish soar.

Emeril's: Bringing Creole and Cajun flavors to everything in sight, Emeril packs a punch with his seafood gumbo and barbecue shrimp. While it may leave you with a fiery tongue, it won't leave you hungry.

Seablue: The aquatic theme is carried throughout the space with a cascading waterfall and blue hues, but the fresh catches flown in daily are what really draw in the seafood-craving crowds.

RESTAURANT GUY SAVOY

★★★TAO

The Venetian Resort Hotel Casino, 3355 Las Vegas Blvd. S., Center Strip, 702-388-8338; www.taolasvegas.com

Part nightclub, part Asian restaurant, Tao packs crowds in nightly with its alluringly sexy Buddha-filled décor, a koi pond and weathered wood, a harmonious combination of ancient culture and contemporary life. You'll find a pan-Asian menu with elements of Chinese, Japanese and Thai cuisine figuring prominently. Sushi is a good choice, and the menu is heavy on trendy maki creations. Entrées are boldly flavored but still familiar, including the wasabi-crusted filet mignon. If you want to linger after your meal, head upstairs to the nightclub—it's one of the hottest Vegas spots for bass-thumping music and celebrity sightings.

Asian. Dinner. $36-85

★★★TOP OF THE WORLD

Stratosphere Las Vegas, 2000 Las Vegas Blvd. S., North Strip, 702-380-7777; www.topoftheworldlv.com

It may not literally be the top of the world, but when the Strip includes the Empire State Building, the Eiffel Tower and the Great Pyramids of Giza, you might think it is. Perched atop the Stratosphere, the tallest point in Las Vegas, Top of the World is best known for its revolving dining room, which offers a complete 360-degree view of the city. On a clear day, you can see straight to Nellis Air Force Base, and at night spy one of the best views of downtown Las Vegas. You'll find classic continental cuisine on the menu, executed with quality ingredients, including the veal chop served with roma artichoke and mushroom demi-glace. Old favorites such as surf and turf are a big hit. But in Vegas you get what you pay for, so don't expect the food to be quite as good as some of the celeb-chef haunts down below. Top of the World can also get a tad tourist-heavy, with gawkers wanting to see that perfect view of Vegas.

American. Lunch, dinner. $36-85

PICASSO

★★★★TWIST

Mandarin Oriental, Las Vegas, 3752 Las Vegas Blvd. S., Center Strip, 888-881-9367; www.mandarinoriental.com

Following in the footsteps of fellow legendary French chefs Joël Robuchon, Guy Savoy and Alain Ducasse, Pierre Gagnaire opened Twist as his first stateside foray. Located on the 23rd floor of the opulent Mandarin Oriental, the views from Twist's 20-foot-high windows are as noteworthy as the chef. But there's plenty to gaze at inside the restaurant as well, particularly the 300 suspended illuminated globes floating throughout the space. Don't-miss dishes include chicken chiffonade with three kinds of tender gnocchi, as well as the signature langoustine five ways, including a seared tail of langoustine with salty ham; a lightly grilled version with creamy avocado; a mousseline with manzanilla; a gelée made with lobster innards; and then tartare with pomegranate. Close with the Grand Dessert Pierre Gagnaire, a twist on traditional French pastries and a meal unto itself. The five-course indulgence features inventive dishes like the savory Evil, a saffron-tequila bavaroise with a scoop of peppered mozzarella ice cream.

French. Dinner. Closed Sunday-Monday. $86 and up

★★★VALENTINO LAS VEGAS

The Venetian Resort Hotel & Casino, 3355 Las Vegas Blvd. S., Center Strip, 702-414-3000; www.venetian.com

Italian cuisine can either be very humble and rustic, or it can be highly refined and extravagant. Sometimes, however, there is a pleasant blending of the two, and Valentino is it. This signature Venetian spot is spacious and beautifully appointed and has six private dining rooms in addition to the main rooms, including an intimate wine cellar room that can seat four and an exclusive chef's table for up to six people. The menu is, of course, Italian, concentrating on traditional flavors with elegant presentations. Many ingredients are imported directly from Italy for optimum authenticity in flavor, and the menu changes seasonally. One of the mainstays, the pollo al

mattone, a simple, flavorful roast chicken butterflied and cooked flat under a brick, served with a creamy spinach risotto. While you're piling on the carbs, go for the three-color gnocchi with rabbit sausage, mushrooms and a cream demi-glace sauce—it's actually lighter than it sounds. The wine list is staggering–with about 2,500 selections—and service is impeccable.
Italian. Dinner. $86 and up

★★★VERANDAH
Four Seasons Hotel Las Vegas, 3960 Las Vegas Blvd. S., South Strip, 702-632-5000; www.fourseasons.com

Four Seasons Hotel Las Vegas is one of those rare spots on the Strip where you don't feel like you're on the Strip at all. Verandah, an open, airy restaurant with plenty of lush greenery and overlooking the exclusive Four Seasons pool is a common destination for both ladies who lunch and those looking for a little break from daily Las Vegas shenanigans. Afternoon tea (you can opt for champagne as well), complete with tiered platters of delicate finger sandwiches, scones and pastries, is popular, as Verandah is one of the few places where you can enjoy this genteel activity without the sound of slot machines in the background. Though the restaurant serves breakfast, lunch and dinner, the weekend breakfast buffet, with its create-your-own-doughnut station, is most popular. Instead of focusing on quantity for the masses, the staff delivers quality for those who are smart enough to dine here rather than the cattle calls that can be found at other hotel buffets.
American. Breakfast, lunch, dinner, Saturday-Sunday brunch, afternoon tea. $36-85

ALSO RECOMMENDED
AMERICAN FISH
Aria Resort & Casino, 3730 Las Vegas Blvd. S., Center Strip, 702-590-8610; www.michaelmina.net

Yet another Michael Mina restaurant (this marks his 17th, and fifth in Las Vegas alone), American Fish focuses on simply prepared seafood dishes in a clean-lined modern space with an intriguing steel ceiling sculpture. Of course, Mina doesn't really do simple; he cooks up a bounty of regional seafood in four signature preparations, including salt baked, wood grilled, cast-iron grilled and ocean-water poached. The ocean water is flown in from Hawaii and used to lightly poach a daily shellfish selection or two other fish filets, like halibut and bass. A highlight is the old-fashioned cornmeal-crusted rainbow trout, which comes from the cast-iron portion of the menu. Sides are required ordering here, including malt vinegar french fries with tartar dipping sauce, truffled mac and cheese and sweet corn with bacon. An extensive wine list is offered, but classic American cocktails like Singapore slings and gimlets are the draw.
Seafood. Dinner. Closed Tuesday. Bar. $36-85

JOËL ROBUCHON

WHAT ARE THE BEST OVERALL RESTAURANTS?

Alex: If walls are lined in Mother of Pearl and the ceiling is made from custom-carved mahogany, imagine how much effort is put into the food. Alessandro Stratta's appreciation for natural flavors makes even the simplest of dishes shine.

Joël Robuchon: You'll feel far removed from the Las Vegas Strip upon entering this epicurean palace. From the caviar to the blinis to the chocolate cake, your taste buds will want for nothing at the hands of this culinary master.

AQUAKNOX

BAR MASA

Aria Resort and Casino, 3730 Las Vegas Blvd., Center Strip, 877-230-2742; www.arialasvegas.com

Chef Masa Takayama follows up his New York success with Bar Masa, located within Aria at CityCenter. The restaurant is actually two in one. At Bar Masa, guests can dine on simply prepared, traditional Japanese fare in a sleek and open space that resembles a large airport hangar. The menu changes seasonally and includes a variety of sushi and sashimi, as well as dishes such as uni risotto with truffles and Peking duck with foie gras. The more intimate Shaboo seats just 54 and offers an omakase menu that focuses on the Japanese variant of a "hot pot," known as shabu-shabu, where guests cook meats and vegetables in a shared pot of bubbling broth. It's an exclusive, tranquil and rare dining experience. Masa's unique talent for omakase will appeal to a variety of discerning palettes.

Japanese. Dinner. Reservations recommended. $86 and up

BARTOLOTTA RISTORANTE DI MARE

Wynn Las Vegas, 3131 Las Vegas Blvd. S., Center Strip, 702-248-3463; www.wynnlasvegas.com

Italian preparations of seafood usually revolve around the freshest fish available, treated with the simplest of ingredients. Bartolotta Ristorante di Mare upholds that practice by flying in shellfish and seafood daily straight from the Mediterranean, which means you're most likely getting choices that aren't available elsewhere on the Strip. The warm and friendly waitstaff walks diners through chef Paul Bartolotta's newest creations and can aptly suggest the perfect wine pairing to complete any meal. The elegant dining room overlooks a romantic lagoon, and the mood is further enhanced by dim lighting and sparkling crystal chandeliers. If the weather is nice, and you can secure a table, dine in one of the chic outdoor private cabanas overlooking the lagoon. Serene, quiet and secluded, this intimate space is a breath of fresh air in Las Vegas. Combine the impossibly fresh seafood with the homemade pastas, or opt for a whole fish simply grilled with

B & B RISTORANTE

minimal accoutrement and a glass of wine, and it's the perfect light, yet still decadent, Italian meal.

Italian, seafood. Dinner. $36-85

BOTERO
Encore Las Vegas, 3121 Las Vegas Blvd. S., Center Strip, 702-248-3463; www.encorelasvegas.com

If you ever doubted the link between food and fine art, an evening spent at Botero is certain to change your mind. This poolside space is visually stunning, with a soaring arched ceiling, padded white columns and, of course, lots of original works of art by Fernando Botero. Celebrity chef Mark LoRusso ensures that the food is equally artistic. Ahi tuna tartare is a study in color and texture with creamy avocado and crispy ginger, while the pinwheel of wild salmon is almost too pretty to eat. There is no lack of masterpieces on the dessert menu either. The signature ice cream cupcakes will have you reminiscing back to your early days, as will the PB & J brioche doughnuts.

Contemporary American. Lunch (Friday-Saturday), dinner. $86 and up

THE COUNTRY CLUB
Wynn Las Vegas, 3131 Las Vegas Blvd. S., Center Strip, 702-248-3463; www.wynnlasvegas.com

Down a long hallway far away from the casino, The Country Club feels exactly as it should: exclusive. But that doesn't mean the space is stuffy. With gorgeous views of the waterfalls on the 18th hole of the Wynn golf course, the restaurant has a supper club vibe to it, with dark woods, plaid carpeting and low lighting. The friendly staff makes you feel like a long-standing member from the moment you enter to your last sip of wine. For lunch, you'll find excellent burgers and more casual offerings such as a French dip and a grilled hot dog. Dinner is more subdued and slightly more formal, with a variety of steaks including a charbroiled 20-ounce rib chop

and a veal T-bone.
Steak. Lunch (Monday-Friday), dinner (Wednesday-Saturday), Saturday-Sunday brunch. $86 and up

DIEGO
MGM Grand Hotel & Casino, 3799 Las Vegas Blvd. S., South Strip, 702-891-3200; www.mgmgrand.com
With hues of red, pink and orange, Diego's atmosphere is vivacious and sexy, adding excitement to your impending night out. You'll find traditional Mexican flavors and dishes given contemporary twists, such as the Diego carne asada, a rib eye steak marinated in red chile adobo and topped with tequila-laced roasted cactus and tangy onion salsa. Guacamole custom-prepared tableside isn't only entertaining, but tasty, too. With an unparalleled tequila selection, Diego makes going out for a taco a livelier experience. After dinner, try the Mexican coffee with Herradura Reposado tequila, Kahlua and fresh whipped cream.
Mexican. Dinner. $36-85

JEAN GEORGES STEAKHOUSE
Aria Resort & Casino, 3730 Las Vegas Blvd. S., Center Strip, 877-230-2742; www.jean-georges.com
Chef Jean-Georges Vongerichten has another modern steakhouse, Prime, nearby at the Bellagio, but his homage to meat at Aria stands out by featuring cuts from all over the world, including Japan, Argentina and Uruguay. The striking space nestled in the promenade level of the casino resort is done up in a bold palette of black, white and gold. Of course steak is the star on the menu, but go for an innovate meat-free appetizer like black pepper beignets with Asian pear as well as rice-cracker-crusted tuna. Not in the mood for steak? The Kobe cheeseburger provides a juicy alternative. Just be sure to finish with Jean George's signature dessert, warm chocolate cake with vanilla ice cream.
American. Dinner. Reservations recommended. Bar. $36-85

JULIAN SERRANO
Aria Resort & Casino, 3730 Las Vegas Blvd. S., Center Strip, 877-230-2742; www.arialasvegas.com
You can do some great people-watching at Julian Serrano. The restaurant opens right into Aria's lobby, where hordes of tourists come and go, but

VERANDAH

your eyes will be fixed on the innovative Spanish tapas. Try signature dishes like a lobster-pineapple skewer, salmon with truffle béchamel sauce and portobello mushrooms, as well as a refreshingly simple apple-manchego salad with chives. Go with a group of high rollers and order away; these plates are meant to be shared. Adding to the convivial atmosphere is the autumn-inspired décor: the dining room's decked out in inviting reds and golds with tall glossy black tree sculptures sprouting between tables. There's also a hopping bar scene, where Spanish wines and housemade sangria keep the mood light and fun.
Spanish. Lunch, dinner. Bar. $36-85

MING'S TABLE
**Harrah's Las Vegas, 3475 Las Vegas Blvd. S., Center Strip,
702-369-5000; www.harrahslasvegas.com**
For hearty Chinese classics, head to Ming's Table. The restaurant provides a casual and authentic Chinese dining experience in a comfortable setting. The bright room takes on a minimalist mystique with a few Asian accents mixed in, but the food is decidedly authentic. Favorites include crab Rangoon, roast duck with plum sauce, Peking duck, spicy hot and sour soup, and kung pao shrimp and scallops. You'll also find dan dan noodles and shark's fin stir fried with black bean or ginger scallion sauce. Sushi and Southeast Asian cuisine are available, but the Chinese fare is definitely the way to go.
Asian. Lunch, dinner. Closed Wednesday-Thursday. $36-85

OKADA
**Wynn Las Vegas, 3131 Las Vegas Blvd. S., Center Strip, 702-248-3463;
www.wynnlasvegas.com**
Japanese cuisine is traditionally elegant, precise and simple, and the food served at Okada at Wynn Las Vegas falls in line with those aesthetics. The dining room has an excellent flow to it and is accented by blond woods

and natural stone, with a giant window offering a view of the waterfall just outside. Sushi is the main attraction, with expert sushi chefs behind the bar preparing some of the freshest raw fish available in Las Vegas. Teppanyaki-style cooking is also a good bet, but don't expect these chefs to theatrically clang their knives against the grill—this is a much more reserved forum, ideal for group dinners.

Japanese. Dinner. $36-85

OSTERIA DEL CIRCO

Bellagio Las Vegas, 3600 Las Vegas Blvd. S., Las Vegas, 702-693-7223; www.bellagio.com

The famed Maccioni family may have made their mark with French cuisine in New York, but at Osteria del Circo, they return to their Italian roots with a Tuscan menu inspired by their matriarch, Egidiana Maccioni. Circo is referred to as the more "casual" sister to Le Cirque next door, but it's still fine dining in our book. The whimsical, colorful décor adds an air of playfulness, making the ambience less stuffy. The menu may look intimidating but in reality, this is pure, honest Italian food at its best. Simple preparations of seafood, such as grilled sea bass served with fennel, cherry tomatoes and zucchini, are presented with style and elegance, allowing the flavors of the dish to shine. If you think all pizza is created equal, forgo the heartier dishes and opt for pizza alla crema bianca, which incorporates Norwegian smoked salmon, onions, capers, crème fraîche and American caviar into a clay-oven-baked, thin-crust masterpiece. Overlooking Lake Bellagio, Circo makes you feel as if you're on Lake Como itself, complete with the authentic Tuscan aromas streaming from the kitchen.

Italian. Dinner. $36-85

PEARL

MGM Grand Hotel & Casino, 3799 Las Vegas Blvd. S., South Strip, 702-891-7380; www.mgmgrand.com

True elegance and sophistication is what Pearl exudes in both its traditional menu and minimalist, but stunning décor. With red lanterns hanging from the ceiling, black lacquered tables and serene blue walls, it demonstrates a combination of modern and classic Asian aesthetics. Here you'll

---

WHERE ARE THE BEST BUFFETS?

The Buffet at Bellagio: The lines can be very long, but it's worth the wait for the huge spread of seafood, Italian, Japanese, Chinese and American delights. Bellagio prides itself on the quality of its buffet, not on the quantity, so dishes are replaced often, which means you'll get fresh food no matter what time you arrive.

MORE The Buffet at Luxor: There is something for every appetite, including omelette stations and a 30-foot salad bar here. The Mexican station is said to be one of the most authentic (and the spiciest) on the Strip.

Spice Market Buffet: Vegetarians love this place at Planet Hollywood because unlike other buffets, there are more than salads and non-meat pizza to choose from, thanks to Mediterranean and Middle Eastern choices such as falafel, hummus and tabbouleh.

discover that Chinese food is more than egg foo young and General Tso's chicken. Fresh seafood is exceptional, dispatched only before it's going to be cooked, and prepared simply to allow the ingredients' true flavors to surface. Signature items such as spider prawn dumplings and roasted Peking duck showcase the chef's talent for Cantonese and Beijing cuisine.
Chinese. Dinner. $36-85

PINOT BRASSERIE
The Venetian Resort Hotel Casino, 3355 Las Vegas Blvd. S., Center Strip, 702-414-8888; www.patinagroup.com
As a classically-trained French chef, Eric Lhuillier feels right at home with the traditional brasserie fare on the menu here. The charming space looks as if it came straight from Paris, with its red leather chairs and banquettes, brass rails and wood walls. Like the décor, the bistro menu is comfortable, yet elegant. Dishes such as the roasted chicken with garlic French fries and braised short rib with potato mousseline are comfort foods at their best. If your evenings are already booked up, try Pinot Brasserie for lunch, as there are hearty sandwiches, including a croque monsieur, that, hit the right note every time.
French. Lunch, dinner. $36-85

RED 8
Wynn Las Vegas, 3131 Las Vegas Blvd. S., Center Strip, 702-770-3380; www.wynnlasvegas.com
Red 8 is the more casual Asian restaurant at Wynn, offering a wider variety of cuisines, but that doesn't mean it resembles your average Chinese take-out place. The red and black dining room is often bustling, as guests schmooze around cozy booths and polished stone tables. In case there's any doubt left as to the cuisine of choice here, a large red lantern hangs majestically in the middle of the restaurant, with tiny lamps around the perimeter of the space. Red 8 offers heartier, more common dishes than its shark's fin-serving counterparts, including Hong Kong-style barbecued beef and soups containing fresh noodles and meaty dumplings. Don't miss the dim sum menu, offering 20 choices of deliciously dense dumplings. And with this more casual dining experience comes a smaller bill—in case you haven't had luck at the tables.
Asian. Lunch, dinner. $36-85

SAGE
Aria Resort and Casino, 3730 Las Vegas Blvd S., Center Strip, 877-320-2742; www.arialasvegas.com
You might think of bypassing Sage for one of the splashier, celebrity-chef

JASMINE

driven restaurants in Aria, but you'd be missing out on a great meal. Sage is a serious restaurant serving provocative farm-driven cuisine in a lively and boldly decorated space that feels worlds away from the slot machines. Chef Shawn McClain is an acclaimed Chicago-based chef, and his experience shows in signature dishes such as savory foie gras brûlée. This unique take of the requisite goose liver dish will have you doing a double take if you are used to the more familiar seared foie gras popular around town. Vegetarians and non-vegetarians alike would be amiss to overlook the slow-poached organic farm egg with smoked potato and black truffle. Desserts are a highlight as well, particularly the warm sugared beignets with the freshest fruit of the season. Time your dinner so you can enjoy one of the inventive housemade cocktails or intriguing beers at the large bar and lounge area before settling down for a modern farm dinner.

American. Dinner. Closed Sunday. Bar. $36-85

SHANGHAI LILLY

Mandalay Bay Resort and Casino, 3950 Las Vegas Blvd. S., South Strip, 702-632-7409; www.mandalaybay.com

With long curtains and walls adorned with vintage photos of Chinese beauties, Shanghai Lilly simultaneously examines the past while looking forward to the future. They don't tell you if Shanghai Lilly was an actual woman or not, but the black and white 1920s-era portraits of anonymous ladies hanging throughout the space make you hope she was. The award-winning design of the room was imagined by Tony Chi, who sought to simulate the elegance and ease of ancient Chinese luxury. The Imperial Peking duck is second to none, as are the lobster lettuce wraps. If you're more of a traditionalist, go for the black-peppered beef tenderloin or kung pao chicken; you won't be disappointed. The four private dining rooms, apart from the main dining area, are ideal for a private affair or a special celebration—just book months out because those tables are often hard to nab.

Chinese. Dinner. Closed Tuesday-Wednesday. $36-85

CUT

SILK ROAD

Vdara Hotel & Spa, 2600 W. Harmon Ave., Center Strip, 866-745-7767; www.vdara.com

Silk Road offers a sleek and sunny spot for breakfast and lunch, thanks to a bold indigo color scheme, undulating waves on everything from the walls to the booths, and bright, natural light that flows inside. Executive chef Martin Heierling has crafted a balanced menu of savory and sweet selections, such as delectable sliders with beef tenderloin, fried egg, bacon and tomato confit as well as addicting blueberry and ricotta pancakes with honeycomb butter and candied rose petals. If you have trouble deciding, try the signature Eggs, Eggs and Eggs, which offers poached, scrambled and fried eggs all in one dish. During lunch, go for the Southern-inspired chicken and waffle basket or the refreshing popcorn shrimp lettuce wraps with mango slaw.

American, Asian. Breakfast, lunch, Sunday brunch. $16-35

SINATRA

Encore Las Vegas, 3121 Las Vegas Blvd. S., Center Strip, 702-248-3463; www.encorelasvegas.com

Encore's signature restaurant pays homage to Ol' Blue Eyes in more than name alone. Framed images of the famous crooner line the cream colored walls and his voice provides a pleasant backdrop for dinner conversation. Celebrated chef Theo Schoenegger continues the salute with sophisticated Italian fare fit for the Rat Packer himself. Pastas read simple and straightforward, though taste anything but. The lasagna Bolognese incorporates veal, pork and beef between layers of heavenly hand-rolled pasta, and the agnolotti stuffed with bufala ricotta is surprisingly light and airy. The chicken saltimbocca is another sure bet, only improved upon with a side of herb-potato gnocchi. The intimate dining room is often filled with two-tops looking for a romantic alternative to the frenzied pulse of Vegas. And what's more romantic than spending a night with Ol' Blue Eyes?

Italian. Dinner. $86 and up

SIRIO RISTORANTE

Aria Resort & Casino, 3730 Las Vegas Blvd. S., Center Strip, 877-230-2742; www.arialasvegas.com

Sirio Maccioni of New York's famed Le Cirque created this restaurant to show off the rustic dishes of his Tuscan childhood. The Italy-inspired design—with proscenium arches, travertine floors, a silver-leaf-patterned inverted dome ceiling and black-and-white photographic murals of Italian architecture—provides the perfect setting for the simple appetizers, pastas and main courses, such as the white-truffle-scented beef carpaccio and the traditional Tuscan tomato bread soup. For a hearty entrée, try the pistachio-crusted lamb with semolina gnocchi. There's no better way to end a traditional Italian meal than with some cannoli. Here, the housemade Sicilian treats are filled with imported buffalo ricotta, candied citrus, pistachios and chocolate chips.

Italian. Dinner. Bar. $36-85

SOCIETY CAFÉ

Encore Las Vegas, 3121 Las Vegas Blvd. S., Center Strip, 702-770-5300; www.encorelasvegas.com

This popular restaurant at Encore Las Vegas is the perfect place to dine at any time of the day. Lavish décor makes you feel like high society, but the casual vibe makes you feel comfortable. With inspiration taken from London during the Victorian era, you'll see high ceilings, archways with black and white striped drapes, bright green light fixtures, oversized hot pink couches that serve as banquette seating and black crocodile chairs. Chef Kim Canteenwalla serves up classic American fare with a fun twist like frosted flake French toast and steak and egg sliders at breakfast, and lollipop chicken wings at lunch. At dinner, warm pretzel bread is brought out with mustard butter while you peruse the menu. Start with tasty tuna tacos or one of their many salads and then move on to an entrée such as the jidori chicken, Mediterranean seabass or build your own burger. For dessert, try the warm donut bites with chocolate, caramel and raspberry dipping sauces.

American. Breakfast, lunch, dinner, late-night. $36-85

STRATTA

Wynn Las Vegas, 3131 Las Vegas Blvd. S., Center Strip, 702-770-3463; www.wynnlasvegas.com

Chef Alessandro Stratta's second restaurant at the Wynn is his more-casual concept of rustic, regional Italian fare. Red-backed chairs, an open

WING LEI

fire hearth and a clear view into the kitchen create an atmosphere that is laid back and welcoming. The restaurant's lounge is a smart place to meet for drinks, and the location makes it an ideal spot to grab a bite before or after catching a show at Wynn. The wood-fired pizzas are great picks (we particularly liked the Bosco, with roasted mushroom purée, white truffle oil and Bel Paese cheese), and the pastas definitely have enough variety to make everyone in your group happy. For a more substantial meal, the roasted pork chop stuffed with fontina cheese and prosciutto is heavenly. *Italian. Lunch (Friday-Sunday), dinner. $36-85*

SW STEAKHOUSE
Wynn Las Vegas, 3131 Las Vegas Blvd. S., Center Strip, 702-248-3463; www.wynnlasvegas.com
SW at Wynn Las Vegas rises above and beyond a classic Vegas steakhouse. You won't find a dimly lit, smoky room here. Instead, an airy dining room opens onto the Lake of Dreams, where light and music shows play nightly. The prime steaks come from corn-fed Nebraskan cows, which results in great tasting beef. Side dishes are where steakhouses always differentiate themselves, and SW's offerings—truffled creamed corn, crisp potato tots with herb cream—are what set it apart. The fairground-gone-luxe funnel cake is a good way to end an indulgent experience—crisp, fluffy funnel cake slices are presented on the branches of a metal tree, and served with sauces of crème anglaise, salty caramel and fudge. *Steak. Dinner. $86 and up*

SWITCH
Encore Las Vegas, 3121 Las Vegas Blvd. S., Center Strip, 702-248-3463; www.encorelasvegas.com
If anything at Encore is kitschy, this restaurant might be it. But as with all things Wynn, even kitsch is done with style, sophistication and a touch of playfulness. The concept behind Switch is that the walls constantly rotate

to provide changing ambience throughout your meal. You won't get through dessert without seeing a few repeats, but at that point your full attention will be on your plate, not the walls around you. Chef René Lenger has created a menu that is as animated as the décor. Jumbo lump crab cakes come alongside a quail egg and fried pickles, while the salmon filet is bathed in a champagne sauce. Serious carnivores will appreciate the charbroiled steak selection, and the black truffle creamed spinach is a side worth splurging on. The service is warm and informed, especially on questions regarding the lengthy wine list.

American. Dinner. $86 and up

TABLEAU
Wynn Las Vegas, 3131 Las Vegas Blvd. S., Center Strip, 702-248-3463; www.wynnlasvegas.com

Don't think you can't secure a table at Tableau just because it's tucked away in the Tower Suites at Wynn. This spacious, airy dining room offers American cuisine for breakfast, lunch and weekend brunch, along with prime views of the Tower Suites pool and gardens. You won't find any frilly nouveau fare here—deep down the menu is meat and potatoes, albeit more elegantly presented. The organic roast chicken BLT sandwich is far from your run-of-the-mill lunch option, with cipolini onions and a warm bacon-shallot dressing. For sweeter palates, the wild blueberry buttermilk pancakes slathered in orange blossom butter is the perfect way to start the day. Service is personable and outgoing, but not obsequious. Tableau certainly offers fine dining, but it's not hard to feel comfortable here.

American. Breakfast, lunch, Saturday-Sunday brunch. $36-85

WING LEI
Wynn Las Vegas, 3131 Las Vegas Blvd. S., Center Strip, 702-248-3463; www.wynnlasvegas.com

The meaning of the Chinese characters that represent Wing Lei is twofold: not only does it mean "forever prosperous" but it also represents "Wynn" itself (Wing in English is "Wynn"). This upscale Chinese offering pulls out all the stops with its decadent menu and French- and Chinese-inspired décor. Red, the color of luck in China, accents the room in the form of curtains and on the backs of chairs, emphasizing the handcrafted black onyx bar in the corner. Executive chef Ming Yu's menu is a blend of traditional Shanghai, Szechwan and Cantonese cuisines, including a five-course Peking duck extravaganza which starts with Peking duck salad with orange truffle vinaigrette and wild duck soup and carries into pan-seared duck noodles and the famed table-carved roasted duck presentation. The Mongolian beef and Sichuan chili prawns are solid entrées. If you simply can't decide (the menu is lengthy), the chef's signature dinner is a five-course affair with dishes like grilled black cod, wok-tossed Maine lobster and braised Kobe sirloin with black pepper au jus.

Chinese. Dinner. $86 and up

OFF-STRIP

★★★ALIZÉ
Palms Casino Resort, 4321 W. Flamingo Road, Off-Strip, 702-951-7000; www.alizelv.com

André Rochat of Alizé is one of the first star chefs to bring his knives to Las Vegas. His restaurant at the top of the Palms features a 180-degree view of

the Strip through 16-foot floor-to-ceiling windows. A two-story wine cellar in the middle of the dining room houses more than 1,700 selections, with a healthy mix of New World and Old, top dollar price points and affordable finds. The intimate bar isn't the place to sling cosmopolitans or Red-Bull-and-vodkas; serious spirits await you, including an impressive collection of cognac gathered by Rochat himself. The menu is a study in contemporary French cuisine and elegant presentation with dishes such as escargots Burgogne with garlic herb butter and pan-seared duck breast with sautéed foie gras in a raspberry vinaigrette. Tasting menus are available and are a nice place to start for those being initiated into French fine dining.
French. Dinner. $36-85

★★★DJT
Trump International Hotel & Tower Las Vegas, 2000 Fashion Show Drive, Off-Strip, 702-982-0000; www.trumplasvegashotel.com
It's all about the art of the meal at this handsome restaurant inside Trump International Hotel & Tower. The dining room, with rich colors and intimate seating, recalls the glamour of the 1930s. The upscale and sophisticated contemporary American fare includes dishes such as the 28-day dry aged bone-in ribeye, slow roasted chicken with broken rice, spinach and adobo sauce, and buccatini carbonara. A three-course tasting menu is also available for $39, which includes a choice between two appetizers, three entrees and a dessert.
American. Breakfast, lunch, dinner. $36-85

★★★N9NE STEAKHOUSE
Palms Casino Resort, 4321 W. Flamingo Road, Off-Strip, 702-933-9900; www.n9negroup.com
It may feel like a nightclub when you walk in, complete with loud, thumping music and a modern metal décor lit by blacklights, but if you can get past the trendy aspect, you're in for a good meal. Starters such as the N9NE rock shrimp are always fun to munch on, and are served in a carnival-style cardboard box with two dipping sauces. Prime aged steaks are expertly done and sides, such as macaroni and cheese and loaded baked potatoes, are above average. There's a high likelihood of a celebrity sighting as sports stars like to drop by before heading out to the big parties. So if part of your Vegas experience includes a solid steak and some star gazing, you'd better get used to the pulsating house music.
Steak. Dinner. $36-85

★★★NOBU
Hard Rock Hotel, 4455 Paradise Road, Off-Strip, 702-693-5090; www.hardrockhotel.com
There's sushi in Las Vegas, and then there's Nobu. One of the pioneers of modern Japanese cuisine, chef Nobu Matsuhisa takes traditional Japanese ingredients and technique and applies to them the knowledge he acquired while working in South America. There may now be about 20 versions worldwide of Matsuhisa's original restaurant, but this outpost at the Hard Rock Hotel is particularly welcoming, with calming green walls behind bamboo stalks, small birch trees and an onyx-tiled sushi bar. The yellowtail sashimi with jalapeños simply melts in your mouth and the lobster salad includes a spicy lemon dressing that will kick-start any meal. You know that black cod with miso that you find on every menu in every trendy Japanese

restaurant across the country? This is one of Matsuhisa's original signature dishes, and there's nothing quite like the original.

Japanese. Dinner. $36-85

ALSO RECOMMENDED

BLUE AGAVE

Palms Casino Resort, 4321 W. Flamingo Road, Off-Strip, 702-942-7777; www.palms.com

Latin flavors collide with prime raw seafood at the Palms' Blue Agave. Top that off with a margarita made from any one of their 150 tequilas behind the bar and you've got yourself the perfect Mexican meal. The circular bar is festive, with stars hanging from the ceiling, and always draws a crowd (we assume the tequila has something to do with it). Expect bold tastes in almost everything that comes out of the kitchen, from the pastas to the roasted seafood, including our favorite: the spicy lobster, shrimp, crab and scallop gumbo. Be sure to utilize the chile bar, a wide assortment of fresh chilies and salsas to add extra heat and even more flavor to your plate.

Mexican. Lunch, dinner, Sunday brunch. $16-35

HAMADA OF JAPAN

365 E. Flamingo Road, Off-Strip, 702-733-3005; www.hamadaofjapan.com

With three locations close to each other by the Las Vegas Strip, Hamada of Japan must be doing something right. Sure, it might play into the stereotypes of what a Japanese restaurant looks like, in addition to pushing specialty cocktails with names like "Geisha" and "Banzai," but they definitely do traditional Japanese cuisine well, if not a little kitschy. Favorites such as teriyaki, tempura and sushi dinners are popular, and special platters groaning under the weight of seafood or shabu shabu prepared tableside can be ordered for two or more to share. With private, low-seated tatami rooms and teppanyaki dinner grilled tableside, Hamada of Japan is great

N9NE STEAKHOUSE

for groups who want to have a good time during their meal at a decent price point.

Japanese. Lunch, dinner. $36-85

RAKU
5030 W. Spring Mountain Road, Off-Strip 702-367-3511;
www.raku-grill.com
Located way off the Strip within a seedy strip mall in the heart of Chinatown, Raku doesn't look like a great spot for dinner. But it's where many big-name Vegas chefs head to eat after cooking all night in their own restaurants. Ignore the underwhelming exterior (and massage parlors) and step inside for some of the most innovative and addictive food the city has to offer. This authentic Japanese charcoal grill restaurant serves an extended menu of small bites that are perfect for sharing while sipping ice-cold Sapporo drafts. The staff is friendly and welcoming and willing to steer novices in the right direction. Grilled asparagus, tomatoes and mushrooms are deceptively simple but delicious, and the fresh tofu in hot broth is a house specialty. The menu offers some delicious surprises you wouldn't ordinarily find at a Japanese eatery, such as a delicious fried chicken and a fluffy cheesecake dessert. Go late at night (it serves until 3 a.m.) to see many of Vegas' top chefs chowing down on the tasty mix of traditional and untraditional eats.

Japanese. Dinner. Closed Sunday. $16-35

VOODOO STEAK & LOUNGE
Rio Hotel & Casino, 3700 W. Flamingo Road, Off-Strip, 702-777-7923;
www.riolasvegas.com
As if the nightclub at the top of the Rio wasn't enough, you can have a good steak up there as well. Formerly known as VooDoo Café, VooDoo Steak has a more refined menu, with premium reserve and dry-aged beef as the specialties. With a gorgeous view of the entire Strip, the restaurant features Creole and Cajun bites such as ham and andouille sausage beignets and

WHAT ARE THE BEST ITALIAN RESTAURANTS?

B&B Ristorante: Mario Batali's menu at this spot is simple, rustic Italian with a gourmet edge. A pasta tasting menu is available for those who can't decide which dish to order.

Fiamma Trattoria: Meatballs take on a whole new meaning when they are made from Kobe beef. Surround them with handmade spaghetti and you have an Italian feast.

Osteria del Circo: The Maccioni family of Le Cirque fame have returned to their Italian roots with a Tuscan menu inspired by their matriarch, Egidiana Maccioni, that is pure, honest Italian food at its best.

Sinatra: Celebrated chef Theo Schoenegger offers sophisticated Italian fare fit for the Rat Packer himself. Pastas read simple and straightforward, though taste anything but.

Stratta: They say New York has the best thin crust pizza, but "they" haven't tried the wood-fired pies from Stratta. Even the traditional margherita pizza provides slice after slice of ooey-gooey deliciousness.

Valentino Las Vegas: With many of the ingredients imported straight from Italy, you know you'll be getting the real thing, whether it's pillowy gnocchi or flavorful roast chicken.

---

delta frog legs and mussels. The VooDoo "Menage a Trois," a surf and turf offering of petite filet mignon, prawns and lobster, puts a sexy spin on your meal. Head out on to the terrace for an after-dinner cocktail, but don't look down (the view of the ground below is not for the weak).
Steak/Cajun/Creole. Dinner. $36-85

SUBURBS

★★★HACHI
Red Rock Casino, Resort & Spa, 11011 W. Charleston Blvd., Summerlin, 702-797-7576; www.ilovehachi.com
Modern Japanese has found its way into the suburbs under the capable hands of Nobu alum chef Linda Rodriguez. One of the few female executive chefs at a major property in Las Vegas, Rodriguez's touch can be seen and felt throughout the dining room and in the kitchen. Hachi's décor is both modern and feminine, with Japanese cherry blossoms incarnated not only in photographs on the wall, but also in the form of 2,500 hand-blown glass blossoms hanging from the ceiling. Presentations of dishes are dynamic, yet delicate and thoughtful. Drawing on her training from Nobu as well as cultural influences from Europe and Latin America, the menu offers twists on classics like seared Kobe beef sashimi with yuzu soy and seared tuna tataki salad with warm bacon vinaigrette. With an outstanding sushi selection and amazing hot dishes under her belt, Rodriguez also is willing to do an omakase tasting menu for tables of six or fewer (a must if you have the time). With her making the decisions based on your personal likes and dislikes, you're in good hands.
Japanese. Dinner. $36-85

★★★MARCHÉ BACCHUS
2620 Regatta Drive #106, Summerlin, 702-804-8008;
www.marchebacchus.com

You don't have to be relegated to the Strip to find excellent French bistro fare. Marché Bacchus, located in the community of Summerlin, 10 miles from downtown, is a perfect way to get a feel for just how good the locals have it here. The restaurant is part wine shop, part restaurant, and diners can select from the shop's 950 labels and have the bottle with their meal at only $10 over the retail price. The outdoor patio sits alongside one of the city's many man-made lakes, and cooling misters and rustic trellises offer a nice respite from the Vegas heat. Executive chef Jean Paul Labadie recently joined the restaurant after stints as head chef at Emeril's in the MGM Grand and Table 10. Labadie's menu features French bistro favorites such as croque monsieur sandwiches, steak frites (which they call "La Piece de Boeuf du Boucher") and baked escargot in garlic herb butter. With a selection of wine platters offering everything from imported cheeses and olives to pâté and French salami, Marché Bacchus is also a stellar pick if you're looking to get away from the casinos for an afternoon.

French. Lunch, dinner, Sunday brunch. $36-85

ALSO RECOMMENDED
SETTEBELLO
140 Green Valley Parkway, Henderson, 702-222-3556;
www.settebello.net

It isn't easy finding good pizza in Las Vegas. Located in a strip mall, like most Vegas venues off the Strip, this Henderson eatery is a hit with locals for its honest-to-goodness Napoletana-style pizza. The brick oven, imported from Italy, is what makes these thin crust beauties so tasty. It gets up to temperatures of 950 degrees Fahrenheit, which chars the bottom of the pizza, while keeping the top warm and gooey. Simple toppings like crushed tomatoes, luscious fresh mozzarella and fruity olive oil are all you need to satisfy your pizza craving.

Pizza. Lunch, dinner. $16-35

LAVO

ON THE TOWN

The Strip offers a brilliantly lit stretch of nightlife opportunities. From little lounges that serve sophisticated cocktails to multi-tiered marvels for dancing, there's something to fulfill any night owl's fantasy. Digitally savvy revelers will rejoice at the tech-toy playground that is Eyecandy at Mandalay Bay. Wine aficionados will encounter a playground of their own at the Palazzo's Double Helix Bar. Surrender at Encore is the place for A-list sightings and, after an evening just about anywhere, a Bloody Mary at Zuri is just what you need to convince you to do it all over again.

THE STRIP

THE BANK

Bellagio Las Vegas, 3600 Las Vegas Blvd. S., Center Strip, 702-693-8300; www.lightgroup.com

You'll find quite the red-hot spot inside The Bank's vaults. A private escalator brings you to the posh club and chandeliers light your way to a Cristal-stacked foyer. Then you'll enter a multi-floored space bathed in black and gold. Elegant VIP booths are layered around the glass-enclosed dance floor, which thumps with hip-hop, rock, house and mash-ups. Both are filled with impeccably (and often barely) dressed crowds looking to cozy up to one another as foam sprinkles down like snow from above. Among those in the crowd, you might bump into J.Lo and Marc Anthony or Rose McGowan and Mariah Carey. You might also spy celebrities such as Good Charlotte's Joel Madden and star DJ Samantha Ronson behind the turntable. It's no wonder the club is a celebrity magnet: The sky-high, luxe European table service—which includes silver trays of strawberries and chocolates—requires a big pocketbook. Nevertheless, you'll want to open an account in The Bank. *Thursday-Sunday 10:30 p.m.-4 a.m.*

BAR VDARA

Vdara Hotel & Spa, 2600 W. Harmon Ave., Center Strip, 702-590-2111; www.vdara.com

Unlike other late-night spots on the Strip, Bar Vdara offers a place to unwind in a chic setting without club kids and all the chaos they bring. With a nature theme corresponding to the hotel's commitment to sustainable design, the bar features a reflecting pool, outdoor swings, and a patio overflowing with flowers. Order one of the specialty cocktails, such as the Red Rose Garden, which mixes Belvedere black raspberry-flavored vodka, sweet and sour mix, fresh raspberries and rosemary, or the Kiss of Pearsuasion, a concoction of Absolut Pears vodka, St-Germaine Elderflower liqueur and champagne. A light menu offers tasty options such as ahi tuna rolls and Kobe beef sliders. *Sunday-Thursday 11 a.m.-1 a.m., Friday-Saturday 11 a.m.-2 a.m.*

THE BEATLES REVOLUTION LOUNGE

The Mirage, 3400 Las Vegas Blvd. S., Center Strip, 702-693-8300; www.thebeatlesrevolutionlounge.com

After Cirque du Soleil created *Love*, the show based on the music of the Beatles, they created Revolution, an intimate space devoted to Fab Four beats. The Abbey Road Bar draws people in from the casino floor and the staff knows a bit of trivia for any diehard Beatles fan. Who knew John Lennon was the cheerleader when the boys were first getting started? (The lanky Lennon would ask "Where are we headed, mates?" after each record

BLUSH

label rejection. "To the top! To the very top!" they would reply in unison.) The cozy 400-person capacity club features a DJ that spins bites of Beatles music as well as the latest hip-hop and Top 40 hits. Adjacent to the Love theater, Revolution features lighted tables with floating psychedelic images that randomly transform on the tabletop screen. Or create your own as you manipulate the images with your fingers. The mood changes from mellow in the early evening to a dance groove well past midnight.
Wednesday-Monday 10 p.m.-4 a.m.

BLUSH
Wynn Las Vegas, 3131 Las Vegas Blvd. S., Center Strip, 702-770-3633; www.blushlasvegas.com
Celebrities regularly descend upon this sleek, exclusive lounge to dance on the lit onyx floor underneath the 300-some Asian-inspired color-changing lanterns, while rock, hip-hop and house boom from the speakers. But it isn't only celebrities who get down at this club situated off Wynn's casino floor. Locals come to sip infused vodkas on the chocolate-brown banquettes. Black-clad tourists, of course, are itching for star sightings. No matter why you end up here (and you better be dressed to impress or don't bother showing up), head to the swanky open-air patio, where you can relax on the olive-brown couches and sip a cantaloupe-honeydew-watermelon vodka elixir, amid twinkling white lights and foliage. At least if you don't spy a Hollywood star, you can get a glimpse of the ones in the midnight Vegas sky.
Tuesday-Saturday 9 p.m.-4 a.m.

CARAMEL
Bellagio Las Vegas, 3600 Las Vegas Blvd. S., Center Strip, 702-693-8300; www.lightgroup.com
This late-night spot is where you should go when you want to savor a drink. You can order wine, champagne, beer or a standard cocktail, but why do a ho-hum beverage when there's such an eclectic list of martinis? For dessert

CARAMEL

in a glass, get the delicious Oreo shake martini, made with Bailey's, Dutch chocolate vodka, Godiva chocolate and a splash of cream with crushed Oreos. While you sip your sugary treat, take in the sophisticated surroundings, which are a nice escape from the nearby casino floor, thanks to marble tables, dark wood, olive leather couches and huge round ottomans. The one-way windows will allow you to keep an eye on the buzzing action outside, but the gamblers can't see into the bar, so you'll have some privacy. The bar is small and far more low-key than neighbor The Bank. It's the place to go to for a cocktail before a show, a post-club pit stop to wind down your evening or any excuse you can think of to drink a tasty libation. *Daily 5 p.m.-4 a.m.*

CENTRIFUGE
MGM Grand Hotel & Casino, 3799 Las Vegas Blvd. S., South Strip, 800-280-8271; www.mgmgrand.com
If you are looking to dance, you'll be drawn to this place, which pulses with Top 40 remixes, hip-hop and techno. Even the employees can't resist the beat; you'll see them jump up on the bar and perform choreographed routines or break out with freestyle numbers. Order one of the bar's fruit-infused cocktails, such as the exotic Stoli Lychée (lychée-infused vodka with lime and pineapple juice). If after hours of shaking it you feel a bit dizzy—the circular bar doesn't help, and neither does the spinning, glowing structure atop the center of the bar—take a break on the gray sofas or in one of the cherry-colored armchairs, and watch the employees work it out. *Sunday-Thursday 4 p.m.-close, Friday-Saturday noon-close.*

CHRISTIAN AUDIGIER THE NIGHTCLUB
TI Treasure Island, 3300 Las Vegas Blvd. S., Center Strip, 702-894-7580; www.treasureisland.com
If you hadn't guessed it from the name on the marquee, this club is a testament to the fabulousness of designer Christian Audigier. From the staff uniforms to the champagne bottles, Audigier's glamorous designs and rock

---

WHICH LOUNGES ARE BEST FOR A QUIET COCKTAIL?
Bar Vdara: Unlike other late-night spots on the Strip, Bar Vdara offers guests a place to unwind in a chic setting without all the club kids fist-pumping. The bar's nature theme, complete with reflecting pool, makes it the perfect place to unwind with a drink.

Mandarin Bar: This sophisticated and spacious lounge on the 23rd floor of the luxurious Mandarin Oriental hotel offers spectacular views, smart cocktails and tasty snacks.

---

and roll sensibility are everywhere. Get cozy on one of the black leather sofas in the VIP section overlooking the dance floor, or embrace your inner pirate—with a glass of Cap'n Morgan's, perhaps—and venture out onto the sizeable patio with a great view of TI's Siren's show. Don't come under-dressed, or you'll be turned away at the door. If you're donning a Christian Audigier design, you're good to go, naturally.
Thursday-Sunday 10 p.m.-4 a.m.

DOUBLE HELIX BAR
The Palazzo Las Vegas Resort Hotel Casino, 3325 Las Vegas Blvd. S., Center Strip, 702-735-9463; www.palazzolasvegas.com
After shopping at Diane von Furstenberg and Christian Louboutin at the Shoppes at The Palazzo, enjoy a glass or two at this wine bar, which sits in the center of the upscale shopping center. With more than 50 by-the-glass offerings (in either taste portions or full glasses) and over 300 bottles, there's a lot to choose from. Join other oenophiles at the circular bar or bring the wine-tasting party to one of the marble-topped tables underneath the domed painted-sky ceiling. A small menu from chef Emeril Lagasse is also available—try the artisanal cheese board. After enough glasses, who knows? You may build up enough courage to continue your shopping spree.
Monday-Friday 11 a.m.-11 p.m., Saturday-Sunday 11 a.m.-midnight.

DRAI'S AFTERHOURS
Bill's Gamblin' Hall & Saloon, 3595 Las Vegas Blvd. S., Center Strip, 702-737-0555; www.drais.net
Drai's has been a classic late-night gathering spot since the early '90s (a lifetime in Vegas), and is one of the best after-hours clubs in the city. Decorated in deep reds and browns with animal print accents, the intimate space attracts performers from Cirque to Jubilee! after the night's final performances. After midnight the place ditches the tables and kisses its restaurant portion goodbye. House music is ramped up, the lights dimmed and lounging on the couches and chairs peppered throughout the club seems to be the only reasonable activity. The best time to get here is around 3 a.m. for a cocktail and a nibble from the limited gourmet menu.
Thursday-Sunday 1-7 a.m.

EVE NIGHTCLUB
3720 Las Vegas Boulevard S., Center Strip, 702-227-3838;
www.evethenightclub.com
Located on the second floor of Beso, Eva Longoria Parker's restaurant with chef Todd English, is the actress's nightclub. Since opening, the club

HAZE

has attracted scores of celebrities—everyone from Kim Kardashian to buddy Mario Lopez. The actress and her husband, Tony Parker, also make regular appearances. The black and gold interior with plush VIP booths and a 50-foot-tall arched ceiling is as elegant and glamorous as you would expect. But perhaps the best part is the large windows that feature views of City Center. The space is intimate but spacious—not a mega-club and not a lounge, and there's plenty of room for dancing.
Wednesday, Friday-Saturday 10:30 p.m.-4 a.m.

EYECANDY SOUND LOUNGE & BAR
Mandalay Bay Resort and Casino, 3950 Las Vegas Blvd. S., South Strip, 702-632-7777; www.mandalaybay.com
There's not only a lot to see at Eyecandy; there's a lot to do. Nestled in the center of Mandalay's casino floor, Eyecandy is a treat with a serious high-tech twist. Interactive tables, revolutionary sound stations and a touch-activated LED dance floor create a sensory haven for clubbers. You can spy on your neighbors with the motorized cameras that sweep the lounge and display the beautiful people around the club. Grab a seat at one of the three tables where you can plug in your iPod and send your favorite songs to the DJ for the entire club to hear. (Airtime is up to the DJ's discretion, so don't

---

WHERE DO THE LOCALS GO AFTER DARK?
Drai's Afterhours: Showing you how the local set lives, Drai's draws an after-work crowd of showgirls, cocktail waitresses and pit bosses nightly.

Frankie's Tiki Room *(1712 W. Charleston Blvd., Off-Strip, 702-385-3110; www.frankiestikiroom)* It doesn't get any more local than this way Off-Strip retro lounge, which locals love for its kitschy Polynesian décor and fruity, potent drinks.

be surprised if you never hear your ABBA request.) The dance floor has an ever-changing landscape paired to the tunes of the resident DJs, pulsating with light in synch with the sounds. The interactive tables are a new way to use those old pick-up lines—you can create visuals and messages on your table's circular screen and watch as the image appears on your neighbor's adjacent interactive touch table.
Daily 11-5 a.m.

FONTANA BAR
Bellagio Las Vegas, 3600 Las Vegas Blvd. S., Center Strip, 702-693-7111; www.bellagio.com
When you need a breather from the overstimulation of the casino floor, head to Fontana. For some fresh air, grab a spot on the lovely patio and watch the majestic fountain display on the eight-acre lake. Classic is this casual bar's modus operandi—no hip-hop or starlets here. Instead, you'll hear the vocal stylings of nightly lounge singers, such as diva Dian Diaz, who hearken back to old-time Vegas entertainers. There is a dance floor in case the music—which ranges from R&B to jazz, and includes covers and original tunes—moves you. Otherwise, you can simply relax in your comfortable chair while drinking a Bellini with fresh peaches or a sidecar sweetened with rock-candy syrup.
Monday-Thursday 5 p.m.-1 a.m., Friday-Sunday 5 p.m.-2 a.m.

GOLD LOUNGE
Aria Resort and Casino, 3730 S. Las Vegas Blvd., Center Strip, 702-693-8300; www.arialasvegas.com
Elvis fans will be drawn to this lounge located directly across from the Viva Elvis Theater in Aria. The Gold Lounge is another tribute to the King. Inspired by Graceland, the lounge includes clusters of comfortable seating areas for bottle service, a chic gold, black and red color scheme, and Elvis references everywhere, such as monkey detailing and a horse lamp (a nod to the stables where Elvis spent much of his time). The menu includes plenty of indulgences, including the 24k, a drink with gold flakes and egg whites, and snacks such as jelly doughnuts, mac and cheese, and of course, a peanut-butter-and-banana sandwich.
Monday-Saturday 5 p.m.-4 a.m.

HAZE NIGHTCLUB
Aria Resort and Casino, 3730 Las Vegas Blvd. S., Center Strip, 702-693-8300; www.arialasvegas.com
Haze Nightclub brings 25,500 square-feet of clubbing space to Aria. Heightening club-goers' sense of perception, the two-level club features a main dance floor with well-known DJs pumping out music through the latest and greatest in sound technology. A kaleidoscope of colors are projected onto huge 20-foot screens, and there are small stages for guest performances and dancers. Huge metal structures hang off the ceiling, while suede walls and plush booths make the club that much more of a sensory experience. Kick back with friends over cocktails and work up a sweat on the dance floor. Or head up to the second level where you can look down on the main floor and just watch the craziness ensue before your eyes.
Thursday-Saturday 10:30 p.m.-4 a.m.

EYECANDY SOUND LOUNGE & BAR

LA SCENA LOUNGE
The Venetian Resort Hotel Casino, 3355 Las Vegas Blvd. S., Center Strip, 702-414-1000, 877-883-6423; www.venetian.com
If you prefer your music live, head straight to La Scena, which offers nightly entertainment that features both a DJ and a band. The bands play everything from rock 'n' roll and Motown to disco and Top 40. The space, with gray chairs, a few tables, a small dance floor and a simple stage, is the place to go if you don't care about the scene and just want to dance. In between sets, hunker down with a beer and play a few rounds of poker until the band hits the stage again. You can always head back into the casino afterward, which is only steps away.
Daily 6:30 p.m.-2:30 a.m.

LAVO NIGHTCLUB
The Palazzo Las Vegas Resort Hotel Casino, 3325 Las Vegas Blvd. S., Center Strip, 702-791-1818; www.lavolv.com
You can choose to hang out in the lounge, where worn wood and low chandeliers set the mood near the curved bar, or if you want to dance, take the glass-and-wood screened bridge upstairs to the club, where vaulted glazed tile arches open to a domed ceiling. House and hip-hop shake the room, a place that's seen everyone from Jamie Foxx and Lebron James to Drew Barrymore and Kristen Dunst.
Tuesday-Sunday 10 p.m.-5 a.m.

MANDARIN BAR
Mandarin Oriental, Las Vegas, 3752 Las Vegas Blvd. S., Center Strip, 702-590-8888; www.mandarinoriental.com
For spectacular views of the city, head to the Mandarin Bar on the 23rd floor of the hotel. The spacious lounge features three sides of floor-to-ceiling windows and comfortable seating from which to take in the city lights. Order small plates of tuna tartar, Spanish chorizo or a lobster cocktail.

WHICH CLUBS HAVE THE BEST SIGNATURE COCKTAILS?
Mandarin Bar: The mixologists here create delightful cocktails such as the The Golden Leaf with Hendrick's gin, Aperol, muddled mandarin, pineapple, and fresh lime juice.

XS: Where else can you find a cocktail that includes a gold necklace and engraved set of silver cufflinks? The champagne and cognac hangover after drinking more than one of these is gratis as well.

For your drink, try The Golden Leaf martini, a mix of gin, Aperol, muddled mandarin, pineapple, fresh lime juice and simple syrup. The lemongrass mojito is another good choice. You'll also find champagne cocktails and a nice wine list.
Sunday–Thursday 4:30 p.m.-1 a.m., Friday–Saturday 4:30 p.m.-2 a.m.

MIX LOUNGE
THEhotel at Mandalay Bay, 3950 Las Vegas Blvd. S., South Strip, 702-632-9500; www.mandalaybay.com
The creative minds behind Mix saw the potential of the spectacular view and used every inch of the space to emphasize it—from the balcony to the bathrooms. Incredible 360-degree views from the 64th floor of THEhotel envelope you in this space-age spot decorated in black leather and red lighting. The view is so stunning, the designers carried the floor-to-ceiling glass walls into the restrooms. But the best seat in the house is undoubtedly on the low lounges on the balcony, where you can sit back and look down on the Luxor pyramid and its bright beam of light shooting from the top. The indoor tables are for bottle service only, and you'll need to make a reservation early as they tend to fill up.
Sunday-Thursday 5 p.m.-2 a.m., Friday-Saturday 5 p.m.-3 a.m.

PARASOL UP/PARASOL DOWN
Wynn Las Vegas, 3131 Las Vegas Blvd. S., Center Strip, 702-770-3633; www.wynnlasvegas.com
With its views of Wynn's Lake of Dreams, snagging a seat at this colorful two-level lounge can be a challenge after dark, when the intermittent sound and light shows begin outside on the lake's faux-mountain-cum backdrop. But when you do find a perch, this is a prime spot for sipping perfectly made cocktails (the freshly muddled mojitos are a standout) or snacking on the nibbles available at either level. Parasol Down has an outdoor patio directly on the lake and is a lovely alfresco spot that will make you forget you're in Las Vegas.
Parasol Up: Sunday-Wednesday 11 a.m.-4 a.m., Thursday-Saturday 11 a.m.-5 a.m.; Parasol Down: daily 11 a.m.-2 a.m.

PURE
Caesars Palace, 3570 Las Vegas Blvd. S., Center Strip, 702-731-7873; www.purethenightclub.com
Pure is the spot where all the stars celebrate big bashes, birthdays and new boyfriends. And there's a reason this is such an A-list attraction. Pure's main room is draped in white, with a VIP area taking center stage close to the DJ booth. The massive room is often packed with dancers—and from

PURE

WHICH SPOTS HAVE THE BEST OUTDOOR SPACE?

XS: The wading pool on the patio allows you to cool off without leaving the club. Just don't forget to remove your shoes—many a Manolo has met its demise here.

Fontana Bar: There's no better seat for catching the aquatic symphony of the Bellagio Fountains than on the charming patio overlooking the lake.

Mix Lounge: An amazing 64th-floor terrace offers sensational views of the Strip. The space includes comfortable sectionals and heating lamps for when there's a chill.

Pure: Bringing the beauty of South Beach to the desert, Pure's enormous terrace provides unparalleled views of the Strip, whether you choose to enjoy them from a private cabana or the open-air dance floor.

Surrender: The dazzling indoor space of one of Las Vegas' hottest clubs extends out into a 45,000 square-foot outdoor extravaganza with a three tiered pool, private bungalows and a glass DJ booth. During the day in summer, the Encore Beach Club is where to get the party started.

TABU ULTRA LOUNGE

the dance floor, you have a straight view into the VIP booths where celebrities drink and dance a few feet above the main floor. It doesn't stop there. Pure sprawls over four areas, each with its own bar, music and style. The adjacent Red Room has a more mellow and intimate feel, while The Terrace amps it up four floors above the Strip with tented cabanas for an alfresco experience. Take in the burlesque show at the Pussycat Dolls Lounge, where the vibe is seriously sexy.
Thursday-Sunday 10 p.m.-4 a.m.

SALUTE LOUNGE
The Palazzo Las Vegas Resort Hotel Casino, 3325 Las Vegas Blvd. S., Center Strip, 702-607-7777, 877-883-6423; www.palazzolasvegas.com
If you leave the Palazzo's open-run production of *Jersey Boys* with the musical's "Big Girls Don't Cry" or "Can't Take My Eyes Off of You" numbers stuck in your head, go to the adjacent Salute Lounge to get more of a music fix. Salute is one of the few casino nightclubs on the DJ-heavy Strip to feature free live tunes from a mix of high-energy bands and local favorites. Plus, it offers live music seven days a week, with two outfits taking the stage every night. You'll hear anything from rock 'n' roll and Motown to disco and today's top hits, but generally smooth jazz and classic rock rule the joint. For those who prefer pre-packaged pop, a DJ spins nightly starting around 11:30 p.m. The bar definitely has a retro vibe, with crystal chandeliers, but plush dark red and black seating and zebra-print pillars give it a contemporary edge. So snag a seat, order up the delicious Pearsuasion (Absolut Pears, Malibu Banana, pineapple juice and a splash of 7UP) and enjoy the music.
Daily 4 p.m.-2 a.m.

SHADOW: A BAR AT CAESARS PALACE
Caesars Palace, 3570 Las Vegas Blvd. S., Center Strip, 702-731-7110; www.caesarspalace.com
Even as casino bars go, Shadow is not for the squeamish. More than a place

to grab a quick cocktail between hands of Hold 'Em, this softly lit lounge features female dancers who perform sexy (and occasionally scandalous) scenes behind sheer screens for your pleasure. Between sets, the girls don clingy clothes to serve cocktails and cigars. You'll find even more action behind the bar, where show bartenders toss and flip colorful bottles as they make your drink. Try one of the signature cocktails with names like Liquid Latex and Blue Bawls. The interior is bathed in purple and gold fabrics, with long, sheer white curtains that muffle the noise from the casino.
Monday-Thursday 4 p.m.-2 a.m., Friday-Saturday 2 p.m.-3 a.m., Sunday 2 p.m.-2 a.m.

STUDIO 54
MGM Grand Hotel & Casino, 3799 Las Vegas Blvd. S., South Strip, 702-891-7254; www.studio54lv.com
One of the most famous New York nightspots from the '70s has been recreated at the MGM Grand with all the retro dance hits you can shimmy to. There's a nod to the club's storied past with displays of oversized black and white pictures shot at the original Studio 54 by famed paparazzo Felice Quinto. A giant man-in-the-moon hangs over the DJ booth, another signature trinket from the NY club. The multi-level club starts the night with disco for dancers on its lighted floors. The DJs spin chart-topping dance music paired with an impressive light-and-sound system, which creates the backdrop for the club's aerialists and professional dancers who perform on podiums throughout the club. It makes for quite a free show.
Tuesday-Saturday 10 p.m.-close.

SURRENDER
Encore, 3212 Las Vegas Blvd. S., Center Strip, 702-770-7730; www.encorelasvegas.com
Surrender coincided with the opening of the Encore Beach Club space, an adults-only pool and party scene during the day (the same space transforms into Surrender at night). The expansive club includes numerous bars and an intimate casino, as well cabanas, a multi-tiered pool and seating from the Encore Beach Club. When walking into the space, you're immediately hit by the pulsing music, the cherry-red lighting, ice blue water and 40-foot palm trees, all of which give the place a sort of chic Candyland atmosphere.

STUDIO 54

The main bar features dancing cocktail servers, while the energy continues outside to the pool area, with two additional bars and a tables-only casino. The outdoor space is smartly designed to encourage moving throughout the space rather than staying put, so bring your designer duds and prepare to be seen.
Wednesday-Saturday 10:30 p.m.-close.

TABÚ ULTRA LOUNGE
MGM Grand Hotel & Casino, 3799 Las Vegas Blvd. S., South Strip, 702-891-7183; www.mgmgrand.com
Taking a hint from its flashy Vegas surroundings, Tabú entertains with inter-active art. The lounge uses its granite-top tables as a canvas for projected images that react to the touch of a finger or a glass. You'll want to hover over the table to play with the images, which change every few seconds: Touch a huge eyeball and see it bounce around, or place your hand on a torso and watch it ripple like water. In addition, you'll see images floating around the surface of the bar. Also floating around the bar are model-serv-ers (and we don't mean servers who look like models, but actual models) dropping off cocktails such as the signature candy-like, strawberry-flavored Tabú. Meanwhile, everyone is grooving to house music in any space they can find in the small lounge—even on top of the tables, making interactive art of their own.
Friday-Monday 10 p.m.-5 a.m.

TAO NIGHTCLUB
The Venetian Resort Hotel Casino, 3355 Las Vegas Blvd. S., Center Strip, 702-388-8588; www.taolasvegas.com
Beautiful girls and guys eagerly wait behind the velvet rope to get into one of the hottest clubs on the Strip, while celebrities breeze right on in. Once you get inside, a nearly nude lady bathing in a petal-filled tub is an obvious hint of the scene that awaits. Inside, throngs of people let loose on the dance

WEDDING CHAPEL AT BELLAGIO LAS VEGAS

WHAT ARE THE BEST PLACES TO GET MARRIED IN VEGAS?

The idea of getting married in Vegas may seem more tacky than tasteful, but with the proliferation of luxury resorts and restaurants in Sin City, that's no longer the case. With no waiting period and no blood tests required, Las Vegas is one of the nation's easiest places to get hitched. **The Clark County Marriage License Bureau** *(702-671-0600)* issues the $60 licenses every day of the year from 8 a.m. until midnight; civil ceremonies are performed at the office by the marriage commissioner daily until 10 p.m.

There are far more upscale places to have a wedding ceremony than a county building. **Wynn Las Vegas** offers a wide range of packages that might include anything from limousine transportation to and from the courthouse to get your license, to flowers, photography, music, champagne, dinner at the Five Star restaurant Alex, breakfast in bed and a variety of spa treatments. The onsite wedding salons (which can accommodate as many as 120 guests) are as elegant as the resort itself, and the private courtyard provides an intimate setting for an outdoor wedding.

While **Bellagio Las Vegas** has its own wedding chapel, its best venue for ceremonies might just be its **Terrazza di Sogno**, which overlooks the Fountains of Bellagio. Up to 34 guests can gather around the happy couple on the terrace as they time their vows to coincide with the watershow's grand finale.

SALUTE LOUNGE

floor among the go-go dancers as DJs pump out hip-hop, house and R&B. The sprawling Asian-inspired complex is just as gorgeous as its clientele, with waterfalls, century-old wood and stone walls that get a sultry touch with rich velvets and silk, and a 20-foot hand-carved Buddha statue that floats above an infinity pool with Japanese koi. If you want something a bit more risqué, head over to the rooftop Tao Beach, which allows "European sunbathing," code for "topless." There's entertainment there as well: DJs spin regularly (go to the Sunday Sunset Sessions to hear some of the best house DJs in the world). You never know who you'll bump into at Tao, as Mandy Moore and Reggie Bush have hung out poolside, probably taking advantage of the luxe cabanas, which come with a plasma-screen TV, a DVD player and movies, an Xbox 360 with games, Internet access, and a custom-stocked mini fridge. You'll see views of the city and the Venetian canals, plus there are hundreds of Buddha statues and candles.

Tao Nightclub: Thursday-Friday 10 p.m.-4 a.m., Saturday 9:30 p.m.-4 a.m. Tao Beach: daily 10 a.m.-6 p.m.

TRYST

Wynn Las Vegas, 3131 Las Vegas Blvd. S., Center Strip, 702-770-3375; www.trystlasvegas.com

This posh place features 90-foot cascading waterfalls that empty into a secluded lagoon. It's so stunning, you'll probably want to spend some time in the outdoor patio that surrounds the falls. But also try lounging in the sensual, crimson-drenched rooms that set the mood with red velvet-covered walls, lush maroon sofas and framed mirrors. Big spenders, take note: For $3,000 you can try the club's signature cocktail. The Ménage à Trois martini is an alcoholic threesome of Cristal Rosé, Hennessy Ellipse and Grand Marnier, combined with 23-karat gold flakes, liquid gold syrup and a gold, diamond-studded straw. Be sure to join the stylish masses who dance to Top 40 hits, hip-hop, mash-ups and house.

Thursday-Sunday 10 p.m.-4 a.m.

TAO NIGHTCLUB

VANITY
Hard Rock Hotel and Casino, 4455 Paradise Road, Off-Strip, 702-693-5555; www.vanitylv.com

The newest nightclub from the Hard Rock Hotel, Vanity, is apparently all about you. Metallic mirror-like walls lead guests into what is supposed to be a real life jewelry box—a club decked out in pearls and hand-cut crystals. It's filled with black chrome, two marble bars and antique mirrors that cover the place in case you need to take a peek at your hair. Deep colors of red, purple, gold and green cover the walls and the plush furniture. The dance floor lies underneath a canopy of 20,000 crystals lit up like a disco ball blanketing the entire ceiling. In the area off the dance floor, mirrors cover the ceiling and velvety booths line the walls. An outdoor terrace with cabanas and a fire pit allows guests to lounge outside and take a break from the sensory overload inside. Celebrities such as P. Diddy and John Mayer have hung out here along with plenty of gorgeous people. Ladies, be sure to pay attention in the washroom, as a huge mural of an eye stares at you while you freshen up in the makeup mirrors provided at separate vanities. And if you need someone to assist you with refreshing your makeup, nails or hair, there's a crew standing by to make you look beautiful.
Thursday-Sunday 10 p.m.-4 p.m

V BAR
The Venetian Resort Hotel Casino, 3355 Las Vegas Blvd. S., Center Strip, 702-414-3200; www.arkvegas.com

This little nightspot often gets overlooked because of its more popular neighbor Tao. The benefits of that are that there's never a line and there's no pretension here. Throw in free cover, a little privacy—a smoked-glass wall lines the bar offering a shield from the casino crowd outside—and exotic martinis, and you won't want to leave the place. Order an absinthe-like Smack martini or a sugary-sweet Crystal martini, sink into one of the white double-sided leather chaise lounges, and tap your foot to the hip-hop or smooth house gently pumping through the bar. It's a lot more relaxed than the scene at Tao, but the people are just as gorgeous and the potent drinks ensure that it's just as much fun.

Sunday-Wednesday 5 p.m.-2 a.m., Thursday-Saturday 5 p.m.-3 a.m.

XS
Encore Las Vegas, 3121 Las Vegas Blvd. S., Center Strip, 702-770-0097; www.xslasvegas.com

The hardest decision you'll have to make at XS (besides what to wear) is whether to set up shop at a VIP booth in the nightclub or in a cabana on the patio surrounding the Encore pool. The youngest sibling in the Wynn nightclub family, XS sprawls over more than 40,000 square feet of indoor and outdoor space and is easily considered one of the Strip's hottest spots. Chandeliers and table lamps set the rich gold and bronze décor aglow, while mirrored mosaics and crocodile-embossed leather booths let you know you're in the presence of luxury. Bottle service is a requisite for getting a seat anywhere near the dance floor, which is always crowded but rarely unpleasantly jammed. If you're looking to live large, order the signature drink, the Ono, which includes a white gold necklace and sterling silver cufflinks along with the champagne and cognac cocktail. (Just be sure you have the $10,000 to foot the bill.)

Friday-Monday 10 p.m.-4 a.m.

ZURI
MGM Grand Hotel & Casino, 3799 Las Vegas Blvd. S., South Strip, 702-891-7433; www.mgmgrand.com

If you are looking for the after-party, this place is it. No matter how late it is, you can always rely on this small-but-chic 24-hour bar to keep the party going with tasty and strong fruity concoctions such as Woodford Reserve Bourbon infused with peaches and Granny Smith apple and cinnamon vodka. If it's really late—or rather, early—go for something off the liquid brunch menu. It offers traditional breakfast cocktails to keep a hangover at bay, such as Bloody Marys and mimosas, plus offbeat choices such as Brandy Milk Punch, with Germain-Robin Alambic brandy, whole egg, milk,

WHICH NIGHTLIFE SPOTS HAVE THE BEST DÉCOR?
Surrender: The focal point of this spacious and sleek club at Encore is a 120-foot long silver snake behind the venue's main bar. Beautiful gold banquettes surround the dance floors and the space extends out into a dazzling pool area.

Tabu Ultra Lounge: There's nothing subtle about the big and bright vibe here. Interactive tabletops, projected imagery and strobe lights provide an ever-changing décor for a true Vegas experience.

Tao: The Asian-inspired interior doesn't do imitation. A 20-foot hand-carved Buddha, century-old wood beams, floating Chinese lanterns and a koi pond are just some of the authentic treats you'll find inside.

Tryst: A 90-foot waterfall cascading into a secluded lagoon makes this nightlife spot visually appealing.

XS

powdered sugar and a dash of nutmeg. Unlike the booming, huge clubs that tired you out earlier in the night, Zuri invites you to kick back in a more relaxed and intimate setting. And unlike those sceney spots, it's pretty casual here, so come as you are. Grab a cigar from the bar's humidor, snag one of the oversized olive chairs and enjoy your liquid brunch.
Daily 24 hours.

OFF-STRIP

GHOSTBAR
Palms Casino Resort, 4321 W. Flamingo Road, Off-Strip, 702-938-2666; www.n9negroup.com
Get whisked to another world atop the 55th floor of the Palms. This space-age room decked out with mod white couches is only accessible via an express elevator that zooms you to one of the best bars in the city, mainly thanks to its fantastic view of the valley and the twinkling lights of the Strip. (You might remember it as a popular haunt of the cast of MTV's *Real World: Las Vegas*.) The bar includes an outdoor space that's filled with plenty of tables and chairs that make for prime alfresco lounging. Prepare yourself for one of the city's most literally breathtaking views—a square chunk of transparent glass in the patio floor 55 stories above the tarmac gives a dizzying view of the people entering the Palms below. Tables with bottle service can be reserved, but most guests gather near the railed edges, drinks in hand. For the best spots outside, get there early, since Ghostbar is bigger on fun than it is on square footage.
Daily 8 p.m.-4 a.m.

HOSTILE GRAPE
The M Resort, 12300 Las Vegas Blvd. S., Off-Strip, 702-797-1000; www.themresort.com
Wine lovers will find their nirvana at this tasting room and wine cellar located within the Off-Strip M Resort. A clever serve-yourself system allows you to pick and choose different sizes of pours from the more than 160 wines

WHICH CLUBS HAVE THE BEST VIEWS OF THE STRIP?

Mix Lounge: At 64 floors above the Strip, it is more a matter of what you can't see at this swank spot. Arrive early to stake your claim for a table on the balcony.

Ghostbar: On a clear night, the posh skydeck is the place to be if 360-degree views of the Strip are on the docket. The glass insert in the floor offers a view straight down to the pavement.

Voodoo Lounge: Perched 50 floors above the Strip, the multi-tiered patios and curving 20-ton staircase provide photo-ops aplenty.

Christian Audigier The Nightclub: People-watching is easy from the patio of this chic locale. When eyeing those strolling the Strip gets tiresome, turn your attention to the adjacent dance floor.

---

available by the glass and keep track of your tipples using a pre-paid tasting card. Wines from just about anywhere grapes grow to good results are on offer, from South Africa to Sonoma. The low-lit space is filled with plenty of comfortable chocolate leather couches for lounging and savoring the fine vintages and mellow jazz music.
Tuesday-Thursday 5 p.m.-11 p.m., Friday-Saturday 4 p.m.-2 a.m.

MOON
Palms Casino Resort, 4321 W. Flamingo Road, Off-Strip, 702-942-6832; www.n9negroup.com
Jet over to Moon in the Palms' Fantasy Tower for a fanciful night of dancing. This space-aged themed club 53 stories above the streets of Las Vegas is a blast from top to bottom. Under your feet is a glass tile floor that changes colors. Glance up at the floor-to-ceiling windows to the retractable roof for a truly spectacular view. When open, the desert night blankets the club from wall to wall, but when the roof is closed, a laser and space show plays above the dancers below. Cocktail servers are done up in tiny metallic silver uniforms and chunky black boots, easy to spot when you're in need of a refill.
Tuesday, Thursday-Sunday 10:30 p.m.-4 a.m.

RAIN
Palms Casino Resort, 4321 W. Flamingo Road, Off-Strip, 702-942-6832; www.n9negroup.com
As you enter through the curved mirrored hallway, the music is the first thing to hit you. But it's the atmosphere inside that will soak your senses. Fire-and-water special effects ring the room around the usually packed dance floor. Above, fire clouds billow out over the crowd throughout the evening. Bars are plentiful in this cavernous space, with tiers climbing to the top VIP area. Private water booths, tented cabanas and skyboxes are available with reservations. Unlike other clubs where the stars are secluded in back rooms or shuttered booths, this is a shared experience, with the VIP areas overlooking the dance floors so you can see celebrities or whoever from wherever in the club. Waits can stretch from two to four hours on most weekend nights.
Friday-Saturday 11 p.m.-5 a.m.

V BAR

VOODOO LOUNGE

Rio All-Suite Hotel & Casino, 3700 W. Flamingo Road, Off-Strip, 702-777-7800; www.riolasvegas.com

This is one of the longest-lasting clubs in Vegas, and for good reason. VooDoo sits atop the 51st floor of the Rio and features some of the best DJs in the city. You can party inside on the small dance floor, but most people head out to dance under the stars. Award-winning bartenders entertain behind the bar in this double-decker nightclub, mixing signature libations such as the enormous Witch Doctor, a fruity, oversized drink with a bit of dry ice for dramatic effect. The drink is something you won't forget (unless you have two). The stunning steel staircase that joins the indoor-outdoor rooms provides amazing views of the city below—just watch out for vertigo as you climb up.

Sunday-Thursday 5 p.m.-2 a.m., Friday-Saturday 5 p.m.-4 a.m.

WASTED SPACE

Hard Rock Hotel & Casino Las Vegas, 4455 Paradise Road, Off-Strip, 702-693-4000; www.hartswastedspace.com

Billing itself as Las Vegas' first "anti-club," Wasted Space is not the place to find DJs spinning top 40 hits and frilly bachelorette party girls swooning over sugary cocktails. Instead, Hard Rock Hotel's newest endeavor—the

---

WHAT ARE THE BEST WINE BARS?

Double Helix Bar: The combined bar and boutique concept allows you to sample more than 50 rare wines before deciding which bottles are worth taking home.

Hostile Grape: With more than 160 wines by the glass, you are certain to find a memorable varietal you've never tasted before at this cellar and tasting room.

combined effort of Carey Hart, Jason Giambi, and Benji and Joel Madden— is all about good old rock. The space is welcoming and surprisingly unpre- tentious with thick floor-to-ceiling curtains, hardwood floors and deep leather banquettes. Nights alternate between live music performances and spinning DJs, and the cover charge fluctuates accordingly, but rarely rises above $30, which is a steal in Sin City. The same holds true with the price of cocktails. Most drinks cost less than $10. Try the signature concoction, the Hart Attack, a blend of Jameson, Red Bull, cranberry and Jagermeister. The attached Wasted Lounge remains rocking for 24-hours a day.
Wednesday-Sunday 9 p.m.-4 a.m.

BLUE MAN GROUP

SHOW BUSINESS

Most people come to Las Vegas with one thing on the agenda: striking it rich in the casinos. But it only takes a few minutes in this adult playpen to realize there's a whole lot more than gambling on offer. The billboards alone prove more star-studded shows than anyone could possibly see in a single visit.

What's more, this desert oasis is a living city, with thousands of residents with an interest in more than just casinos and nightlife. Vegas has its share of fine art museums and galleries waiting to be explored.

Whether you're curious about the desert art scene, looking for a laugh or in the mood to hit the links (on one of the poshest courses in the country), you'll find plenty of excuses to get up from those slots, and head out on the town for a dose of culture.

WHERE CAN YOU FIND THE CITY'S BEST ART?
THE BELLAGIO GALLERY OF FINE ART
3600 Las Vegas Blvd., Center Strip, 702-957-9777; www.bellagio.com
If you think a casino is a strange bedfellow for a museum, you haven't been to Bellagio Gallery of Fine Art. Sure, critics harrumphed when they heard about a highbrow museum in "low-brow" Las Vegas, but they've since given BGFA an all-approving nod. Exhibits at this small space, located near the pool area, change throughout the year and display paintings, sculpture and other artistic mediums. Past exhibits have included American modernism, Claude Monet's masterworks, Faberge treasures, Picasso's ceramics and more. A recent installation, *Figuratively Speaking: A Survey of the Human Form*, featured the work of artists who helped define figurative art.
Admission: adults $15, seniors $12, students $10, children under 12 free. Sunday-Tuesday, Thursday 10 a.m.-6 p.m., Wednesday, Friday-Saturday 10 a.m.-7 p.m.

FIRST FRIDAY
Charleston Boulevard and Casino Center, Downtown;
www.firstfriday-lasvegas.org
Break out those horn-rimmed glasses—the first Friday of every month is your time to look artsy. Galleries, bars and shops keep their doors open late as visitors and locals mix, mingle and get to know this under-appreciated part of town. Located just under a mile from the north end of the Strip, this art-fair-meets-street-fair fills the cordoned-off streets of downtown with music, food, beer and, of course, art. No need for a map. Every first Friday, a trolley makes the rounds to notable spots, including local favorite The Fallout Gallery *(1551 S. Commerce St., Downtown, 702-678-6278; www.thefallout. net)*, Atomic Todd Gallery *(1541 S. Commerce St., Downtown, 702-386-8633; www.atomictodd.com)*, The Arts Factory *(101-07 E. Charleston Blvd., Downtown, 702-676-1111; www.theartsfactory.com)* and The Funk House *(1228 S. Casino Center Blvd., Downtown, 702-678-6278; www.thefunkhouselasvegas.com)* antique shop and gallery, among others. Area bars such as Dino's Lounge *(1516 Las Vegas Blvd. South, Downtown, 702-382-3894; www.dinoslv.com)* and Frankie's Tiki Room *(1712 W. Charleston Blvd., Downtown, 702-385-3110; www.frankiestikiroom.com)* bring in bands and will keep you entertained until dawn.
First Friday of each month 6-10 p.m.

PENN AND TELLER

WHERE IS THE BEST COMEDY ON THE STRIP?

CARROT TOP
Luxor, 3900 Las Vegas Blvd. S., South Strip, 800-557-7428;
www.carrottop.com

Few need to spy the bulky biceps, unruly red mane and black eyeliner to know that they're in the presence of Carrot Top. What started as a way to differentiate himself is now just part of his act, as is his self-deprecation and self-flagellation. Like a modern-day Gallagher—without the watermelon—Carrot Top's show is based around an endless array of props that he creates himself. From an "Amish blow dryer" to a telephone made from paper cups and string (with a third cup for call waiting), expect a slew of energetic gaffes and song parodies. This isn't a show for the easily offended, and those not sodden by the water-throwing opening act will be in the minority.
Tickets start at $50. Monday, Wednesday-Sunday 8:30 p.m., 18 and over only.

GEORGE WALLACE
Flamingo Las Vegas, 3555 Las Vegas Blvd. S., Center Strip, 800-221-7299; www.georgewallace.net

George Wallace has more than "Yo Mama" jokes to thank for his success. After years of TV appearances and a long ride on the stand-up circuit, Wallace has gotten comfortable at the Flamingo, but not too comfortable. The show constantly changes according to the day's headlines and current political fodder, so even repeat visitors can expect to laugh at Wallace's deadpan delivery and hilariously logical, occasionally envelope-pushing humor (To wit: "A 700-foot wall for the immigration problem? First of all, who's going to build that wall?"). And if getting a good chuckle out of an evening isn't enough, what about a new car or a diamond necklace? That's right. The entertainer gives prizes away to lucky audience members during each performance.
Tickets start at $50. Tuesday-Saturday 10 p.m.

THE IMPROV

Harrah's Las Vegas Hotel and Casino, 3475 Las Vegas Blvd. S., Center Strip, 702-369-5223; www.harrahslasvegas.com

Sit down at a cocktail table with a stiff drink and prepare for old-fashioned stand-up at this long-standing venue, where comedians take the stage and serve up their best material during raunchy, raucous 60-minute shows. Each week sees two to three different jokesters in residence, with some of the nation's top names in comedy performing before the simple, bare-brick backdrop. Because the evening is entirely unscripted, you might hear diatribes on topics such as national politics, gloabl warming and pretty much whatever is top of mind in shows that are reserved for those 18 and older.
Tickets start at $29.05. Tuesday-Sunday 8:30 and 10:30 p.m.

PENN AND TELLER

Rio All-Suite Hotel and Casino, 3700 W. Flamingo Road, Off-Strip, 702-777-7776; www.pennandteller.com

The brash one (Penn) and the silent one (Teller) have been mystifying and cracking up audiences for more than 30 years. The duo breaks the magician's code again and again, by sharing magical secrets with the audience. Well, at least partial magical secrets, because they still manage to baffle, and entertain—where else can you see a fire-eating showgirl and a duck? The duo's running commentary about how they came up with the tricks adds depth to the production, placing it on a higher plane than your typical rabbit-out-of-a-hat magic show. This is a performance for those prone to raised eyebrows.
Tickets start at $75. Saturday-Wednesday 9 p.m.

RITA RUDNER

Harrah's Las Vegas Hotel and Casino, 3475 Las Vegas Blvd. S., Center Strip, 702-369-5222; www.ritafunny.com

When she turned 50, Rita Rudner admitted that it took quite a while before she could even say her age. Instead, it came out, well, "filthy." But it's not just her sense of humor that makes Rudner funny. It's her dainty, wide-eyed delivery that really seals the deal. Dressed in a blindingly bedazzled gown and heels, Rudner is as girly as they come, and that's, in part, the focus of her material. Take *Men Are From Mars, Women Are From Venus*, shake it up with a splash of *Defending the Caveman*, and sweeten it with the fresh wit and pizzazz of Rudner, and you've got a show that makes you wonder whether the two genders are really that different after all.
Tickets start at $54. Monday-Saturday 8:30 p.m. See website for specific dates.

WHAT ARE THE BEST VENUES FOR LIVE MUSIC?
HOUSE OF BLUES

Mandalay Bay, 3950 Las Vegas Blvd. S., South Strip, 877-632-7600; www.hob.com

Calling the Mandalay Bay home for more than a decade, this HOB outpost is far from your typical concert venue—even by Vegas standards. From the voodoo-esque art on the walls to the worn-in wood and corrugated tin surrounding the place, you'll feel as though you've stepped into the heart and soul of New Orleans. And that's not a bad thing. House of Blues is one of the coziest and most comfortable places in town to catch bands, which range from lesser knowns like Cancer Bats to classics like Joe Satriani and

WHICH IS THE BEST CIRQUE DU SOLEIL SHOW?

Sin City may as well change its nickname to Cirque City. With six permanent **Cirque du Soleil** *(www.cirquedusoleil.com)* shows and more on the horizon, the question remains: How many is too many? The answer: We'll know it when we see it, but it hasn't happened yet. These theaters keep packing them in for surreal productions that take place in the water, air, or on land and always on elaborate sets. Here's the rundown.

With a score made up of snippets of Beatles songs selected by original group producer Sir George Martin and his son Giles, *The Beatles LOVE* at The Mirage, arguably has the best musical soundtrack ever made for a production show. You'll be humming Fab Four tunes while the scenery and action floats from *Lucy in the Sky with Diamonds* to *Octopus' Garden*. Even middling Beatles fans will find their toes subconsciously tapping to *All You Need is Love*.

Cirque purists love the sheer strength involved in *Mystere* at Treasure Island (TI). This is classic Cirque du Soleil, with bright costumes, intriguing sets and acrobatics that make soaring through the air and scaling the walls look effortless. The show is a whirlwind of activity: cast members hop up ropes feet first, flip atop human totem poles and swing horizontally across the stage, and that's just in the opening number.

If ever a stage was the main character in a production, it is so in *Kà* at MGM Grand. The custom-designed platform shifts seamlessly from a horizontal battleground to a vertical mountain to an underwater adventure. It's just as mesmerizing as the acrobats dressed in elaborate costumes who frolic upon it; if you're a stickler for plots, this Cirque show has the

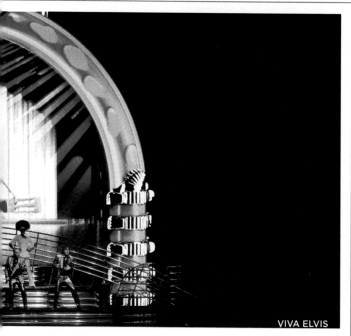

VIVA ELVIS

most distinct storyline. *Kà*, whose story takes its premise from the ancient Egyptian belief in an invisible spiritual duplicate, follows a pair of twins who embark on a tumultuous journey full of battles of physical and spiritual proportions.

Fans of grace and fluidity (over sheer strength) fall in love with *O* at the Bellagio. The show focuses on the concept of infinity and how it applies to time and water (and, on a more literal level, the letter O and the French word for water, eau). The cast of Cirque characters is complemented by world-class synchronized swimmers and divers who take to a 1.5 million gallon pool, which doubles as a stage. Bodies slip in and out of the water like amphibians, and the high-dive takes on an entirely new meaning. Comic relief in the form of two oddly paired clowns reminds you that you're still at a circus, but as sideshows go, this certainly is the big top for waterworks.

Zumanity shows a darker, sexier side of Cirque. The 18-and-up show at New York-New York peers into the "human zoo" through sensual vignettes. With erotica accenting its usual cast of contortionists, clowns and acrobats, this is Cirque du Steamy.

Criss Angel Believe opened at Luxor in 2008 to much acclaim. The show takes on a dark dreamlike reverie, mixing the world of illusion with the dramatic tradition of Cirque. Those craving a concise plot may be disappointed, but the visual elegance and fluidity of Angel and his various muses is pure pleasure to watch.

The new Cirque show, *Viva Elvis*, opened at Aria in CityCenter in December 2009. This show mixes dance, live music and acrobatics, paying tribute to the King.

headliners like Jay-Z and The Black Crowes. Multiple levels (tip: check out the comfortable and semi-secret theater seating upstairs) and various bars make for varied vantage points and convenient cocktail grabbing throughout the shows. The best people-watching happens during Sunday's Gospel Brunch. While the singers on stage get down for Jesus, hundreds of guests praise the lord and pass the biscuits in rockabilly style.

THE JOINT
Hard Rock Hotel & Casino, 4455 Paradise Road, Off-Strip, 800-693-7625; www.hardrockhotel.com
Considering its location in the Hard Rock, a resort built around the theme of good music, the bar remains high for talent at The Joint. The rocking stage and sound system have blasted the likes of Bob Dylan, The Killers, Tom Petty and Coldplay, and succeed in bringing in varied acts of a high caliber (don't expect to find lesser known bands and singers here, unless they're an opening act). The space blends down-home charm with state-of-the-art technology—25-foot-tall speaker bays and multiple plasma screens—to create an authentic rock club vibe.

THE PEARL AT THE PALMS
Palms Casino Resort, 4321 W. Flamingo Road, Off-Strip, 702-944-3200; www.palmspearl.com
With only 2,500 seats, this concert hall at the Palms delivers a uniquely intimate environment for seeing major performers who normally never set foot in venues so small. With a stage that's only four feet off the floor (and the farthest seat 120 feet away from the stage), performers interact with audiences here like nowhere else. That's what makes a show at The Pearl so fun, and tickets so hard to come by. You might see celebrities like Jay-Z or Rihanna camped out in the private boxes, which have their own bars and powder rooms. Recent acts have included Norah Jones, David Gray and Melissa Etheridge.
See website for show times and ticket prices.

WHAT ARE THE TOP LAS VEGAS SHOWS?
THE COLOSSEUM SHOWS
Caesars Palace, 3570 Las Vegas Blvd. S., Center Strip, 702-866-1400; www.caesarspalace.com
Hail Caesar—or at least his performance space. The long-time home of Celine Dion's award-winning show has also hosted Cher in *Cher* with her countless costume changes; the divine Ms. M and her showgirls in *The Showgirl Must Go On*; and the man who made famous the Soup Nazi and beltless trench coats in *Jerry Seinfeld*. The state-of-the-art acoustics make any show here great, and unobstructed sightlines allow you to catch every costume change and comedic raised eyebrow. Even if you're just a casual fan, you'll be laughing or singing along, or both, by the curtain call. And in case you missed Celine Dion on her first go-round, the popular singer is back at Caesars in March.
Tickets are $95-$250. Daily 7:30 p.m. See website for dates.

JERSEY BOYS

GARTH BROOKS AT ENCORE

Encore Las Vegas, 3121 Las Vegas Blvd. S., Center Strip, 702-770-1000; www.encorelasvegas.com

Recently, the country crooner announced he would come out of his self-imposed retirement (Brooks had taken a break from performing to spend time with his children) to play a series of weekend concerts at Encore, and he ended up signing to play for the next five years. The concept is simple: Just Brooks, his guitar and 1,500 fans who might be treated to renditions of favorites such as *Friends in Low Places*. Expect a set list that covers all of Brooks' greatest hits and a venue that's comfortable and intimate.

Tickets $125. Friday 8 p.m., Saturday 8 and 10:30 p.m., Sunday 8 p.m.

JERSEY BOYS

The Palazzo Las Vegas Resort and Casino, 3325 Las Vegas Blvd. S., Center Strip, 702-414-9000; www.palazzolasvegas.com

Newark is a long way from Las Vegas, but that doesn't stop the actors portraying Frankie Valli and The Four Seasons from delivering time and again in this shortened rendition of the Tony-winning blockbuster musical. Hit songs like *Sherry*, *Big Girls Don't Cry*, and *Can't Take My Eyes Off You* will have you musing about your days in poodle skirts and letter jackets. The Palazzo stage was custom-built—the acoustics are top-notch—and laden with memorabilia from The Rock and Roll Hall of Fame, making it a unique theatrical experience all around.

Tickets start at $72.10. Thursday-Friday, Sunday-Monday 7 p.m., Tuesday, Saturday 6:30 p.m. and 9:30 p.m. See website for availability.

LEGENDS IN CONCERT

Harrah's Las Vegas Hotel and Casino, 3475 Las Vegas Blvd. S., Center Strip, 888-777-7664; www.legendsinconcert.com

Impersonation is practically a high art form in Las Vegas. There's so much competition—and we're not just talking Elvis—that a show has to be exceptional to have any kind of shelf life. Legends in Concert has been, well,

"LIONESSES DANCE" IN THE LION KING LAS VEGAS

legendary at impersonation since 1983. After more than 25 years at the Imperial Palace, the show moved down the strip to Harrah's Theater in 2009, adding VIP booths and table cocktail service to its list of selling points. Each show still includes performances from multiple artists, all of whom belt out their own songs and medleys—no lip-synching here. The line-ups change frequently, so you never know what you'll get, but Elvis, The Blues Brothers, Tom Jones and Marilyn Monroe are staple performers. Dazzling costumes and dancers and a live orchestra round out the faux-superstar show.
Tickets start at $59. Thursday-Tuesday 7:30 p.m. and 10 p.m.

LE RÊVE
Wynn Las Vegas, 3131 Las Vegas Blvd. S., Center Strip, 702-770-9966; www.wynnlasvegas.com
A fantastical production of water, acrobatics and dramatic flair, this permanent show at Wynn Las Vegas showcases choreography and athelticism at its best. The concept follows a dreamworld journey (le rêve is French for dream) that has dozens of actors swimming, diving, twirling, dancing and performing incredible feats of strength in a specially designed aquatic theater. Make an evening of the experience with the VIP package ($179 per person), which includes champagne and chocolate-covered strawberries, luxury lounge seating with screens that provide a glimpse of the real-time backstage action, and a special VIP pass for use at the resort's restaurants and nightclubs on the day of the performance.
Tickets start at $99. Friday-Tuesday 7 p.m. and 9:30 p.m.

DISNEY'S THE LION KING
Mandalay Bay Resort and Casino, 3950 Las Vegas Blvd. S., South Strip, 877-632-7400; www.mandalaybay.com
The long-running and much loved production, with its impressive, towering shadow puppets and colorful sets, has a home in Las Vegas at Mandalay Bay. You might recognize the score by Elton John and Tim Rice, which includes songs such as *Can You Feel The Love Tonight?* and *Hakuna*

Matata. Even if you come without kids in tow, the family-friendly play's parable about the ebb and flow of the life cycle is an entertaining one.
Tickets start at $64. Monday-Thursday 7:30 p.m., Saturday-Sunday 4 p.m. and 8 p.m.

PHANTOM—THE LAS VEGAS SPECTACULAR
The Venetian Resort Hotel Casino, 3355 Las Vegas Blvd. S., Center Strip, 702-414-9000; www.phantomlasvegas.com

Leave it to Vegas to add glitz, glamour and pyrotechnics to improve the most successful theatrical production in history. The $40 million stage is practically a character in itself, and the $5 million chandelier, which falls at a breakneck 45 feet in three seconds, will have the faint of heart gripping their seats—or ducking under them for cover. *Phantom—The Las Vegas Spectacular* was shortened to 95 minutes to cut out intermission and quicken the pace (the shortening of shows has become a Las Vegas tradition, since it's a way of getting you back on the casino floor more quickly) but includes all of the original songs. In the hands of original director Harold Prince, Andrew Lloyd Webber, and, well, Las Vegas, the version is true to its name—spectacular.
Tickets start at $59. Monday-Saturday 7 p.m. See website for availability.

WHAT ARE THE BEST GOLF COURSES?
BALI HAI
5160 Las Vegas Blvd. S., Off-Strip, 888-427-6678;
www.balihaigolfclub.com

Your first inclination might be that golf and the desert don't make a great pair. But when that desert happens to be in Las Vegas, they do. Courses like Bali Hai show mans' triumph over nature (and then nature's triumph over man, when it comes to the $200 to $300 rates). The name elicits visions of a tropical paradise immortalized in the Rodgers & Hammerstein musical *South Pacific*, and this lush golf club doesn't disappoint. The Lee Schmidt- and Brian Curley-designed course has seven acres of water features and the type of service you'd expect in paradise.

WYNN GOLF COURSE
3131 Las Vegas Blvd. S., Center Strip, 888-320-7122;
www.wynnlasvegas.com

Built in 2003, Wynn Golf Course actually has a historic reputation. It's located on the former Desert Inn Golf Club site that for 50 years hosted PGA, Senior PGA and LPGA tournaments. Nearly 1,200 of the 50-year-old trees still stand on the 7,042-yard par-70 course, which was designed by Tom Fazio and Steve Wynn. A 37-foot waterfall is just one of the many water details that meander throughout the course. Wynn has something of the Midas touch when it comes to development, and Wynn Golf Club is no exception. To emphasize its exclusivity, the course was previously open to Wynn hotel guests and invited visitors only, though that requirement was lifted in November of 2007, and fees reach $500.

WHERE IS THE BEST RACETRACK?
LAS VEGAS MOTOR SPEEDWAY
7000 Las Vegas Blvd. N., Off-Strip, 702-644-4444; www.lvms.com

You may not understand the appeal, but that shouldn't deter you from feeling the power, smelling the oil and reveling in the grit of NASCAR at the Las Vegas Motor Speedway. Every March the city's neck turns a touch redder, as more than 100,000 fans fire up their grills and head to NASCAR's Sprint Cup and Nationwide Series races. The $200 million track, which was built in 1995, extends 1,500 acres and includes the 1.5-mile super speedway, in addition to a 2.5-mile road course, a half-mile dirt oval and a drag strip. Technicalities aside, the people-watching here is priceless. So when your eyes tire of following the blurry left turns on the track, grab a hot dog and check out your neighbor's head-to-toe Jimmie Johnson-themed wardrobe. *Admission: adults $8, children under 12 and seniors $6. Daily. Race prices vary. Tours: Monday-Saturday 9 a.m.-4 p.m., Sunday 11-4 p.m.*

WHAT ARE THE BEST BOXING VENUES?

Boxing and casinos go together like Texas and Hold 'Em. (Especially in Las Vegas, also known as the Boxing Capital of the World.) This is, after all, where Mike Tyson got an earful. Muhammad Ali, Sugar Ray Leonard, Oscar De La Hoya, Floyd Mayweather—the list goes on, but anyone worth their weight class has fought in Vegas.

MANDALAY BAY EVENTS CENTER
3950 Las Vegas Blvd. S., Center Strip, 702-632-7777;
www.mandalaybay.com

The Events Center at Mandalay Bay gets top billing when it comes to boxing bouts. The 12,000-seat complex is relatively small in comparison to other venues, providing good sightlines from nearly every seat. Consequently, it often draws a packed house, so secure tickets in advance. If sitting ringside isn't in your cards, head to the casino's sports bar to get in on the action, flat-screen style.

MGM GRAND GARDEN ARENA
3799 Las Vegas Blvd. S., Center Strip, 877-880-0880;
www.mgmgrand.com

Perhaps the best-known boxing venue in Las Vegas, the MGM Grand Garden Arena, is also one of the largest, comfortably seating 16,800 eager fans. State-of-the-art acoustics let you hear every swing of the glove—a necessity since many seats are too far away from the action in the ring to watch except on the jumbo screens. If you care about seeing the bout up close, be prepared to shell out some heavy coinage.

BEYOND LAS VEGAS

MOUNT CHARLESTON

BEYOND THE BRIGHT LIGHTS

Many forget that Las Vegas, the city of lights and millionaire-making possibilities, is in the middle of a desert. What does this mean for you? Besides having to bathe in sunscreen daily and drink a lot of water, it ensures that you'll have plenty of unique day trips to enjoy once you tire of Vegas's warped reality. Why not explore Las Vegas's aquatic lifeline, otherwise known as Hoover Dam? Or head to one of the hottest places on earth—the Valley of Fire. Those with a bit more time on their hands can even make it to one of the seven Natural Wonders of the World.

WHAT ARE THE BEST DAY TRIPS FROM THE STRIP?

HOOVER DAM AND LAKE MEAD

Imagine Las Vegas without the Fountains of Bellagio, without the Sirens of TI, without any of the mega-hotels and casinos. That's how it would be if it weren't for the **Hoover Dam**: dry, dusty and dull. The fate of Las Vegas was forever altered in the early 1930s, when the dam became the giant camel of the West, catching and storing water, and making the land truly habitable for the first time.

Just 30 miles southeast of Las Vegas, Hoover Dam can offer a much-needed reality check from the monopoly-money mentality of the Strip. It was named a Monument of the Millennium by the American Society of Engineers and is a designated National Historic Civil Engineering Landmark, and even with the more than one million annual visitors, you're sure to feel rightly insignificant and diminutive in comparison to its massive concrete stature. A tour takes you inside the belly of the beast, more than 500 feet underground to emerge near the hydroelectric power plant and its genera-tors. Feel the rush of water as you stand above a pipe that's 30 feet in diameter, carrying 22,500 gallons of water per second—per second—from Lake Mead to Hoover Dam. Trade the hydro-electrics for the vistas of the observation deck 800 feet above the rushing Colorado River, and you'll notice that this is far more than a functional slab of concrete. Artists and architects framed the dam in the Art Deco style popular during the era it was built, and a bronze sculpture of a worker scaling the rocks near the dam could just as easily grace the grounds of a gallery. You'll hear the stories of the 21,000 laborers who came to the desert seeking jobs in the Great Depression, and how they toiled through triple-digit temperatures to create this unprecedented water barricade—and did all of it in less than six years. Keeping in line with the two-for-one deals so common in Las Vegas, you should drive out to see Hoover Dam, but stay for Lake Mead, the largest man-made lake in the United States and a direct result of Hoover Dam.

Spanning 157,900 acres and boasting depths of 589 feet, **Lake Mead** *(www.nps.gov)* is more than just a mirage in the desert. It's the aquatic lifeline for landlocked Las Vegas. But before you imagine strolling along sandy beaches and frolicking in the cool waves, know that Lake Mead is a utilitarian lake, first and foremost. The shores are rocky and don't lend them-selves to lounging. That said, there are other ways to enjoy the water. Zip across the lake in a personal watercraft, float along on a fishing boat or enjoy a water-filled weekend on a houseboat. If you'd prefer someone else play captain, make a reservation on the **Desert Princess** *(www.lakemeadcruises. com)*. A throwback to the days of Huckleberry Finn, the Desert Princess is

LAKE MEAD

a three-level, Mississippi-style paddlewheeler that takes passengers across Lake Mead to Hoover Dam and back.

The less aquatically inclined will find plenty of good trails around the lake. One of the best walks is the nearly seven-mile roundtrip **Historic Railroad Tunnel Trail** *(www.nps.gov)* along the rim of the lake. The easy hike gives way to stunning views of the blue water and its craggy surroundings. If you left your hiking shoes behind and aren't inspired to leave your vehicle, the road surrounding the lake is a lovely drive. The hour-plus route takes you through drastically changing scenery, transforming from lake views to red sandstone areas to fields of teddy bear cholla. The road takes you to Overton, and from there you can hop on the I-15 and return to Las Vegas. Or for more sightseeing, take S.R. 167 to the Valley of Fire.

How to get there: From Las Vegas Boulevard, take NV-589/Sahara Avenue and make a left. After three miles, turn right on NV-582 and merge onto I-515 South (which becomes US-93 South). Continue for 11 miles before seeing signs leading to Hoover Dam.

VALLEY OF FIRE

If you're looking for a *Fear and Loathing in Las Vegas* experience without the hallucinogens, head to the **Valley of Fire State Park** *(www.parks.nv.gov)*, located about 55 miles northeast of the Strip. Known for its flame-colored rocks, shadowy geological pockets and trippy formations, this place feels almost moon-like. Hollywood has certainly taken note. A long list of movies have been filmed here, including *Star Trek: Generations*, *Total Recall* and *Transformers*, using the fiery sandstone as a striking backdrop.

The area was formed about 150 million years ago by shifting sand dunes, and has been shaped by wind and water. Who knew wind had such an artistic bent? Have fun matching names to formations, like Beehives, Arch Rock, Elephant Rock and Silica Dome. Though today the sandstone is used for recreational activities, like hiking and rock scrambling, you can still see evidence of its previous purpose as a canvas. The early inhabitants

KOLB STUDIO

of the area, the Basket Maker people and later the Anasazi Pueblo people, communicated with one another by drawing petroglyphs. Many of the drawings on the rocks remain today, and can be seen along the hiking trails (which are relatively short and easy, and make a great alternative if your kids tire of the Strip). If you visit in the summer, keep in mind that you're in the desert, and temperatures can reach 120 degrees in the daytime. Bring plenty of water and sunscreen.

For a bit of heat relief, head to **Mount Charleston** (also known as Spring Mountains National Recreation Area, *www.fs.fed.us*). Just 30 minutes away from Las Vegas, this cool, green playground boasts temperatures that are about 30 degrees cooler than they are on the desert floor. At 11,918 feet, Mount Charleston is the second highest peak in Nevada. Its surrounding Spring Mountain Range offers a tempting escape once the mercury hits the triple digits. Hike past bubbling streams and up to waterfalls, amid wildflowers and clean air while inhaling the fresh scent of ponderosa and bristlecone pines. If you look closely, you may see burros, elk, coyotes and even bobcats. Hikes range from one mile to 17 miles, and cater to all ability levels. Mary Jane Falls is one of the more popular, and takes you through the forest and up to the falls.

In the winter, the mountain is the closest spot to Las Vegas to show off your skiing and snowboarding skills. That's right—even desert dwellers cherish a little downhill recreation, and are proud to have plenty of powder so close by. The **Las Vegas Ski and Snowboard Resort** *(www.skilasvegas. com)* is home to a half-pipe and 11 trails, all flaunting Vegas-appropriate names like Slot Alley, Jacks and High Roller. Its season runs from October through April, and unless you like spending more time on lift-lines than on the runs, aim to visit during the week (weekends can be brutally crowded).

How to get there: From Las Vegas Blvd., make your way onto NV-582 and merge onto I-15 North. Continue on I-15N for 53 miles before exiting at Highway 169 (exit 93). Follow signs for Overton/Logandale; merge onto NV-12. After 23 miles, watch for signs for the Valley of Fire.

DEATH VALLEY NATIONAL PARK

The names of the areas and formations at **Death Valley** *(www.nps.gov)* set the tone: Furnace Creek, Devil's Golf Course and Desolation Canyon don't leave much room for surprise. Still, no one can prepare for the 120-plus degrees that Death Valley reaches in the summer. It's an area best described by superlatives like "hottest" and "driest." And yet, this barely inhabitable spot that's 282 feet below sea level is beautiful.

At 3.1 million acres, Death Valley is the largest park in the contiguous United States. It straddles Nevada and California, and is located about 120 miles northwest of Las Vegas. With its rolling mud hills, colorful mineral deposits and pockets of hardy plants, the national park attracts visitors year round—even in the blazing summer heat. The second hottest temperature in the world was recorded here at a sweltering 134 degrees Fahrenheit, and a ground temperature of 201 degrees Fahrenheit has also been taken (that's 11 degrees short of water's boiling point). It makes sense that most visitors come during the cooler season, from October through April, when the sandy valley starts cooling off (in relative terms), although the park's busiest season is in the spring.

Regardless of when you visit, **Scotty's Castle** *(www.nps.gov)* is worth a detour. It's an ornate mansion, complete with towers and gables, located in the middle of nowhere. The former home is about an hour north of Furnace Creek. A tour guide, dressed in period attire, leads you through the castle, sharing the history of "Death Valley Scotty," a drifter who made his living by convincing investors he found gold in Death Valley. The tour gives you a unique peek into the desert's lore, and insight into the odd character drawn to a land of such extremes.

Following your desert exploration, take State Highway 127 south to the tiny trailer-filled town of Tecopa, which is famous for its hot springs and date shakes. Follow the yellow signs to **China Ranch** *(www.chinaranch.com)*, a verdant valley and date farm. You can hike to waterfalls and streams, and even walk along a portion of the Old Spanish Trail. Before high-tailing it back to Vegas, stop at the store across from China Ranch, and treat yourself to the best date shake you've ever had. Served in simple Styrofoam cups, these chunky shakes taste like caramel, thanks to the perfect combination of vanilla ice cream and freshly picked China Ranch dates. As remedies for the desert's heat go, they can't be beat.

How to get there: From Las Vegas Boulevard, head west on I-215 to exit 10B to merge onto I-15 South toward Los Angeles. Take exit 33 toward Pahrump before merging onto NV-160. Stay on NV-160 for 56 miles and make a left at E. Bell Vista Avenue. After 11 miles, turn right at Ash Meadows Road (and cross the California border). Turn right at CA-127 and left at CA-190 and look for signs for Death Valley National Park.

HOW FAR AWAY IS THE GRAND CANYON?

Though it's about 300 miles from Sin City, too far a distance for a driving day trip, you can get to the **Grand Canyon** and back to your hotel in as little as three to four hours by helicopter. If you need any other incentives to go this route, many companies offer additional adventures like boat rides along the Colorado River, picnics, Hummer treks and more. This isn't the cheapest way to see the canyon, and rides fill up fast. But what better way to view this massive 6-million-year-old canyon than from above?

It's not surprising that nearly 5 million visitors travel to see this world wonder and World Heritage site every year. (Compare that to the 44,173 tourists the park welcomed in 1919, when it was established.) People from all over the globe come here to hike the trails, travel down to the base by mule, camp, backpack, raft the Colorado River or simply stare in admiration from the rim.

The entire park is 1,904 square miles in size, with 277 miles of the Colorado River running through it. Draining water systems have carved dramatic canyons throughout the walls, making every rock in every direction worthy of a look. Forests descend from upper elevations at the rim and give way to desert basins below. At its widest point, the north and south rims are 15 miles across, with average elevations of 8,000 feet and 7,000 feet, respectively. The canyon averages a depth of one mile. At its base, 2 billion-year-old rocks are exposed.

Not quite as old as those rocks, but pretty ancient, are the 12,000-year-old human artifacts found in the park. Archaeologists say that people have used and occupied the area since that time, known as the Paleo Indian period. Nomadic groups hunted animals like mountain goats and bison and gathered plants around the Canyon.

Grand Canyon National Park essentially encompasses two distinct parks: the South Rim and the North Rim. The two sides of the canyon are only about 10 miles apart as the crow flies, but for us grounded creatures, they are realistically a five-hour drive, or 215 miles, from each other—and very different places at that. The scenery, climate and vegetation are all noticeably different between the two sides of the canyon because of the contrast in elevation.

The South Rim, open year-round, is 60 miles north of Williams, Arizona, and has many more tourist services than the North Rim, including day and overnight mule trips, horseback riding and air tours. In addition, there are a variety of museums and facilities on the South Rim. A good starting point is the South Rim Grand Canyon Village, which is the park headquarters and heart of park activity and transportation. Heading north on the South Entrance Road, you will reach a curve toward the left near the rim of the canyon and find the Canyon View Information Plaza, a short walk from Mather Point. This visitor center provides information, a bookstore and outdoor exhibits and is the transportation hub for free shuttle bus tours of the South Rim. They go in both directions from the visitor center, hit all of the hot spots and are a convenient way for families to get around. The West Rim and East Rim drives out from the Village are equally rewarding.

Tours of all kinds are available on both the North and South Rims of the canyon. If you've got a day or two, opt for a hiking tour that leads you into the canyon to camp for the night. For those less inclined to build up a sweat, there are air and bus tours that provide a thorough sense of the history, preservation and sheer magnitude of the country's most beautiful hole. The South Rim, open all year, has the greater number of services, including day and overnight mule trips through Xanterra Parks & Resorts and horseback riding through **Apache Stables** *(928-638-2891)*. The North Rim is usually blocked by heavy snows in winter, and is only open from mid-May to mid-October. Due to the higher elevation, mule trips from the North Rim do not go to the river.

Fall and spring are the best times to trek into the canyon, when it's less crowded. Hiking to the base and back up in one day is a feat accomplished only by the most fit. It's best to camp in the canyon overnight (plan on an additional night if hiking from the North Rim). Fifteen main trails provide access to the inner canyon.

Rafting the Colorado River through Grand Canyon National Park is another great way to see the area, but it requires reservations far in advance. **Hualapai River Runners** *(928-769-2119)* offers one-day whitewater trips, while **Wilderness River Adventures** *(800-992-8022; www.riveradventures. com)* organizes longer whitewater tours of three-and-a-half days or more.

Besides tours, there are a variety of museums and facilities on the South Rim. The **Kolb Studio** in the Village Historic District at the **Bright Angel Trailhead** features art displays and a bookstore. It was once the home and business of the Kolb brothers, who were pioneering photographers here. The Yavapai Observation Station, one mile east of Market Plaza, contains temporary exhibits about the fossil record at Grand Canyon. Also on the South Rim is the historic **El Tovar Hotel** *(1 Main St., South Rim, 928-638-2631; www.grandcanyonlodges.com),* built in 1905 just 20 feet from the edge of the canyon in a style reminiscent of a Swiss chalet with rustic log siding. The storied hotel has hosted everyone from Theodore Roosevelt to Barack Obama, and includes a restaurant where you can have a reliable lunch served up with incredible canyon views.

How to get there: There are numerous helicopter companies that provide tours to the Grand Canyon. Ask your concierge for price information and availability.

SECRET GARDEN AND DOLPHIN HABITAT

WHAT IS THE BEST WAY TO ARRIVE AT AND DEPART LAS VEGAS?

More than 900 flights come in and out of **McCarran International Airport** *(5757 Wayne Newton Blvd., Off-Strip, 702-261-5211; www.mccarran.com)* every day. The airport is busiest on Sunday and Thursday, as those are the days when the city's two main types of travelers (leisure and meeting-goers) are crossing paths. If your plans allow you to fly in and out on a Tuesday, Wednesday or Saturday, your chances of avoiding gridlock and long lines at check-in and security are greatly enhanced.

McCarran recently underwent a number of changes, including a nine-gate addition to its D concourse and 12 more lanes for Transportation Security Administration screening for its C concourse, which should alleviate lines at the security checkpoint. A new terminal with 14 gates (and all the amenities that go with a 14-gate terminal) is expected to open in 2012. Until then, expect to see a lot of construction.

The rumor that concierges at the high-end hotels can somehow get guests past security quicker is just that—a rumor. However, Continental offers a club lounge (outside security, unfortunately). Day passes are available.

Flying isn't the only way to access Sin City. Las Vegas sits at the intersection of four states: Nevada, California, Utah and Arizona, with highways I-15, 95 and 159/160 all heading into or around the city and providing easy access to visitors who choose to drive.

WHAT SHOULD YOU PACK?

During the day, you should wear comfortable clothes and—even more important—comfortable shoes if you plan on doing a lot of walking around the Strip or downtown areas. Las Vegas is one of the few places where a little glitz goes over well. In general, people dress up a bit more at night in the restaurants and at clubs and shows—although, really, anything goes. Just remember that even if it's over 100 degrees outside, it'll still be heavily air-conditioned inside.

WHERE CAN YOU GET MEDICAL TREATMENT IN LAS VEGAS?

There are quite a few hospitals and urgent-care centers in Las Vegas—with many on or near the Strip and the downtown area. **St. Louis Medical Center** *(530 E. St. Louis Ave., Off-Strip, 702-699-8190)* is closest to the Strip, a block north of the Sahara Hotel & Casino. All major casinos and hotels also have a paramedic or nurse either on the property or on call. You should contact security for any immediate medical assistance.

One of the ways to avoid needing medical attention is to remember that Las Vegas is in the Mojave Desert, with a capital D. Make sure to drink enough water—and remember that those cool, frothy drinks by the pool contain alcohol, which can lead to dehydration. Wear sunscreen (and look for shade) if you're going to be walking outside or out by the pools.

ARE HOTEL RATES NEGOTIABLE IN LAS VEGAS?

Everything is flexible in Las Vegas—especially the price for a hotel room. The rates can vary widely depending on the time of year, day of the week (weekday versus weekend) and if there is a convention in town. Even the

LAKE OF DREAMS

swankiest properties are known to cut rates to get people in during slow times, so check often and be flexible. This is not to say you should call and try to haggle the reservations clerk. Instead keep checking hotel websites, where they will list special dates and rates. If you are a gambler—especially if you are a rated player at a particular casino—special casino rates or complimentary nights are often available through the casino marketing department.

WHICH NEWSPAPERS AND MAGAZINES SERVE LAS VEGAS?

The *Las Vegas Review-Journal (www.lvrj.com)* is one of the city's two daily newspapers and grew out of Las Vegas' first newspaper, the *Clark County Review*, which was established in 1909. Official Las Vegas guides are available from the **Las Vegas Convention and Visitors Authority** or at its official website *(www.visitlasvegas.com)*. Another popular (and well-publicized) website is *www.vegas.com*, which is run by the same people who publish *LVM (www.lasvegasmagazine.com)*, which is found in 90 percent of the hotel rooms; along with *Vegas Magazine (www.vegasmagazine.com)*; *Las Vegas Weekly (www.lasvegasweekly.com)* and *In Business Las Vegas (www.inbusinesslasvegas.com)*, and others. Other publications that list shows, restaurants and attractions include *What's On* magazine *(www.whats-on.com)* and *Where* magazine *(www.wheretraveler.com)*, with both available at most hotels and other public venues.

HOW SAFE IS LAS VEGAS?

Pickpocketing is not unique to Las Vegas, but that doesn't mean you should be careless. If you've had some luck in the casinos, do yourself a favor and keep your bounty in the hotel room safe. Something that is unique to Vegas, though not illegal or a scam per se, are the kiosks trying to sell time-shares by enticing you with promises of free show tickets or other incentives. Again, while these are legitimate businesses and perfectly legal,

HOW DOES TIPPING WORK IN LAS VEGAS?

Las Vegas is all about service, and it is appropriate to compensate those hospitality-industry employees who help create a pleasant experience. Here are some recommended guidelines for tipping:

Restaurant servers: 15-20 percent

Bell captains and bellmen: $1-$2 per bag

Valet parking attendants: $2

Housekeeper: $2 per day

Concierge or VIP services: $10 and up for making travel plans or show reservations

Casino: Small tips for dealers, keno runners and slot attendants

For show rooms without assigned seating, a $5-$20 tip to the maître d' will usually ensure a good seat.

people who aren't educated about time-shares and how they work may not know what they're getting themselves into.

WHAT IS THE BEST WAY TO GET AROUND LAS VEGAS?

There are plenty of ways to get around the city, including the **Deuce** *(702-676-1500; www.rtcsouthernnevada.com/transit)*, the Strip's double-decker public bus system; the **MAX** *(702-676-1500; www.rtcsouthernnevada.com/transit)*, a hybrid bus/rail system; and the **Las Vegas Monorail** *(702-699-8200; www.lvmonorail.com)*. The Monorail runs from 7 a.m. to 2 a.m. Monday through Thursday and 7 a.m. to 3 a.m. Friday through Sunday, and makes stops at the MGM Grand Hotel & Casino, Bally's/Paris Las Vegas, the Flamingo Las Vegas, Harrah's/Imperial Palace, Caesars Palace, the Las Vegas Convention Center, the Las Vegas Hilton and the Sahara Hotel & Casino.

IS IT NECESSARY TO RENT A CAR?

Cars aren't necessary in Las Vegas unless you are planning trips away from the Strip or Downtown. If so, rental cars are available at the airport, and many of the hotels have rentals available onsite. Many of the higher-end hotels offer free car service as part of the amenities for their VIPs and casino-invited guests. These include your typical limos and town cars—or perhaps a Maybach (in the case of the Skylofts at MGM Grand) or a Bentley (favored by the Tower Suites at Wynn).

HOW MUCH DOES IT COST TO GET TO THE STRIP FROM THE AIRPORT?

Taxis from the airport cost approximately $9-$13 to the Strip and approximately $16-$20 to Downtown. Shared-ride vans are also available and cost a few dollars less, but charge per person and will not only attempt to fill the van before leaving the airport, but will also most likely hit more than one hotel. In other words, if time is more important than money, take a cab. Those who want to start their trip in style can book a limousine for about $50. Hotels are also happy to arrange towncar service to and from the airport.

VOLCANO AT THE MIRAGE

IS LAS VEGAS A WALKABLE CITY?

Save for the blistering summer heat, Las Vegas is a very walkable city, especially if you are staying along the Strip or Downtown near Fremont Street. The Strip has become more pedestrian-friendly in recent years, with pedestrian bridges now located at the intersection of Las Vegas Boulevard and Tropicana Avenue, and Flamingo and Spring Mountain roads. The bridges go in all four directions of these intersections, so you're never stuck on any particular side of the street (though you may grow a bit tired of riding escalators up and down). As with any major city, it is advisable not to wander off these streets and into neighborhoods with which you are not familiar.

WHAT IS THE WEATHER IN LAS VEGAS?

From May to October, the weather in Las Vegas can be summed up in one word: hot. Or maybe to add an adjective: very hot. Temperatures average in the 100° Fahrenheit range and can get as high as 117° in late-July/August. The rest of the year is mild, with temperatures rarely getting below the 40° to 60° range in the winter and hovering at a comfortable 70°-85° in the spring. The city boasts more than 300 sunny days a year and very little precipitation. Because the casinos, hotels, malls, meeting venues, restaurants, nightclubs and entertainment venues are heavily air-conditioned, have another layer ready for those rooms where they're keeping their temps in the 60s.

BELLAGIO GALLERY OF FINE ART

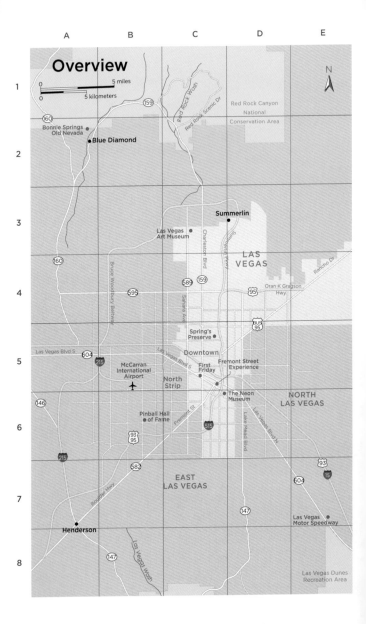

Overview

0 _____ 5 miles
0 _____ 5 kilometers

N

1

159

Red Rock Scenic Dr

Red Rock Wash

Red Rock Canyon
National
Conservation Area

160

Bonnie Springs
Old Nevada

Blue Diamond

2

3

Las Vegas
Art Museum

Charleston Blvd

Summerlin

Summerlin Pkwy

LAS
VEGAS

Rancho Dr

160

Bruce Woodbury Beltway

599

589 **159**

Sahara Ave

95

Oran K Gragson
Hwy

4

BUS
95

5

Las Vegas Blvd S

604 **215**

Las Vegas Blvd S

Spring's
Preserve

Downtown

Downtown

McCarran
International
Airport

North
Strip

First
Friday

Fremont Street
Experience

6

146

Pinball Hall
of Fame

93
95

Fremont St

515

The Neon
Museum

Lake Mead Blvd

Las Vegas Blvd N

NORTH
LAS VEGAS

7

215

582

Boulder Hwy

EAST
LAS VEGAS

147

604

93

15

Las Vegas
Motor Speedway

Henderson

147

Las Vegas Wash

8

Las Vegas Dunes
Recreation Area

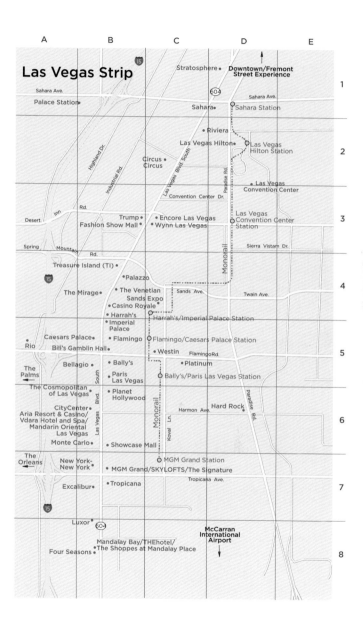

Las Vegas Strip

Stratosphere • Downtown/Fremont
Street Experience

Sahara Ave.

Palace Station •

Sahara • Sahara Station

• Riviera

Las Vegas Hilton • Las Vegas
Hilton Station

Circus
Circus

Las Vegas Convention Center

Convention Center Dr.

Desert   Inn Rd.

Trump • • Encore Las Vegas   Las Vegas
Fashion Show Mall • • Wynn Las Vegas   Convention Center
Station

Spring   Mountain Rd.

Sierra Vista Dr.

Treasure Island (TI) •

• Palazzo

The Mirage • • The Venetian   Sands Ave.   Twain Ave.
Sands Expo
• Casino Royale
• Harrah's   Harrah's/Imperial Palace Station
• Imperial
Palace

Caesars Palace • • Flamingo   Flamingo/Caesars Palace Station

Rio   Bill's Gamblin Hall •   • Westin   Flamingo Rd.

The   Bellagio • • Bally's   • Platinum
Palms
• Paris   Bally's/Paris Las Vegas Station
Las Vegas

The Cosmopolitan
of Las Vegas • • Planet
Hollywood

CityCenter •   Harmon Ave.   Hard Rock •
Aria Resort & Casino/
Vdara Hotel and Spa/
Mandarin Oriental
Las Vegas

Monte Carlo • • Showcase Mall

The
Orleans   New York-   MGM Grand Station
New York • • MGM Grand/SKYLOFTS/The Signature

Excalibur • • Tropicana   Tropicana Ave.

Luxor •

McCarran
International
Airport

Mandalay Bay/THEhotel/
Four Seasons • • The Shoppes at Mandalay Place

179

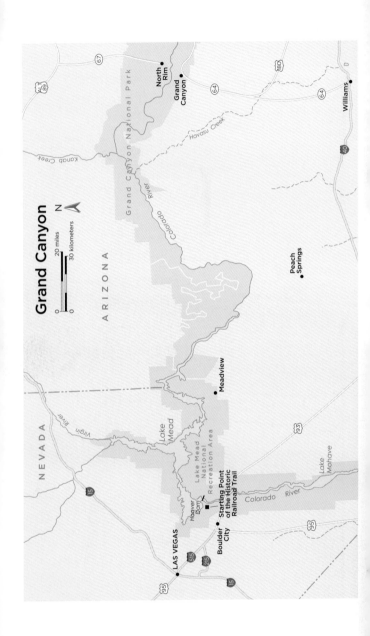

FLAMINGO LAS VEGAS HOTEL & CASINO

A

Activities in Las Vegas, *21*
The Adventuredome, *25*
Alex, *11, 98*
Alizé, *127*
American Fish, *115*
Aquae Sulis Spa, *62*
Aquaknox, *98*
Aria Resort & Casino, *9, 83*
Aria Skysuites, *85*
The Atomic Testing Museum, *39*
The Attic, *53*
Aureole, *12, 98*

B

Bali Hai, *163*
Bally's Las Vegas, *68*
The Bank, *134*
Bar Masa, *11, 117*
Bartolotta Ristorante di Mare, *117*
Bar Vdara, *134*
The Bathhouse, *56*
B&B Ristorante, *99*
The Beatles Revolution Lounge, *134*
The Beatles LOVE, *158*
Bellagio Conservatory & Botanical Gardens, *26*
The Bellagio Gallery of Fine Art, *155*
Bellagio Las Vegas, *10, 46, 68*
Blue Agave, *129*
Blush, *135, 141*
BODIES: The Exhibition, *26*
Bonanza "The World's Largest Gift Shop, *27*
Bonnie Springs Old Nevada, *43*
Botero, *11, 118*
Bouchon, *100*
Bradley Ogden, *100*
Bright Angel Trailhead, *171*

C

Caesars Palace, *9, 69*
Canyon Ranch SpaClub, *56*
Caramel, *135*
Carnevino, *101*
Carrot Top, *156*
Centrifuge, *136*
China Ranch, *169*
Christian Audigier the Nightclub, *136*
Cirque du Soleil, *158*
CityCenter, *9*
The Clark County Marriage License Bureau, *146*
The Colosseum Shows, *160*
The Cosmopolitan of Las Vegas, *86*
The Country Club, *118*
Craftsteak, *11, 101*
Criss Angel Believe, *159*
Crystals Retail and Entertainment, *12*
CUT, *102*

D

David Burke, *11*
Death Valley, *169*
Delmonico Steakhouse, *102*
Desert Princess, *166*
Deuce, *175*
Diego, *119*
Celine Dion, *10*
DJT, *128*
Double Helix Bar, *137*
Drai's Afterhours, *137*

E

The Eiffel Tower Experience, *27*
El Tovar hotel, *171*
Embassy Suites Las Vegas, *91*
Emeril's, *102*
Encore Esplanade, *46*
Encore Las Vegas, *9, 69*
Eve Nightclub, *137*
Excalibur, *9, 35*

CITYCENTER

Eyecandy Sound Lounge & Bar, *10, 138*

F

Fashion Show, *12, 47*
Fiamma Trattoria, *103*
First Friday, *155*
Flamingo Las Vegas, *10, 85*
Fontana Bar, *139*
The Forum Shops at Caesars Palace, *48*
Founding of Las Vegas, *14*
Fountains of Bellagio, *28*
Four Seasons Hotel Las Vegas, *70*
Fremont Street Experience, *41*

G

George Wallace, *156*
Ghostbar, *150*
Golden Nugget Las Vegas, *93*
Golden Gate Casino, *32*
Gold Lounge, *139*
Gondola Rides, *28*

The Grand Canal Shoppes at The Venetian, *48*
Grand Canyon, *169*
Green Valley Ranch Resort, Spa and Casino, *94*
The Griffin, *32*

H

Hachi, *131*
Hamada of Japan, *129*
Hard Rock Hotel Casino, *87*
Harrah's Las Vegas, *70*
Haze Nightclub, *139*
Historic Railroad Trail, *167*
Hoover Dam, *16, 166*
Hostile Grape, *150*
Hotel Rates, *173*
House of Blues, *157*
Hualapai River Runners, *171*

I

Imperial Palace Auto Collection, *29*

CIRQUE DU SOLEIL'S *O*

J

Jasmine, *104*
Jean George Steakhouse, *11, 119*
Jersey Boys, *10, 161*
Joël Robuchon, *104*
The Joint, *160*
Jubilee!, *10*
Jubilee! Backstage Tour, *29*
Julian Serrano, *11, 119*
JW Marriott Las Vegas Resort & Spa, *95*

K

Kà, *158*
Kolb Studio, *171*

L

Lake Mead, *166*
Lake of Dreams, *29*
La Scena Lounge, *140*
Las Vegas and the Mob, *18*
Las Vegas Convention and Visitors Authority, *174*
Las Vegas' cuisine, *22*
Las Vegas Hilton, *87*
Las Vegas Marriott Suites, *89*
Las Vegas Monorail, *175*
Las Vegas Motor Speedway, *163*
Las Vegas Outlet Center, *50*
Las Vegas Premium Outlets, *50*
Las Vegas Review-Journal, *174*
Las Vegas Ski and Snowboard Resort, *168*
Las Vegas Weather, *176*
Las Vegas Weekly, *174*
L'Atelier de Joël Robuchon, *12, 105*
Lavo Nightclub, *140*
LAVO, *105*
Le Boulevard Shops, *49*
Le Cirque, *106*

Legends in Concert, *161, 162*
Le Rêve, *162*
Lion Habitat, *31*
Loews/Lake Las Vegas Resort, *95*
Luxor, *71*
LVM, *174*

M

The M Resort Spa & Casino Las Vegas, *89*
Mac King Comedy Show, *34*
Main Street Antiques, Art & Collectibles, *53*
Main Street Station Casino Brewery & Hotel, *94*
Mandalay Bay Resort & Casino, *71*
Mandalay Bay Events Center, *164*
Mandarin Oriental Las Vegas, *9, 72*
Mandarin Bar, *140*
Marché Bacchus, *132*
MAX, *175*
McCarran International Airport, *173*
MGM Grand Garden Arena, *164*
MGM Grand Hotel & Casino, *9, 72*
Michael Mina, *106*
The Midway at Circus Circus, *31*
Ming's Table, *120*
Miracle Mile Shops, *12, 49*
The Mirage, *73*
The Mirage Spa and Kim Vo Salon, *63*
MIX in Las Vegas, *11, 107*
MIX Lounge, *141*
Monte Carlo Resort & Casino, *73*
Moon, *151*
Mount Charleston, *168*
Mystere, *158*

N

N9NE Steakhouse, *128*
Natural beauty in Las Vegas, *23*
The Neon Museum, *42*
New York-New York, *74*
Nobhill Tavern, *107*
Nobu, *128*
Not Just Antiques Mart, *54*

O

O, *159*
Okada, *109, 120*
Olives, *109*
O'Sheas, *30*
Osteria del Circo, *121*
Over-the-top Las Vegas, *21*

P

The Palazzo Resort Hotel Casino, *9, 10, 74*
The Palm, *109*
Palms Casino Resort, *90*
Paris Las Vegas, *75*
Paris Spa by Mandara, *63*
Pearl, *121*
The Pearl at the Palms, *160*
Penn and Teller, *157*
Penske-Wynn Ferrari/ Maserati Las Vegas, *33*
Phantom-The Las Vegas Spectacular, *163*
Picasso, *110*
Pinball Hall of Fame, *40*
Pinot Brasserie, *122*
Planet Hollywood Resort & Casino, *75*
Planet Hollywood Spa by Mandara, *64*
The Platinum Hotel & Spa, *90*
Popular Casino Games, *21*
Postrio Bar & Grill, *110*
Prime Steakhouse, *111*
Pure, *10, 141*

Q

Qua Baths & Spa, *57*

R

Rain, *151*
Raku, *130*
The Rat Pack, *17*
Red 8, *12, 122*
Red Rock Casino, Resort & Spa, *96*
Red Rock Canyon National Conservation Area, *43*
Restaurant Guy Savoy, *111*
Rio All-Suite Hotel & Casino, *93*
Rita Rudner, *157*
The Roller Coaster, *33*

S

Sage, *122*
Salute Lounge, *143*
Scotty's Castle, *169*
Seablue, *111*
Secret Garden and Dolphin Habitat, *36*
Seeing Las Vegas in One Day, *30*
Seeing Las Vegas in Three Days, *32*
Settebello, *132*
Shadow: A Bar at Caesars Palace, *143*
Shanghai Lilly, *123*
Shark Reef Aquarium, *37*
Shibuya, *112*
The Shoppes at The Palazzo, *12, 50*
Showcase Mall, *37*
The Signature at MGM Grand Las Vegas, *76*
Silk Road, *124*
Sinatra, *124*
Sirens of TI, *37*
Sirio Ristorante, *125*
Skylofts at MGM Grand, *9, 77*

HOOVER DAM

Slots-A-Fun, *30*
Society Café, *125*
The Spa at Mandarin Oriental, Las Vegas, *59*
The Spa at The Four Seasons Hotel Las Vegas, *59*
The Spa at Wynn Las Vegas, *61*
Spa at Aria, *64*
The Spa at Encore Las Vegas, *58*
The Spa at Green Valley Ranch, *64*
The Spa at Red Rock, *60*
The Spa at The Four Seasons Hotel Las Vegas, *59*
The Spa at Trump, *60*
The Spa at Wynn Las Vegas, *61*
Spa Bellagio Las Vegas, *61*
Spa Mio, *62, 65*
Spa Moulay, *65*
Springs Preserve, *40*
St. Louis Medical Center, *173*
Stratosphere Rides, *38*
Stratta, *11, 125*
Studio 54, *144*
Sugarcane, *144*

Switch, *126*
SW Steakhouse, *126*

T

Table 10, *112*
Tableau, *127*
Tabu Ultra Lounge, *145*
The Tank, *42*
Tao, *113*
Tao Nightclub, *10, 145*
Terrazza di Sogno, *146*
THEhotel at Mandalay Bay, *77*
Tipping in Las Vegas, *175*
Titanic: The Artifact Exhibition, *38*
Top of the World, *113*
Tower Suites at Encore Las Vegas, *9, 79*
Tower Suites at Wynn Las Vegas, *9, 79*
Town Square, *51*
Treasure Island (TI), *81*
Tropicana Las Vegas, *82*
Trump International Hotel & Tower Las Vegas, *91*
Tryst, *147*
Twist, *11, 114*

MORE THAN 50 YEARS AGO, WE CREATED THE
VERY IDEA OF THE FIVE STAR EXPERIENCE.

THIS IS STAR POWER.

Mandarin Oriental, Hong Kong, A Five Star winner

V

Valentino Las Vegas, *114*
Valley of Fire State Park, *167*
Vanity, *148*
V Bar, *148*
Vdara Hotel & Spa, *9*, *86*
Vdara Health & Beauty, *65*
Vegas Indoor Skydiving, *41*
Vegas Magazine, *174*
The Venetian Resort Hotel
    Casino, *9*, *82*
Verandah, *115*
Via Bellagio, *12*
Viva Elvis, *159*
The Volcano, *39*
VooDoo Lounge, *152*
VooDoo Steak & Lounge, *130*

W

Wasted Space, *152*
WELL Spa, *66*
The Westin Casuarina Las
    Vegas Hotel Casino &
    Spa, *91*
What are the best celebrity
    chef restaurants?, *108*
What's On, *174*
Where magazine, *174*
Wilderness River Adventures,
    171
Wing Lei, *127*
Wynn Golf Course, *163*
Wynn Las Vegas, *9*, *10*, *83*,
    146
Wynn Las Vegas Esplanade,
    12, *52*

X

XS, *10*, *149*

Z

Zumanity, *159*
Zuri, *149*

ART CREDITS

The Center for Hospitality Research
Hospitality Leadership Through Learning

The source for hospitality industry research

Shaping the global knowledge base in
hospitality by linking academics and industry

www.chr.cornell.edu

489 Statler Hall
hosp_research@cornell.edu
607.255.9780

Senior Partners
Hilton Worldwide • McDonald's USA • Philips Hospitality • SAS • STR
• Taj Hotels Resorts and Palaces • TIG Global

Partners
Davis & Gilbert LLP • Deloitte & Touche USA LLP • Denihan Hospitality Group • eCornell &
Executive Education • Expedia, Inc. • Forbes Travel Guide • Four Seasons Hotels and Resorts •
Fox Rothschild LLP • French Quarter Holdings, Inc. • HVS • Hyatt • InterContinental Hotels Group
• Jumeirah Group • LRP Publications • Maritz • Marriott International, Inc. • Marsh's Hospitality
Practice • PricewaterhouseCoopers • Proskauer • Sabre Hospitality Solutions • Schneider Electric
• Southern Wine and Spirits of America • Thayer Lodging Group • Thompson Hotels • Travelport
• WATG

Friends
4Hoteliers.com • American Tescor, LLC • Argyle Executive Forum • Berkshire Healthcare • Center for Advanced Retail
Technology • Cody Kramer Imports • Cruise Industry News • DK Shifflet & Associates • ehotelier.com • EyeforTravel •
Gerencia de Hoteles & Restaurantes • Global Hospitality Resources, Inc. • Hospitality Financial and Technology
Professionals • hospitalityInside.com • hospitalitynet.org • Hospitality Technology Magazine • Hotel Asia Pacific • Hotel
China • HotelExecutive.com • Hotel Interactive • Hotel Resource • HotelWorld Network • International CHRIE
• International Hotel Conference • International Society of Hospitality Consultants (ISHC) • iPerceptions • JDA Software
Group, Inc. • J.D. Power and Associates • The Lodging Conference • Lodging Hospitality • Lodging Magazine • LRA
Worldwide, Inc. • Milestone Internet Marketing, Inc. • MindFolio • Mindshare Technologies • PhoCusWright Inc. • PKF
Hospitality Research • RealShare Hotel Investment & Finance Summit • Resort and Recreation Magazine • The Resort Trades
• RestaurantEdge.com • Shibata Publishing Co. Ltd. • Synovate • TravelCLICK • UniFocus • USA Today •
WageWatch, Inc. • The Wall Street Journal • WIWIH.COM

Cornell University
School of Hotel Administration

Pg. 43: Bonnie Springs Ranch © Las Vegas News Bureau/LVCVA

Pg 45: Wynn Esplanade © Wynn Las Vegas

Pg. 47: Fashion Show © Las Vegas News Bureau/LVCVA

Pg. 48: Grand Canal Shoppes at the Venetian © The Venetian Resort Hotel Casino

Pg. 51: The Shoppes at the Palazzo © The Palazzo Las Vegas Resort Hotel Casino

Pg. 53: Town Square © Las Vegas News Bureau/LVCVA

SPAS

The Spa at Wynn Las Vegas © Wynn Las Vegas

The Spa at Trump © Trump International Hotel Las Vegas

The Spa at Encore Las Vegas © Russell MacMasters/Encore Las Vegas

Canyon Ranch SpaClub © The Palazzo Resort Hotel Casino/The Venetian Resort Hotel Casino

The Mirage Spa © The Mirage

Well Spa © The Platinum Hotel and Spa

WHERE TO STAY

The Lobby at the Palazzo © The Palazzo Las Vegas Resort Hotel Casino

Bellagio Las Vegas © Bellagio Las Vegas

Encore Las Vegas © Russell MacMasters/Encore Las Vegas

Mandarin Oriental Las Vegas © Mandarin Oriental Las Vegas

Wynn Las Vegas © Wynn Las Vegas

The Signature at MGM Grand © MGM Grand Hotel & Casino

Four Seasons Hotel Las Vegas © Four Seasons

Palms Casino Resort © Palms Casino Resort

Caesar's Palace © Las Vegas News Bureau/LVCVA

The Venetian Resort Hotel Casino © The Venetian Resort Hotel Casino

Aria Resort & Casino Lobby © Aria Resort & Casino

Bellagio Pool © Bellagio Las Vegas

The Palazzo Las Vegas Resort Hotel Casino © The Palazzo Las Vegas Resort Hotel Casino

Trump International Hotel Las Vegas Lobby © Trump International Hotel Las Vegas

Liquid Pool Lounge at Aria © Aria Resort & Casino

Four Seasons Hotel Las Vegas Lobby © Four Seasons

MGM Grand Hotel & Casino © MGM Grand Hotel & Casino

New York-New York © New York-New York

The M Resort Spa & Casino Las Vegas © The M Resort Spa & Casino Las Vegas

Mandalay Bay Resort & Casino © Mandalay Bay Resort & Casino

WHERE TO EAT

Carnevino © The Palazzo Las Vegas Resort Hotel Casino

Aureole © Mandalay Bay Resort & Casino

Bradley Ogden © Caesar's Palace

Fiamma Trattoria © MGM Grand Hotel & Casino

Joël Robuchon © MGM Grand Hotel & Casino

Le Cirque © Bellagio Las Vegas

Craftsteak © MGM Grand Hotel & Casino